A Serpent's Tale

A Serpent's Tale

DISCOVERING
AMERICA'S
ANCIENT
MOUND BUILDERS

Lorett Treese

WESTHOLME
Yardley

Facing title page: The Serpent Mound, Adams County, Ohio. (*Ohio History Central*)

Westholme Publishing, LLC
904 Edgewood Road
Yardley, Pennsylvania 19067
Visit our Web site at www.westholmepublishing.com

ISBN: 978-1-59416-364-7
Also available as an eBook.

Printed in the United States of America

For MAT

Contents

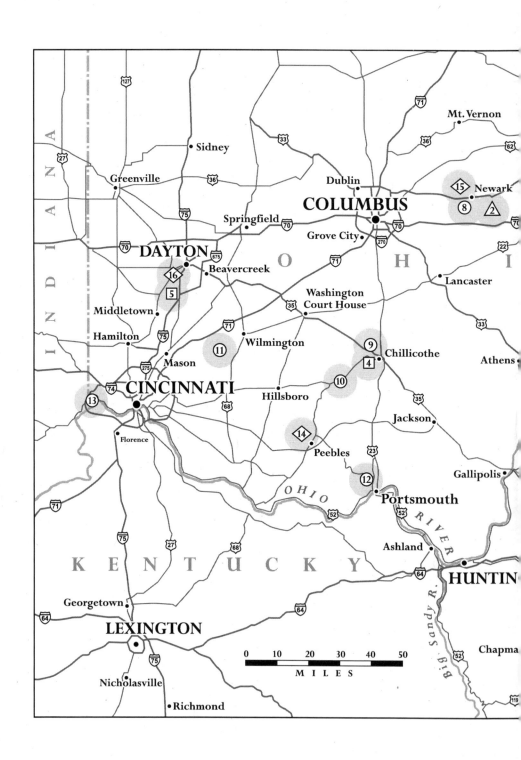

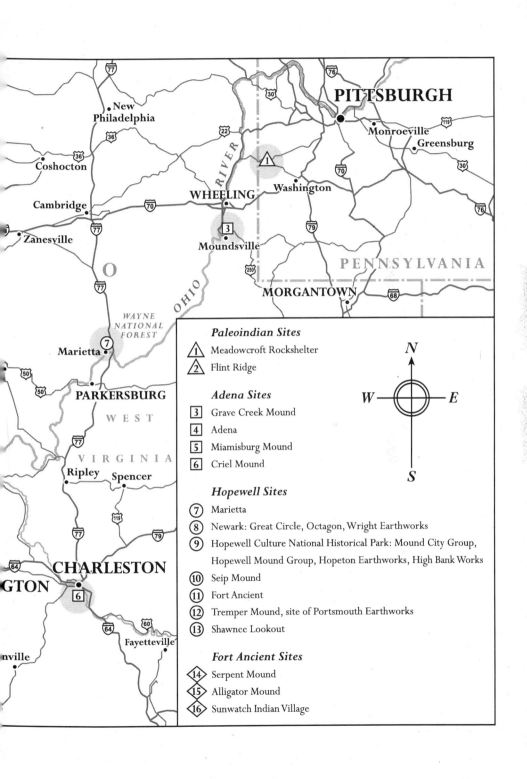

Paleoindian Sites

△ 1 Meadowcroft Rockshelter
△ 2 Flint Ridge

Adena Sites

3 Grave Creek Mound
4 Adena
5 Miamisburg Mound
6 Criel Mound

Hopewell Sites

7 Marietta
8 Newark: Great Circle, Octagon, Wright Earthworks
9 Hopewell Culture National Historical Park: Mound City Group, Hopewell Mound Group, Hopeton Earthworks, High Bank Works
10 Seip Mound
11 Fort Ancient
12 Tremper Mound, site of Portsmouth Earthworks
13 Shawnee Lookout

Fort Ancient Sites

◇ 14 Serpent Mound
◇ 15 Alligator Mound
◇ 16 Sunwatch Indian Village

1

A Serpent's Tale

For several days in August 1987 numerous visitors arrived at a small memorial park in Adams County, Ohio, to enjoy the sight of a rare alignment of the sun, moon, and a number of planets known as the Harmonic Convergence. True believers from all walks of life came to chant, dance, meditate, and celebrate what was supposed to be a cleansing of the planet that would usher in a New Age of understanding. They were generally peaceful and caused no damage that some additional topsoil couldn't fix.

But how did this very rural spot outside a tiny burg called Peebles get on the list of "power centers" for Harmonic Convergence celebrants along with attractions like Mount Shasta and Mount Fuji? Because a narrow promontory rising some ninety feet above a winding river called Brush Creek has been a special place for a very long time. There a prehistoric people built the Serpent Mound, one of North America's largest and best examples of a prehistoric animal effigy mound. Over thirteen hundred feet long, the Serpent Mound is an earthwork shaped like an undulating snake which appears to be in the act of swallowing an egg. It is draped over the slightly angled and convex surface of the elevated plain as though its architects had placed it carefully upon a natural altar.

The Serpent Mound also may well be the poster child for the several pre-Columbian Native American cultures collectively known as Mound Builders. These peoples who left no written records have fired the imaginations of Americans ever since the first white explorers and pioneers ventured west of the Alleghenies and discovered the evidence of their prior occupation writ large on the landscape in the form of abandoned earthworks and mounds.

If the Serpent Mound made the place historic, other reports and rumors made this corner of Ohio even more interesting. Before and following the 1987 Harmonic Convergence, some visitors have claimed to experience odd feelings or energies at the Serpent Mound, particularly if they happened to be alone. Others have reported vivid dreams following a Serpent Mound visit. In an interview in 2009 the site's acting assistant manager reported that those who might be called New Agers arrive regularly at the Serpent Mound, usually in warmer weather and often in groups. They conduct their own ceremonies and activities and are generally respectful of other visitors, who in turn are tolerant of them. The site's management welcomes the New Agers so long as they don't try to climb on the mound or harm it in any way.

For some reason Erich von Daniken excluded the Serpent Mound from his popular 1968 book titled *Chariots of the Gods?* in which he claimed that a variety of ancient works had been constructed by aliens, but this effigy has been cited as evidence for a number of other fabulous theories. In the late nineteenth century Ignatius Donnelly wrote of its resemblance to an effigy in Scotland, adding this to other evidence that survivors from the sunken continent of Atlantis might have migrated to both loca-

Ephraim George Squier (1821–1888), left, and Edwin Hamilton Davis (1811–1888): the journalist and doctor who introduced the Serpent Mound to the American reading public through their 1848 study published by the Smithsonian Institution.

tions. Around the turn of the twentieth century, an Ohio minister named Landon West claimed that the Serpent Mound had been placed where it was by God himself, or through his divine inspiration, to mark the location of the Garden of Eden and provide a lasting symbol of humans' sinful disobedience provoked by the wiles of Satan.

The earliest description of the Serpent Mound by authors who could claim to be men of science was published in the mid-nineteenth century by the then fledgling Smithsonian Institution. Ephraim George Squier and Edwin Hamilton Davis had undertaken the daunting task of mapping and describing all the known earthen antiquities still standing in the midsection of the United States. Their book titled *Ancient Monuments of the Mississippi Valley* appeared in 1848. According to Squier and Davis, at that time only the locals knew where the Serpent Mound lay, sheltered and hidden by vegetation. Many folks thought it was some sort of prehistoric fort, but Squier and Davis immediately recognized it as an effigy. "The true character of the work was apparent on the first inspection," they wrote. Their book was full of startling illustrations and their full-page diagram of the Serpent Mound is among its most intriguing.

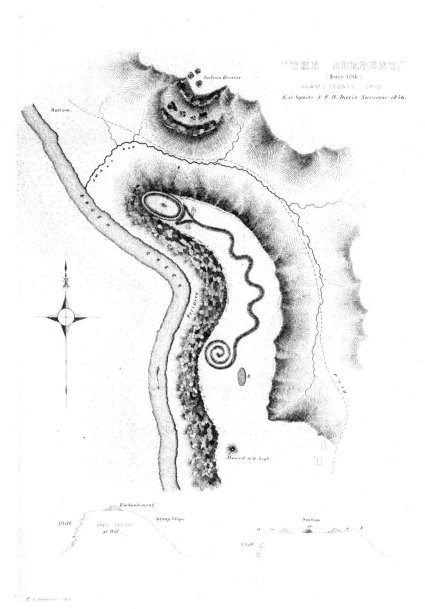

The Serpent Mound, appearing for the American public for the first time in Squier and Davis's *Ancient Monuments of the Mississippi Valley*, one of the most dramatic and intriguing illustrations from the 1848 volume.

Precisely when and how the Serpent Mound was first discovered remains a mystery. Adams County was formed in 1797, with its first county seat located at Adamsville a few miles above the mouth of Brush Creek. Later the town of West Union, laid out in 1804, became the county seat. The earliest map with Brush Creek identified as such was drawn in 1807. The earliest map showing the modern boundaries of Adams County appeared in an atlas published in 1814. In earlier maps Adams County is just an indistinct portion of a larger tract identified as the Virginia Military Lands. On none of these early maps is there any indication of the Serpent Mound's location. A survey on antiquities in Ohio published in 1820 by local resident Caleb Atwater, who lived in Circleville less than fifty miles away, included no mention of the Serpent Mound.

Yet the northern boundary of Adams County has an interesting feature. Instead of being a straight line like the boundaries of so many other Ohio counties, it starts at the county's western boundary running more or less due east, then it swings northeast, then east again, then southeast. There was no town in the area thus defined, so what were the surveyors surrounding and containing within Adams County if not the general location of the Serpent Mound? Were that the case, no one seemed in a hurry to claim the Serpent Mound or do anything to protect it, and the hills in this area remained for years government property used as free range for the cattle and hogs of local pioneers, as well as hunting ground for squatters.

Although his material was published a decade after that of Squier and Davis, author William Pidgeon claimed to have visited the Serpent Mound in 1832 in a book whose lengthy title can be abbreviated as *Traditions of De-coo-dah* (the name of his Native American friend and traveling companion). Pidgeon reported that his attention had been called to the structure by a Mr. James Black, another local resident and celebrated bee hunter. Pidgeon climbed the hill and had no trouble identifying the effigy: "It can not fail to present to the eye of the most skeptical observer, the form of an anaconda or huge snake, with wide distended jaws, in the act of devouring its prey."

Pidgeon, however, identified the oval structure at the very point of the serpent's plateau not as an egg, but as the effigy of another animal: a tortoise (do snakes eat tortoises?) that carried on its back an altar constructed of rocks. Pidgeon removed its surface stones and found larger stones "bearing the impress of intense heat." Thinking he might have discovered a furnace used to smelt ores, Pidgeon obtained a crowbar and some hand spikes and proceeded to excavate. He failed to find the "relic of metal" he was looking for and "was compelled to leave without coming to any satisfactory conclusion relative to the origin or use of the work."

When Squier and Davis arrived they noticed that some sort of stone structure had once existed in the middle of the oval in front of the serpent's open mouth, but they did not credit its destruction to scientific research. They recorded that the stones had been "thrown down and scattered by some ignorant visitor, under the prevailing impression probably that gold was hidden beneath them."

Little had changed at the Serpent Mound when Frederic Ward Putnam arrived with four fellow archaeologists in 1883. Putnam, born in Salem, Massachusetts, in 1839, had studied natural history at Harvard before turning his attention to the study of anthropology. He became curator of Harvard's Peabody Museum of Archaeology and Ethnology in 1875. He would later become curator of anthropology at the American Museum of Natural History in New York City. If Squier and Davis were the first to publish information on the Serpent Mound, Putnam became the Serpent Mound's popularizer when his article titled "The Serpent Mound of Ohio" appeared in the April 1890 volume of *The Century Magazine*, which had a much larger audience than the Smithsonian's publications.

Putnam and his colleagues traveled by wagon from the town of Hillsborough in neighboring Highland County, approaching the cliff where the serpent lay by fording Brush Creek. Putnam wrote that his party left their wagon and "scrambled up the steep hillside, and pushing on through brush and brier were soon following the folds of the great serpent along the hilltop."

The illustrations that accompanied Putnam's article were far more dramatic than the straight down, bird's-eye view used by Squier and Davis in their book. Putnam's illustrations clearly showed the height of the cliff and the slight angle of its plateau. They showed the graceful way that the serpent conformed to its location and provided some sense of its scale.

Frederic Ward Putnam (1839–1915), the scholar who popularized the Serpent Mound in a magazine article and became instrumental in its preservation.

Some of these same illustrations were used by E. O. Randall a few years later in his thin volume titled *The Serpent Mound: Adams County, Ohio*, which had the honor of being the first book entirely about the Serpent Mound written for tourists and published by the Ohio State Archaeological and Historical Society. In the prefatory note to his second edition, printed in 1907, Randall referred to himself as the book's "preparer" rather than author, noting that he was citing information from other authorities. This second edition, he added, had become necessary because his first thousand copies had sold out, so thirsty had the public then become for information on this particular antiquity.

Both Randall and Putnam observed that Nature had already placed a serpent image in this location long before prehistoric man arrived. When the edge of the promontory's cliff is viewed in profile from ground level, a jutting portion resembles a reptile's head. Perhaps this natural feature had caused ancient worshippers to regard the cliff as a sacred place worthy of a shrine, and inspired the construction of the effigy mound.

Randall thought that the serpent's promontory would have been easy to spot from a distance and that the serpent's builders had exploited another natural feature, the slightly slanted or tipped nature of the plateau, to make their effigy more of a beacon. He wrote that the structure had been positioned so that it

Two views of the Serpent Mound used to illustrate Frederic Putnam's article in the April 1890 issue of *The Century Magazine*. The illustrations show how the Serpent Mound was located on a cliff whose edge suggested the head of a snake.

"would easily be seen in all his majestic length and snake splendor from far and near on the plains below."

According to Squier and Davis, the Serpent Mound occupied an area pretty much devoid of other antiquities. Besides a single earthen mound and what they called a "platform, or large oval terrace," both located near the serpent's coiled tail, they could find only a few other mounds within six or eight miles, and no earthworks at all on the alluvial terraces of nearby streams, which were frequently the setting for other large-scale ruins elsewhere in Ohio.

Putnam's more extensive research in the area showed that people had indeed once lived nearby and they had left plenty of evidence of their habitation. Putnam discovered ashes, broken pottery, and chips and pieces of flint, jasper, quartz, and other rocks, evidently the detritus of tool making. He also unearthed completed tools such as hammers, knives, and what looked like long spear points. He found graves in which the skeletons appeared to have been deposited in a bundle. Putnam wrote, "All these things showed beyond question that there had been an ancient village... . As our explorations were continued we discovered that there had been dwellings and burials of different times."

At the oval or egg at the serpent's open mouth, Putnam also noticed the mess that Pidgeon had left behind. Putnam wrote, "Near the center of the inclosed area is a small mound of stones which was formerly much larger, since it was thrown down over fifty years ago by digging under it in search of supposed hidden treasure." From an "old gentleman," he learned that more vandalism had followed. At the base of the cliff there were stones that showed the same signs of fire as those left from the mound in the oval's center. Apparently it had become a local custom to heave the serpent's altar stones over the cliff. The various disturbances sometimes led other observers to identify the construction at this end of the monument as something other than an egg, including the effigy of another animal or an eye in the serpent's head.

Farther away from the effigy Putnam excavated a conical earthen mound. Beneath its soil he found a clay platform bearing evidence that a fire had been kindled and kept burning to produce a bed of ash. Putnam wrote, "When this ceremony was finished and enough ashes for the desired purpose had been obtained, the body of an adult man, nearly six feet tall, was placed, with the head to the east, at full length upon the hot ashes, and at once covered with the clay, smothering the still smoldering logs and changing the embers to charcoal." Putnam concluded that following this individual's funeral ceremonies the mound had been raised as a grave marker. He noted that nine other burials had been subsequently made in higher elevations of the same mound, identifying them as intrusive graves.

On a knoll commanding a nice view of the valley Putnam located a low oblong mound with four more burials under beds of ashes. East of this mound on a point of land extending south of the serpent plateau Putnam found several irregular groups of stones covering graves, as well as other stones marking the positions of ancient fireplaces that contained fragments of bone and stone splinters.

As for the Serpent Mound itself, Putnam exposed the edges of the effigy and excavated cross sections in both the oval and the body. He concluded that the effigy had been very carefully designed, its architects first creating an outline for their monument which they constructed in places with stones and elsewhere with clay mixed with ashes. Nearby he located the pits which had probably been the source of the clay.

Putnam did not report any occult dreams or visions in all his years of work in the area, but he did record that the place had a general spookiness. Putnam wrote, "Late in the afternoon, when the lights and shades are brought out in strong relief, the effect is indeed strange and weird; and this effect is heightened still more when the full moon lights up the scene, and the stillness is broken only by the 'whoo-whoo, hoo-hoo' of the unseen bird of night."

In Putnam's opinion, religious worship would have been the only possible motivation for the construction of something so carefully planned and executed. He suggested that the Serpent Mound was a shrine visited by pilgrims at specific times, its general vicinity also serving as a VIP cemetery where people honored certain individuals by burying their remains with ceremonial fanfare. Over time it might have become a place inhabited by later Native Americans "without any legendary knowledge or thought of the earlier worshipers at the shrine."

Putnam noted that serpents frequently served as religious symbols in ancient Mexico, Central America, South America, and the American Southwest. Nor did he fail to mention that the serpent was a common religious symbol in the ancient Old World. However Putnam declined to speculate on any possible connections, merely asking, "Is it all to be taken as mere coincidence in the development of a faith in America and in the Old World?"

In his book published a few years later, Randall mentioned that many primitive peoples regarded snakes with fear and awe. He, too, assumed a religious use for the Serpent Mound, proposing that sacrifices had been made at the site where fires were lighted which "would be seen for a great distance down the valley and would cast a glare over the whole region, producing a feeling of awe in the people who dwelt in the vicinity."

However to Randall the real purpose of the Serpent Mound would remain always a mystery. He wrote, "The great serpent still holds within his coils the secret of his existence as silent and impenetrable as the midnight hush of his solitary abode on the mountainside far above the plains and valleys."

In the course of the nineteenth century other ancient earthen mounds shaped like animals had been discovered in North America, mainly in Wisconsin. Squier and Davis included descriptions of many of them as well as a description and diagram of one other effigy mound located in Ohio popularly called the "Alligator," though their diagram made it look more like a bear rug with a long coiled tail. Squier and Davis noted that the effigy mounds in Wisconsin bore "some resemblance" to the effigy mounds in Ohio, but they stated firmly that the Ohio effigies "seem clearly of a different origin and dedicated to a different purpose."

Other mounds that could be snake effigies have been discovered more recently in Ohio, such as two possible structures in the valley below the hilltop earthwork known as Fort Ancient. Some have already been destroyed, like the one in Warren County that fell victim to the gravel excavation industry. Other possible remains of what might once have been serpent effigies have been identified elsewhere in the Midwest by persons flying in planes or studying photographs of terrain taken from the air.

The Serpent Mound still stands in Adams County mainly because Putnam made it his business to preserve it. In the time between Squier and Davis's visit and Putnam's arrival, a tornado had moved through the vicinity, taking down most of the trees. Although nature was reclaiming the area with an underbrush of redbuds and briers, the land had become much more attractive for cultivation since it had been relatively cleared. Learning that the landowner, a Mr. John Lovett, was planning to sell, Putnam agreed on a price and got a one-year option to come up with the money. Putnam was very grateful for the assistance of Miss Alice C. Fletcher, who together with other ladies of Boston solicited subscriptions during the winter of 1885–1886 and turned over approximately six thousand dollars by June. Roughly sixty acres of Ohio subsequently became the property of the Peabody Museum of Archaeology and Ethnology at Harvard University.

By the time Putnam's magazine article appeared in print, this acreage had been transformed into Serpent Mound Park, open to all visitors and exempt from taxation thanks to an act of the Ohio legislature. For the refreshment of picnickers, with whom the park was very quickly becoming popular, a spring house was constructed to protect the park's clear spring.

The Peabody returned the park to local management in 1900 by deeding it to the Ohio State Archaeological and Historical Society, which made further improvements. In 1908 the society constructed an observation tower so that visitors could get a clear view of the entire structure. In the 1930s the visitor facilities were improved, and in the 1960s the society added interpretive exhibits.

Today the Serpent Mound State Memorial is open year round during daylight hours. Its small museum closes during the winter. Besides the serpent, you can view several burial mounds located near the parking lot. There are a number of annual events, many coordinated by a local group called Friends of the Serpent Mound. Since 2009, the site has been managed by the Arc of Appalachia Preserve System in partnership with the Ohio History Connection.

A path allows visitors to follow the undulations of the Serpent Mound, over a quarer mile long. The best view is from the observation platform at this Ohio state memorial park and nature preserve. (*Author*)

In the later years of the twentieth century an interdisciplinary field of study called archaeoastronomy became popular, and a glance at the Serpent Mound's current website shows that the archaeoastronomers have not ignored this spot. One sentence reads, "There is some evidence for astronomical correlations that suggest an earthly acknowledgement of cosmic celestial events."

The team of Clark and Marjorie Hardman, who surveyed the Serpent Mound in the 1970s and published their findings in 1987, made the argument that the ancient builders of the effigy had so carefully designed and constructed it because it was an astronomical observatory that worked as a calendar to indicate the proper timing for planting, harvesting, or other annual events. The Hardmans speculated that the builders might have first constructed the oval, or egg, and then used its short and long diameters as units of measure for the length of the snake's undulations as well as the spacing between them. Sighting through the middle of each of these undulations put one in position to view the major solar horizon positions throughout the year, including the summer and winter solstices and the spring and autumn equinoxes.

From their vantage point at the serpent's elevated plateau, ancient celebrants could also watch the sun touch a knob on the distant horizon at sunset on the summer solstice and see it progress along a ridge at sunset from the autumn equinox to the winter solstice. The Hardmans suggested that archaeologists examine these two locations for evidence of prehistoric activity such as the construction of markers that might have been visible from the Serpent Mound.

Other scholars have examined the Serpent Mound for solar alignments, including Robert Fletcher and Terry Cameron, who published an article in 1988 demonstrating that a line drawn from the middle of the serpent's gaping jaw through the middle of the egg would also point to the position of the sun at sunset on the summer solstice and run right through the spot where both Pidgeon and Putnam had discovered evidence of a pile of stones with burn marks that seemed like an altar. Fletcher and Cameron also argued that some of the serpent's undulations were aligned with certain solstice and equinox solar events.

The archaeoastronomers have not been without critics. Civil engineer James A. Marshall, who had spent many years mapping and surveying the remains of prehistoric constructions in the Midwest, criticized the Hardmans in a 1999 article mainly because they had examined only the Serpent Mound, which to him constituted a "completely inadequate database." In Marshall's opinion they and others had gone too far with their assumptions by not starting with accurate and thorough topographic maps.

Regardless of how you may feel about the profession of archaeoastronomy, you can celebrate the solstices at the Serpent Mound. There are various events at the summer solstice, and on the evening of the winter solstice the Friends of the Serpent Mound organize the placement of hundreds of luminaries surrounding the serpent, which brightly outline its shape after the sun goes down. Many folks also visit to celebrate the autumn and spring equinoxes.

Putnam was looking not at the sky but at the ground when he attempted to date the Serpent Mound. Having found no artifacts when he dug around or through the effigy, he concluded it had been constructed by the same people who had built some of the nearby burial mounds, one of two separate peoples that he realized had occupied the general area at different times. By the turn of the twentieth century these particular burial mound builders had been christened the Adena Culture by scholars. Up through the middle of the twentieth century, archaeologists examining the artifacts found by Putnam or found elsewhere at the site tended to agree that the Serpent Mound had been an Adena structure.

In 1985 when the Fletcher and Cameron team were studying the Serpent Mound's possible astronomical alignments, they were also trying to date the effigy. One way to accomplish this would be to compare its alignments with astronomical data for different time periods, but by this time in the history of archaeology, radiocarbon dating was a superior alternative. The technology had long been in use and by then could be applied to carbon samples that were very small. Knowing that the Serpent Mound had a layer of clay, ash, and stone, Fletcher and Cameron worked with Bradley Lepper of the Ohio Historical Society and Dee Ann Wymer of Bloomsburg University on limited excavation and core sampling in July 1991.

Having found several pieces of charcoal in what appeared to be undisturbed sections of the mound, they submitted them for radiocarbon dating. The results indicated that the Serpent Mound was a little over nine hundred years old, having been built around AD 1070, plus or minus seventy years.

This meant that the Serpent Mound had nothing to do with the earlier Adena people. It had not existed then. The Serpent Mound belonged to another people who had inhabited a village whose remains were about one hundred yards south of the effigy, a people whom archaeologists had since named the Fort Ancient Culture.

The Serpent Mound is a good fit with what is known about Fort Ancient society. Fort Ancient peoples were centrally governed by chiefs and ruling families, an organization that would have facilitated a large-scale building project like the Serpent Mound. The Fort Ancient peoples were known to have cultivated maize, and therefore might have found an astronomical calendar useful. And among the artifacts that Fort Ancient peoples left behind elsewhere were a number of gorgets, or ornaments worn at the throat or on the breast, that were sometimes decorated with snake motifs.

If the 1070 date is correct, inspiration for the Serpent Mound might have come from the cosmos itself. Its builders might have witnessed light from the supernova that produced the Crab Nebula which reached earth in 1054 and remained visible for two weeks. Then in 1066 Halley's Comet made its regular appearance that occurs every seventy-six years.

On the other hand, anyone who wanted to hang on to an earlier date for the Serpent Mound could claim that Fort Ancient peoples had stumbled across an existing effigy just as Pidgeon, Putman, and Squier and Davis had. This might have inspired them to settle down in the area and patch up the monument for their own ceremonial use. Author Ross Hamilton makes such a claim in his book titled *The Mystery of the Serpent Mound* published in 2001. According to Hamilton, the presence of charcoal that can be dated to AD 1070 simply means that someone happened to be burning a fire at the site at that time. His own estimate for the age of the Serpent Mound is forty-five hundred to five thousand years: "as old as the pyramids of Egypt, perhaps older."

Hamilton concurred with other scholars that the Serpent Mound had a religious purpose and provided some insight into his own spiritual studies. He wrote of having been initiated by a "Master of Spiritual Science" and said he had experienced insights and visions. In the 1970s he studied alchemy. He got interested in the Serpent Mound through the Great Serpent Mound Chapter of the American Society of Dowsers, who argued that there were present at points on the serpent's body what they called "blind springs," or subterranean collections of water and magnetic energy, as well as lines of energy converging in the oval at the serpent's head.

When I started reading *The Mystery of the Serpent Mound*, I expected to dismiss Hamilton as some crackpot like von Daniken or the folks who predicted with confidence that the world would end on December 21, 2012, based on the ancient Mayan calendar. However the sheer volume of his research made this impossible. Also, in cases where Hamilton and I had examined the same sources, I could find nothing to complain about. For example, Hamilton correctly identified Putnam and synopsized his research and writings.

Hamilton respects the practitioners of archaeoastronomy and what they can teach us about prehistoric science. He acknowledged that his study of the Serpent Mound was helped along by his acquaintance with William F. Romain, who published a map of the Serpent Mound in 1987 and discovered that a line drawn from the tip of the serpent's tail through the apex of the roughly triangular shape in its head would run true north and point to the North Star, Polaris.

However, at the time that Hamilton reckoned the Serpent Mound to have been built, the Earth's polestar, or star located directly over the North Pole that appears not to move in the night sky, was not Polaris but a star called Thuban, or Draconis-alpha. Hamilton had been comparing maps of the Serpent Mound to astronomical charts and had discovered that the star pattern of the constellation Draco matched the shape of the Serpent Mound. As for the star Thuban, it could be mapped to a point not on the mound itself, but at the center of the undulation equidistant from both ends of the serpent, or at the dead center of a circle one could draw around the effigy touching its outermost points. Hamilton wrote, "Thus the so-divided Great Serpent, imagined as a mythological constellation, would have rotated with precision around the highest point of the northern sky, like clock hands sweeping the dome."

Hamilton acknowledged that serpent icons had been employed in many ancient cultures, but for him the appearance of serpents in Greek cosmology was more than coincidental. Hamilton argued that the Serpent Mound was a repository of not only astronomical lore but also Pythagorean geometry. He also managed to find the various symbols of the Greek alphabet among the serpent's curves and angles. He stopped short of stating that the ancient Greeks built the Serpent Mound, simply noting that there's some sort of connection we do not now understand. Elsewhere in his book he suggested that the builders of the Serpent Mound had been the ancient and mysterious race who had lived on in the oral history of the Lenape or Delaware Indians as the Allegewi.

If you want to question or debate Ross Hamilton, you just might run into him at the Serpent Mound. In 2009 the site's acting assistant manager reported that during warmer weather Hamilton was frequently at the site, where he was willing to chat with visitors and give informal talks. Sometimes he draws quite a crowd. In 2011, he was one of the speakers at the summer solstice celebration. I have never heard him speak, but I was able to watch video clips of one of his on-site lectures that appeared on one episode of a television program called *Telepathic TV* which had been uploaded to YouTube.

The question of the Serpent's age is still not settled. As recently as 2011 a team of scientists that included William F. Romain obtained more charcoal samples for testing which suggested that the Serpent Mound had been constructed about twenty-three hundred years ago but renovated some fourteen hundred years later. So while that still would not make it as old as Ross Hamilton supposed, the Serpent Mound could have been originally built by Adena people and spruced up by Fort Ancient folks. Or perhaps it was really constructed by Fort Ancient builders using debris they dug out of old Adena fire pits.

Hamilton was not the only scholar to note that the Serpent Mound had been constructed in a geologically special place, not only upon an elevated plateau, but at the edge of a crypto explosion feature, or an area where the bedrock was fractured and deformed. Crypto explosion features exist in several places on the globe, and geologists have two theories as to how they are formed: by impact from an asteroid or meteorite, or by a powerful underground explosion of gases. No one has ever witnessed the process taking place.

It was not until 2003 that the Ohio Department of Natural Resources released the news that a team of geologists concluded that it had been a meteorite that created what had come to be called the Serpent Mound Disturbance. The impact would have occurred between 248 to 286 million years ago, back when the modern continents were joined together in one big continent that today's scholars have named Pangea. Though dissenters exist, it's the general consensus that the builders of the Serpent Mound did not become inspired by or even recognize this geological anomaly.

My husband and I first visited the Serpent Mound in 2007, about the time that I was starting in earnest my research on Mound Builder cultures in the Midwest. The state memorial's signage reflected what was then accepted knowledge: that the effigy had been constructed circa AD 1000 by peoples of the Fort Ancient Culture on the edge of a massive asteroid crater. Another sign commemorated the part Putnam had played there. We visited the small museum and shop then walked the path that winds around the serpent. Our fellow visitors included no New Agers but rather families with children who seemed less interested in the effigy mound than in looking down from as close as they could possibly come to the edge of the cliff. We experienced nothing supernatural.

We had a difficult time seeing a serpent or any other shape in the low curving mound of earth until we climbed the observation tower. Then we saw it: a giant twisting snake. We both wondered how Pidgeon, or Squier and Davis, or anybody else had figured out what it was if they could view it only from ground level.

I had been studying the Mound Builder cultures on and off since the winter of 1993 when my husband and I were briefly residing in Warren County, Ohio, while he was on a consulting assignment for a business there. As I would regularly drive to a shopping center outside the town of Lebanon, I'd pass a sign pointing the way to Fort Ancient. At the time I was writing a book about Valley Forge, so I assumed Fort Ancient had to be some old fort constructed during the Indian wars that had been fought in this area in the wake of the American Revolution. I would have stopped in to see Fort Ancient, but the site was closed for the winter season.

A member of the county convention and visitors' bureau heard that an author who wrote about history and travel was visiting, and kindly called to ask if there were any local attractions I wanted to see while I was in town. When I brought up Fort Ancient, she called back to confirm that the site's outdoor facilities were closed, but that the site manager would be glad to meet me at the visitors' center.

I had studied Classical and Near Eastern archaeology in college. I had read books and viewed documentaries about the Incas and the Aztecs, as well as the pre-Columbian Native American societies of America's Southwest. But I had not grown up in Ohio, where kids study about Mound Builder cultures in grade school and folks picnic in the parks surrounding Mound Builder sites just like people in the Philadelphia area do at Valley Forge. East Coast gal that I was, it amazed me to find a man-made structure in Ohio that had been there for over two thousand years.

Wanting to learn more, I asked the Fort Ancient site manager for a bibliography, which he mailed to me a few days later. It was six pages long, so there was plenty of material, but most of it was in books on state and local history, or in the publications of state and local historical societies. A lot of the material dated from the 1880s to the 1930s. There were two national magazines on the bibliography, namely *American Heritage* and *National Geographic*, but the articles with information on Fort Ancient dated from 1953 and 1972, respectively. No wonder I had never heard of the place.

As I began to read about Fort Ancient, both the site and the culture, and the two other Mound Builder cultures now known as Adena and Hopewell, I came to appreciate the evolution of their interpretation. Eighteenth- and nineteenth-century traders, soldiers, missionaries, and prospective farmers entering the Midwest had shared my wonderment that it had ancient ruins. Since the Indians then living among these ruins failed to claim credit, America had engaged in an intellectual debate over who might have built them. Among the many creative theories advanced was the idea that they were the work of colonists or refugees from the Eastern Hemisphere, possibly Egyptians, Romans, Hindus, or you name it, who somehow got lost and ended up in America.

It so happened that the earthen antiquities were being discovered at just the time that the Western world was developing a fascination with the history of its own civilization. During the eighteenth and early nineteenth centuries the ruins of Greece and recently rediscovered Roman Pompeii inspired artists and architects. Napoleon's brief conquest of Egypt and the wonders that his attendant scholars recorded brought the ancient pharaohs to the attention of Europeans and Americans. Many people purchased furniture and knickknacks inspired by the ancient world to decorate dwellings embellished with architectural ornament that looked like it came from classical temples. In America, settlers had taken to naming their new towns after ancient cities, such as Memphis, Athens, Syracuse, and Rome. Abraham Lincoln grew up not far from an Illinois river town called Cairo.

In 1862 when President Lincoln delivered what we now call the State of the Union address, he brought up the vast territory that he called the "body of the Republic" which was bordered by the Allegheny Mountains, the Rockies, Canada, and the "line along which the culture of corn and cotton meets," warning what a dissolution of the Republic might mean to the ten million people living there. What phrase did he use to suggest the rich potential of this area? He called it "this Egypt of the West."

As the nineteenth century progressed, archaeology and anthropology matured into scholarly professions. Their more modern practitioners reexamined and overturned the theories about pre-Columbian European lost civilizations, embracing the notion that Native Americans had constructed the Midwestern earthworks, mounds, and effigies. Like Putnam, other scholars began to realize that the remains had been left behind by different groups at different times. The peoples who had collectively been called Mound Builders evolved into three distinct groups. New scientific techniques allowed scholars to begin assigning time frames to the Adena, Hopewell, and Fort Ancient cultures and speculating on the relationships among them.

Today's archaeologists have remarkable new, and often noninvasive, technologies at their disposal enabling them to gather new data and reassess long held interpretations, but even though archaeology can claim a greater lay following than any other science, the general public hears very little about what is going on. Scholars in academia spend a great deal of time reviewing each other's arguments, thus refining and advancing them, but then they produce articles fraught with jargon that are published in professional journals that the layman does not read. Thanks to legislation passed from the 1960s to the present, federal and state agencies have hired or contracted archaeologists to identify and mitigate the destruction of cultural resources when public money is spent on development. These archaeologists produce their own reports and data bases that academic scholars may disdain as "gray" (that is, un-peer-reviewed) literature, if they ever even see them. Needless to say, the layman does not read these, either.

Now and then someone comes up with an intriguing theory that may be brilliant, or may be totally unjustified, but one that catches on with the public and sells a lot of books and videos. The professionals may or may not give it the time of day. Fourteen years following its publication, the only reviews I could find of Ross Hamilton's *Mystery of the Serpent Mound* were customer reviews on Amazon. Don't get me wrong; I am not buying Hamilton's theory that the Greek alphabet was encoded in the body of the Serpent Mound, but like the work of Putnam, Squier, Davis, Fletcher, Cameron, Lepper, Wymer, and the Hardmans, his thesis, right or wrong, is part of the site's fascinating history.

My focus is on how we came to think what we do rather than the wisdom currently prevailing, which can change with the next significant discovery. This book grew out of my research into the writings and interpretations made by those Americans who discovered the Mound Builders as well as those who subsequently shaped our understanding of these particular Native American cultures, and their place in the larger story of prehistoric humans in the Western Hemisphere. And it's also my personal journey through a physical and intellectual landscape that can confidently be called the birthplace of American archaeology.

2

Genteel Virginia Gets
News from the Frontier

While serving in the Continental Congress, Thomas Jefferson was among its members to receive a questionnaire from a man named François Marbois, secretary of the French legation to the United States of America. Since that title made Marbois extremely important to anyone interested in the success of America's Revolutionary War effort, Jefferson took the time to gather information that would answer Monsieur Marbois's questions. In 1781 and 1782 Thomas Jefferson drafted and finalized the manuscript that would eventually be recognized as one of the most important books written by an eighteenth-century American. Today's historians call it *Notes on the State of Virginia*, a convenient abbreviation of its original lengthy title.

Among other information, Marbois had asked that his respondents provide "a description of the Indians established in [the] State." The facts and figures Jefferson collected told a sad story of steeply declining populations. He replied that when the first British settlements had been created in 1607, over forty Indian tribes were living between the colony's mountains and sea coast. The most powerful among them he identified as the Powhatans, the Mannahoacs, and the Monacans. Jefferson summarized a census conducted in 1669 indicating that by that time only about one third of the original known Indian population was left. Jefferson attributed the trend to "spirituous liquors, the small-pox, war, and an abridgement of territory."

Another statement in *Notes on the State of Virginia* shows that Jefferson was convinced that America's disappearing Indians had not left very much behind. He wrote, "I know of no such thing existing as an Indian monument; for I would not honor with that name arrow points, stone hatchets, stone pipes and half-shapen images. Of labor on the large scale, I think there is no remain as respectable as would be a common ditch for the draining of lands." Within a few more years, Jefferson was probably wishing he had never put into print a statement so demonstrably false, but at the time that he was working on *Notes on the State of Virginia*, news was just beginning to be published by men who had traveled beyond the frontier of British civilization to places in North America where they had come face to face with the mysterious remains of "labor on the large scale." Jefferson apparently missed the first few opportunities to learn about them.

David Zeisberger was a member of the Moravian Church, which was among the first Protestant churches to send missionaries to the American Indians. After Zeisberger immigrated to America, he spent over sixty years in the backwoods of New York and Pennsylvania. In 1771 he traveled to the Muskingum River, a tributary of the Ohio River, where he founded three missions and remained until 1781 when he was driven away by soldiers during the hostilities of the American Revolution. He returned to the area in 1798 and stayed there until his death in 1808.

Zeisberger described earthworks constructed along the Muskingum which he assumed to have been fortifications around a long vanished town. He also described nearby earthen mounds as "not natural, but made by the hand of man." To Zeisberger, they seemed to be crowned with hollow depressions which he interpreted as places of refuge for women and children in times of enemy attack. Jefferson might have found his speculations interesting, but Zeisberger was just in the process of compiling them at his mission on the Muskingum in 1779 and 1780. They would not be published until many years later.

The wilderness experiences of the Rev. David Jones were already a matter of public record, the author having published a book in 1774 shortly before he became pastor of the Great Valley Baptist Church in Pennsylvania. Jones had been born in Delaware in 1736 and ordained in 1766. The missions he undertook in 1772 and 1773 took him into territory northwest of the Ohio River where he attempted to preach to Shawnee and Delaware Indians then living there. He abandoned his missions after having enjoyed little success, but he published his experiences for an intended audience of other pastors to inspire them to take up the task of converting Indians.

Just north of the Shawnee town Jones spelled "Cillicaathee" he reported seeing what he took to be an old wall enclosing a square-shaped space of about fifteen acres. It had openings at each corner and in the middle of its sides, one of which connected to a ten-acre space with a spring that was enclosed by a circular entrenchment. Jones concluded that the area had been "inhabited by a martial race of mankind enjoying the use of iron, for such entrenchments, as appear in various places, could not have been made otherwise: but of this part of antiquity we shall remain ignorant."

Jones is also believed to have been the author of an unsigned letter published in the *Royal American Magazine* in 1775 describing another structure which he had heard about from a local trader. This letter describes a fort "situated towards the head waters of the River Sciota [sic] which empties into the Ohio on the N.W." Although the author had not seen this fort himself, he did possess a plan drawn by a man he trusted who had explored it on horseback. The accompanying drawing, perhaps the first published dia-

"A Plan of an Old Fort and Intrenchment in the Shawnee Country, Taken on Horseback, by Computation Only," appeared in the January 1775 issue of the *Royal American Magazine*. This map, dated October 17, 1772, may have been the first plan of an ancient earthwork published in America. Compare this with Caleb Atwater's map on page 56. This diagram is much cruder, but illustrates the orientation of the earthwork with the bank of the Scioto River.

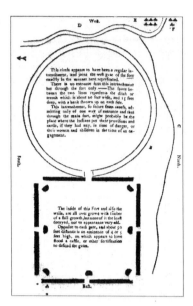

gram of Mound Builder remains, showed a square "fort" pierced by eight openings, one of which led to a circular "intrechment" where the writer assumed the builders had stored their provisions and livestock, as well as their women and children, when under attack. The writer also made the point that the Delaware and Shawnee who now lived nearby had not built the remains, nor could they explain them; moreover, those who had built them were "doubtless better skilled in the arts of fortification and architecture than the present inhabitants."

Jonathan Carver wrote a book called *Travels Through the Interior Parts of North-America in the Years 1766, 1767 and 1768*, which was widely read and discussed in Europe and America following its initial publication in London in 1778. Unlike Jones and Zeisberger, Jonathan Carver was a military man whose career had begun in the Massachusetts militia in the 1750s. He had expected to be paid by the British army for his explorations, and probably conceived the idea of publishing his travel journals when reimbursement no longer seemed to be forthcoming.

Carver wrote about an earthwork he had discovered on the shore of the Mississippi about four feet high and covered with grass that he supposed had been a military breastwork, noting that it was oriented with its rear to the water and its front poised to oppose enemies approaching by land. His conversations with backwoods traders confirmed that they had seen similar structures and reached the same conclusions. Carver mused, "How a work of this kind could exist in a country that has hitherto (according to the general received opinion) been the seat of war to the untutored Indians alone, whose whole stock of military knowledge has only, till within two centuries, amounted to drawing the bow, and whose only breast-work even at present is the thicket, I know not."

Unfortunately Carver died in 1780 and was not on hand to defend his book against questions that would later be raised about the accuracy of his descriptions, not to mention whether he was their actual author.

Jefferson would not have had to read a book to learn about the frontier from a fellow Virginian with firsthand experience, namely George Washington. Jefferson had probably been acquainted with Washington since 1769 when he first entered Virginia's House of Burgesses, and the events of the American Revolution would give him far more opportunity to work with this man whose presidential administration he would serve as secretary of state.

In 1748, while Jefferson was still a boy and Washington just sixteen, the future father of our country was already embarked on a career as surveyor of the large estate of Lord Thomas Fairfax. Washington traveled via pack horse through the Blue Ridge Mountains into the Shenandoah Valley, gaining the experience that might have led to his appointment in 1753 by Governor Robert Dinwiddie to reconnoiter the system of forts that the French had constructed in the Ohio Valley. French officials graciously received Washington when he visited Fort Venango, but firmly declined the British suggestion that they withdraw from the region. Washington returned to the area during the resulting French and Indian War in 1754 and 1755 as a lieutenant colonel in the Virginia militia serving in two failed military campaigns: the confrontation at Fort Necessity and Braddock's defeat.

Having become familiar with the area, Washington became anxious to get it opened for settlement and linked with British ports on the East Coast. As a member of Virginia's House of Burgesses, he advocated a plan to connect the Potomac to the Monongahela River with a canal. Washington was among the many Americans who thought that the decisive British victory over rebellious Native Americans at Bushy Run in 1763 should have opened the West for British expansion, and he joined with others to petition the British crown for land grants in America's interior. They were stymied by the British Proclamation Line of 1763, which was intended to placate the Indians by prohibiting white settlement beyond the Appalachians.

Remaining interested in western real estate development, Washington again journeyed into the interior in the fall of 1770. In the previous year, a number of powerful and important Englishmen and Americans had joined forces to form the Grand Ohio Company to establish a new western colony to be called Vandalia. This project would incorporate land claimed by the earlier Ohio Company of Virginia as well as land intended as bounty for the veterans of the Virginia Regiment, plus one other land company of which Washington was a member. Washington traveled from Mount Vernon to Fort Pitt, and down the Ohio to the Great Kanawha.

Washington's journey took him past the mouth of the Muskingum, where Zeisberger would record the existence of ancient earthworks just a few years later. Washington's party spent several days exploring the Kanawha, some members venturing about twenty miles upstream. They also gathered information from the local Indians about what the land was like as far as the river's falls, located about fifty or sixty miles farther upstream, in the general area where ancient remains would later be recorded in West Virginia. Washington made detailed daily notes about this journey, noting the location of fertile bottom land, possible mill sites, and the flora and fauna that he encountered. He wrote that the Muskingum was 150 yards wide at its mouth and navigable by canoe a good distance upstream. He also noted what kinds of timber grew on the banks of the Kanawha. Yet Washington's personal diaries are completely lacking any descriptions of ancient ruins that he might have witnessed himself or heard about from other members of his party. It's not possible that Washington was ignorant of them; more likely their existence simply made no difference to his plans to develop the area.

In the years following victory in the American Revolution, the government of the new United States began to lay the groundwork to accomplish Washington's dream: to settle the West. These efforts increased the number of explorers heading in that direction, often in more official capacities. Thomas Jefferson was by that time in Paris where he had agreed to go in 1784 to spend the next five years as American minister to France. It's a tribute to the reputation of Jefferson that during his tenure much news coming in about ancient American ruins is preserved in his correspondence, as though by that stage in his life, any extraordinary or intellectually mystifying discoveries had to be reported to him.

Ezra Stiles, president of the educational institution that would become Yale University, wrote to Jefferson enclosing a letter from a General Samuel Holden Parsons dated April 1786. Parsons had spent the previous winter in the region bordering the Ohio River. He had ventured to a place called Big Bone Creek where he had gathered several hundred pounds of bones of extinct animals. He happened to mention "numerous remains of fortifications in that country" and artifacts that included pottery and even bricks. The size of the trees growing on the structures suggested that they had been abandoned before Columbus sailed. He enclosed a diagram of the complex at the mouth of the Muskingum River, not far from where Americans by then had established a military post called Fort Harmar. Parsons also mentioned "numerous mounds of Earth erected in conical forms, to the height of 70 or 80 F. [feet], containing the bones of the Dead." In his cover letter, Stiles set down his opinion that such evidence showed "that there have been European or Asiatic Inhabitants there in antient ages, altho' long extirpated."

In April 1787, Charles Thomson, who had been secretary of the Continental Congress, enclosed a letter from John Cleves

Symmes that he thought Jefferson might find interesting. In February of that year Symmes, who lived in a remote town called Louisville in what was then still Virginia, wrote about what he had seen himself in the wilderness and what he had heard from others including "Captain Carver." He described extraordinary "temples" at Grave Creek, which emptied into the Ohio River, similar to those discovered by the Spaniards in Mexico, and the remains of a town near the banks of the Monongahela which had been surrounded by an earthen wall. He included news of entrenchments on the banks of the Muskingum and the Mississippi. He wrote of graves of uncommon size that yielded up "many human bones" when opened. Symmes's letter added his thesis that the ancestors of the natives of Mexico had once resided in the Ohio Valley, but had been cleared out by more savage nations of the North. He commented, "Their laudable struggle and patriotism appear very evidently from the numerous lines of fortifications, forts, and strongholds, that remain in many parts of the Country, for it is well known that the modern Indians of North America never fortify." He suggested that these proto-Mexicans had descended the Ohio and then the Mississippi to the Gulf of Mexico, where they had reestablished themselves and flourished.

The ancient remains on Grave Creek and the Muskingum were also described by a young medical student named Benjamin Smith Barton in his 1787 monograph titled *Observations on Some Parts of Natural History*. Barton called attention to "the artificial mounts or eminences which are scattered over the Western Parts of North America." A large mound at Grave Creek he described as a "stupendous eminence . . . composed of huge quantities of earth." While the local Indians could not explain the Grave Creek mound, Barton recorded that they regarded it with "veneration," though he also observed that they tended to be a superstitious lot inclined to accord the same degree of awe to natural features like mountains and waterfalls that they had for technological manmade objects like timepieces. Barton included a map of the earthworks on the Muskingum which he interpreted as the remains of an ancient town. Its ten-foot walls were punctuated at the sides and corners by "chasms," enclosing three "elevations" each about six feet high.

Nearby there were mysterious caves and a burial ground.

Barton's own conclusion was that these structures had been built by ancient Danes. He speculated that these people, who were famous as seafarers, might have voyaged across the Atlantic to Labrador and gradually migrated south where they became incorporated into the Toltec civilization in Mexico.

Barton did not communicate directly with Jefferson, but he might have been hoping that Jefferson would read his book since he went out of his way to describe Jefferson in the text as "a gentleman of distinction, and of profound philosophical as well as of political knowledge."

By that time, the American Philosophical Society, whose members were learned scientists and scholars, had come into being from an earlier idea for an academy of scholars proposed by Philadelphia's Quaker botanist John Bartram in 1739. Following a few meetings in the 1740s, interest had lagged until the 1760s when an attempted revival was soon sidelined by the American Revolution and its aftermath. Benjamin Franklin finally got the American Philosophical Society up and running in the mid-1780s and served as its president until his death in 1790. It occurred to Jefferson that the members of this organization were precisely the people who should be studying the kind of information that had been coming in to him. In 1787 he wrote to Charles Thomson with a suggestion that the American Philosophical Society collect descriptions of all known Indian monuments. However Jefferson wanted more fact-gathering and less speculation. He expressed his wish that "the persons who go thither [West] would make very exact descriptions of what they see of that kind, without forming any theories.... It is too early to form theories on those antiquities."

John Bartram's son William had been a corresponding member of the 1760s version of the American Philosophical Society as well as a student of Charles Thomson. He moved to Cape Fear River in North Carolina where he set up a trading post and a base for extensive travel to research natural history in the southeast during the 1770s. His 1791 book, *Travels Through North and South*

Carolina, with its exciting accounts of camping out alone in alligator country, also informed Americans that ancient remains could be found in that part of the country.

Bartram wrote about a visit to Lake George years before when "all appeared wild and savage." There a "magnificent Indian mound" was linked by an "Indian highway" three-quarters of a mile long through an orange grove and a live oak forest to an artificial lake. He also discovered conical mounds and earthen terraces while traveling up the Savannah River. One large mound forty or fifty feet high had a flat top reached by a spiral path from ground level. Bartram interpreted niches carved into the mound facing the four cardinal points as sentry boxes where lookouts could be stationed.

In 1793 the *Transactions of the American Philosophical Society* published a 1791 letter from a Major Jonathan Heart to Benjamin Smith Barton, who was by that time a medical school professor in Philadelphia nurturing a lifelong interest in Native Americans. Heart had heard of the ancient artifacts on and near the Mississippi and had himself seen the ancient works at the mouth of the Muskingum and at Grave Creek. The major reinforced the idea that ancient remains were more numerous and widespread than previously imagined, writing, "The common mounts, or Indian graves, or monuments (for they are not always found to contain bones), are scattered over the whole country, particularly along the Ohio, and its main branches: indeed, I have scarcely ever seen an handsome situation on an high flat, adjoining any large stream, where there were not some of the above mentioned vestiges of antiquity."

Jefferson might have appreciated Heart's very restrained speculation regarding the identity of the builders. "I can only give my opinion negatively," Heart wrote, declaring that the earthworks could not have been constructed by explorer Hernando de Soto, nor any other European, Asian, or African in the years since America's discovery by Columbus. He did not think they had been constructed by "present Indians or their predecessors; or some traditions would have remained as to their uses." Heart did allow that the builders "were not altogether in a state of uncivilization: they must have been under the subordination of law, a strict and well governed police, or they could not have been kept together in such numerous bodies, and made to contribute to the carrying on of such stupendous works."

By 1799 Jefferson had himself become president of the American Philosophical Society, which by then had established a "Committee to Collect Information Respecting the Past and Present State of this Country." The society's transactions published that year contained a circular letter listing the priorities of this committee, which included obtaining "accurate plans, drawings and descriptions of whatever is interesting, (where the originals cannot be had) and especially of ancient Fortifications, Tumuli, and other Indian works of art: ascertaining the materials composing them, their contents, the purposes for which they were probably designed, &c." By the time Meriwether Lewis and William Clark were about to begin their famous voyage of discovery, Jefferson was president of the United States, using the power of his office to instruct them to gather information on Indian monuments.

In the 1790s, people began sending Jefferson not just news and descriptions of artifacts, but actual artifacts that had been unearthed by the region's first farmers and laborers. A land agent in Kentucky sent a small stone figurine of a woman kneeling to give birth. From Tennessee came male and female busts. Jefferson displayed the artifacts in the entrance hall at Monticello, later adding specimens collected during the expedition of Lewis and Clark. Jefferson began to call this space "an Indian Hall," arguably America's first Native American museum, thereby elevating the "half-shapen images" he had once disdained to works of art.

There's a family tradition that several objects at the modern Monticello were part of Jefferson's original Native American collection. However what happened to the contents of Jefferson's Indian Hall remains unclear. There is evidence that Jefferson planned to donate materials to the University of Virginia where they could be preserved in a real museum setting, but no formal records were kept of the disposition of Jefferson's Native American artifacts after his death.

When the Thomas Jefferson Foundation planned to decorate

Monticello's entrance hall so that it would look like it did during Jefferson's residence, the foundation partnered with the Peabody Museum of Archaeology and Ethnology at Harvard University to have new pieces created by Indian artists. Today visitors see examples of hide painting, weaponry, decorated smoking pipes, and quillwork, which the guides describe as being similar to objects collected by Lewis and Clark.

In Jefferson's book *Notes on the State of Virginia*, his statement that he knew of no Indian monument as impressive as a common drainage ditch is followed by a colon and the qualifying phrase, "Unless indeed it be the Barrows, of which many are to be found all over this country [meaning Virginia]." Eighteenth-century Englishmen used the word *barrows* to describe the mass burial mounds they had discovered when they began establishing plantations in Virginia's Piedmont region.

Jefferson also included in his book a description of an incident that had occurred when he was a boy. Whether he witnessed the event himself or simply heard it reported, it made a profound impression that stayed with him a very long time. Jefferson wrote that some Indians passing through Albemarle County had strayed off the main road and made a six-mile detour through the woods to visit one such barrow. There they had remained for some time with sorrowful expressions on their faces before continuing on their way. His implication was that they knew exactly where to find the graves of their ancestors and had a tradition of paying their respects to the dead.

In *Notes on the State of Virginia*, Jefferson described this particular mound (which came to be called the Jefferson Mound) as being forty feet wide and seven and a half feet high, surrounded by a ditch five feet deep and five feet wide. He called it "spheroidical" and stated that before this piece of ground had been placed under cultivation, trees twelve inches in diameter had covered it. Jefferson estimated that the mound had once been twelve feet high and noted that it had been situated "on the low grounds of the Rivanna [River], about two miles above its principal fork, and opposite to some hills on which had been an Indian town."

Jefferson went on to describe digging into several parts of this mound and finding masses of human bones, not neatly laid out as the English buried their dead, but "in the utmost confusion ... entangled and held together in clusters by the earth," as though they had been dumped there "from a bag or a basket," and subsequently covered with dirt. The bones of adults and children were jumbled together, some so decayed that they disintegrated at the touch. Jefferson next dug a cut through the mound wide enough to walk through, so that he could examine the layers of earth forming the mound. He concluded that the Indians had created the mound by covering the bones of their dead (which had been cleaned of flesh at some other place by some other process) with stones from a nearby cliff and river, fol-

Charles Willson Peale's 1791 portrait of Secretary of State Thomas Jefferson. Jefferson's exploration of one of Virginia's Native American "barrows" prompted some biographers to call him the Father of American Archaeology. (*Independence National Historical Park*)

lowed by a layer of earth. Jefferson estimated that they had repeated this process frequently enough to bury the remains of a thousand humans in this mound. He also was convinced that contrary to prevailing British opinion, this was not a mass grave of warriors fallen in some battle, due to the absence of wounds that might have been made "with bullets, arrows, or other weapons."

Jefferson's groundbreaking employment of the now universal practice of what modern archaeologists call stratigraphy and his intelligent conclusions about the remains he examined show he was thinking like a scientist. Such an attitude also explains why he had been warning about premature speculation on the question that was obviously on everyone's mind: what was the relationship, if any, between burial mounds visited by contemporary Indians and the abandoned and seemingly older mounds and earthworks farther west? It certainly explains why Jefferson was the go-to guy on antiquities in his own day and has since earned a mention in just about every book on the history of archaeology and sometimes the title Father of American Archaeology.

Jefferson's mound was located in what had been the territory of the Monacan tribes, whom earlier British settlers had been studying for the sake of their own continued wellbeing. Early explorers had identified five Monacan villages named Mowhemcho, Monahassanugh, and Massinacack on the James River, Rassawek at the junction of the James and the Rivanna, and Monasukapanough on the Rivanna. They had observed that these Indians hunted, fished, farmed, and constructed their villages on fertile bottom land. They had learned that their mortuary rituals included the custom of burying their dead twice: first to begin rotting off flesh, then in an earthen mound ossuary located in a place that seemed to have been selected for its commanding view.

The British had also discovered that the Monacans tended to be standoffish. Not long after they had been discovered and studied by Englishmen, they began moving away. Modern scholars have speculated that the British inadvertently disrupted the market for the copper that the Monacans had mined or traded by providing an alternate source of this commodity to the coastal Indians who had been the Monacans' best customers. In *Notes on the State of Virginia*, the 1669 census that Jefferson referred to had indicated that there were then only thirty Monacan warriors left in the area. By 1735 an Englishman owned the land on the Rivanna River that included the abandoned burial mound that Jefferson would later excavate.

Some Monacans who remained in Virginia began slipping deeper into the wilderness that would become Amherst County. Many interrelated Monacan families settled on Bear Mountain, where itinerant Protestant ministers were among the few who ever reached out to them.

In the early twentieth century, scholar David I. Bushnell, Jr. "rediscovered" the Monacans. In an article published in *William and Mary Quarterly* in 1914, he wrote, "At the present time there are living along the foot of the Blue Ridge, in Amherst, a number of families who possess Indian features and other characteristics of the aborigines. Their language contains many Indian words; but as yet no study has been made of the language. While these people may represent the last remnants of various tribes, still it is highly probable that among them are living the last of the Monacan."

Antebellum Virginia had classified all descendants of Indians as mulatto, but in 1924, Virginia's Racial Integrity law reclassified Virginia's Indians as colored, essentially changing their race on paper. Many Native Americans moved out of the state during the years it would take for them to even begin reclaiming their racial identity.

In the last two decades of the twentieth century, Virginia recognized the Monacans as an indigenous tribe, and the Monacans began fundraising to purchase land, fund scholarships, and preserve their artifacts in a museum. Today the Monacan Indian Nation numbers about two thousand individuals, many of them intensely interested in researching their heritage in conjunction with sympathetic scholars from the University of Virginia, where their chief ally and champion is Professor Jeffrey L. Hantman.

In 2003 the professional journal *American Antiquity* published an article by Hantman and coauthors Debra Gold and Gary Dunham about the excavation of a Piedmont mound known as the Rapidan Mound located on a floodplain of the Rapidan River during three summer sessions of field work conducted between 1988 and 1990. It was one of twelve known mounds located in the floodplains of Virginia's rivers, including the north and south forks of the Shenandoah, the Rapidan, the Roanoke, and several tributaries of the James. The Jefferson Mound would make thirteen, but owing to floods on the Rivanna River and continuous cultivation in the area, archaeologists have yet to relocate it. The authors concluded that between one and two thousand individuals of both sexes and all ages had been buried in the Rapidan Mound, probably in several episodes spanning several centuries.

The authors decisively linked the Virginia mounds with Monacan Indians, but made no mention of any links to the prehistoric mound-building peoples of Ohio. They did consider possible connections and parallels with other groups practicing collective burials in other areas, specifically the Great Lakes region, the Atlantic coastal plain from North Carolina to Maryland, Pennsylvania, and the Florida Gulf Coast.

Earlier scholars had looked into this issue but somehow the line of inquiry had gone out of vogue. In 1891 and 1892 Gerard Fowke of the Smithsonian Institution's Bureau of Ethnology conducted an archaeological survey of the area drained by the James and Potomac rivers in Maryland, Virginia, and West Virginia. He described existing mounds, deteriorating mounds, and the former locations of obliterated mounds. Significantly, Fowke had been recently conducting research in the Midwest and he happened to notice that some of the artifacts found in the East Coast mounds "closely resemble in style, finish, and material those considered typical of the mound-building tribes of Ohio." In the 1950s, there had been some speculation that the prehistoric Adena people, who were known for building conical mounds over burials in the Ohio River valley, may have migrated east. Adena-like artifacts and evidence of Adena-like customs were discovered at sites in New York and New England, not to mention two sites in Maryland: outside Cambridge on the Eastern Shore of the Chesapeake Bay, and in Anne Arundel County south of Baltimore on the Western Shore.

Wondering what modern-day Native Americans thought on this topic, my husband and I drove south to Virginia in the summer of 2006. We entered Monacan territory as we drove through the valley of the Shenandoah River toward Charlottesville on Route 340. At one point near Compton, my atlas told me we were right across the river from a place named Indian Grave Ridge, but there were no signs directing us to visit any mound or barrow. As it turned out, there's only one artifact identified by a Virginia highway marker as an "Indian Mound," but it's farther west in Lee County, it's a different kind of mound, and no one is buried there. We did observe considerable evidence that the route we were traveling had been used by generations of white Americans, including the railroad viaducts that dominated the scenery and a lot of small square buildings, now either boarded up or renovated for other uses, that had been constructed as gas stations during the 1920s and 1930s.

After lunching in Luray and visiting Jefferson's Monticello, we continued toward Lynchburg on Route 29, parts of which bore the name Monacan Trail. We exited the highway in Amherst and followed Kenmore Road for several miles as it wound about the base of Richardson Mountain and Bear Mountain. A sign planted by Virginia's Adopt-a-Highway program informed us that the Monacan Indian Tribe had taken upon themselves the maintenance of this twisting, shaded, narrow road.

Finally I recognized a log cabin I had seen in book illustrations, originally built as a church for the Indians in the late nineteenth century, and now on the National Register of Historic Places. The Monacan Ancestral Museum had been constructed next door. We turned into the parking lot and got out of our car, prompting two horses in a nearby field to walk toward us, as if they thought we had come to visit them and were hoping we had brought them a treat. We could see there was still a small church just across a brook in a tiny hollow that was so profoundly quiet we could hear the water babbling over rocks in the creek bed.

What we did not see that day were any Monacan Indians. A sign on the museum's door informed us that it was closed for a festival being held at Natural Bridge that weekend.

We arrived early the next day at Natural Bridge, a natural wonder where Cedar Creek runs through a gorge beneath a huge rock arch formed over two hundred million years ago. Natural Bridge has been a landmark and a tourist attraction ever since British colonists discovered it, and probably much longer if Native Americans ever indulged in any sort of tourism. Thomas Jefferson once owned the land on which it stood. George Washington carved his initials in the area when he was working there as a young surveyor.

Soon after we had walked beneath the arch, taking many photographs and making sounds that expressed our awe, we came to the reproduction village that modern Monacans had constructed in the Cedar Creek gorge, where members of the tribe now conduct living history demonstrations. One costumed Monacan interpreter welcomed us in his native language and invited us to examine the longhouse that was under construction as well as the communal cooking fire where slabs of venison and fat turkey thighs were roasting. The tiny fire in a sleeping lodge helped us to shake off some of the early morning Virginia mountain chill, and we were very impressed by the skill of another Monacan who demonstrated how the Indians had hunted game with bow and arrow.

We found a Monacan in Native American dress and a Caucasian interpreter costumed in colonial garb who were on hand to answer historical questions. Both were well aware of Jefferson's story about watching Indians mourn at an earthen burial mound. But before we had time to discuss possible connections between Virginia's mound builders and those of Ohio, our conversation took another turn. Our Monacan costumed interpreter politely but firmly expressed his opinion that graves ought never to be disturbed or exploited, and that we'd all do better to leave Native American burial mounds alone.

Many, but not all, Native Americans believe that grave sites, however ancient, are places where the departed should be able to rest in peace, not sources of curiosities or skeletal remains destined for storage in some laboratory or, even worse, display in some museum case for the benefit of the gawking curious. To many Native Americans, archaeologists are simply looters, desecrating not only their ancestors' graves but also the places where they lived or worshipped which might continue to have spiritual meaning to them or be valuable for maintaining or passing down cultural traditions. Native Americans may be even more at odds with physical anthropologists who literally violate the deceased when they handle and study skeletal remains.

In the 1970s climate of social unrest, Native Americans began speaking out about what many considered a civil rights issue. This resulted in passage of the Native American Graves Protection and Repatriation Act (NAGPRA) in 1990, which created a process whereby Native Americans could reclaim human remains and funerary objects when they could be reasonably associated with specific families or tribes. NAGPRA does not apply to finds on private property or to institutions that receive no federal funding.

In 1996 a nearly complete human skeleton was discovered on federal land in Washington State near the town of Kennewick. Radiocarbon dating indicated that the individual had lived eight or nine thousand years ago. A federal agency planned to transfer the skeleton to a coalition of local tribes for burial, but a number of scientists objected and sued for the right to study the remains beforehand. Two court decisions favored the scientists based on the form and structure of the skull that demonstrated no cultural affiliation between Kennewick Man, whom the Indians had named the Ancient One, and the local tribes or any other tribe. The court decisions repolarized the entire repatriation issue for years, but by 2015 DNA testing showed that Kennewick Man was genetically more closely related to modern Native Americans than any other population worldwide.

Toward the end of our discussion at the Natural Bridge Monacan festival, our Native American interpreter questioned my reflexive use of the word "ownership" when it came to Virginia land. The modern Monacans preferred to say that Englishmen had "possessed" the soil on which Jefferson's mound had stood at the time of his excavation. We finally agreed that Europeans had "acquired" Monacan land. "But we're still here as you can see," observed my Monacan interpreter with a grin.

Tourists in Virginia have no trouble locating mounds constructed by white men, specifically the eighteenth-century Englishmen who were purposely adding them to the landscape as garden ornaments at their elegant country estates. Jefferson and Washington were both among America's Colonial "mound builders."

At Mount Vernon one can witness exactly what Americans wanted to create in America when they began settling the West following the American Revolution. Mount Vernon is England, only better. Much better, in fact, because this elegant Arcadian retreat, worthy of a British lord, was the home of a man who had had to work for a living at the age of sixteen.

The atmosphere was rather hectic on a Sunday morning in June when we visited, because the entire school district from Knoxville, Tennessee, was there for a spring excursion, and no less than thirty buses were lined up outside the main entrance. Yet when we walked around the mansion to its famous portico and witnessed the panoramic view of the Potomac below, we began to experience the restorative peace of this gentrified landscape. Later when we took the landscape and garden tour, our guide would explain how all quotidian evidence of George Washington's working farm had been carefully kept from interrupting this view. A wall that the eighteenth-century English called a "ha ha" (intended to keep farm animals from wandering into this area) had been constructed so that it was completely invisible from anyone relaxing on George Washington's back porch.

Washington hired gardeners from Europe and followed the published gardening principles of Batty Langley of Twickenham. Washington's "upper and lower" gardens, the sites of his greenhouse, botanical garden, and kitchen gardens, were also carefully screened from the sight of anyone standing at Mount Vernon's front door. What visitors see instead, then and now, is what Washington called his bowling green, a vista of lawn shaped like a Queen Anne–style cartouche and framed with trees, inviting the visitor to gaze west.

Far in the distance but impossible to miss are two small symmetrically placed mounds. Washington had intended these to be platforms on which to display some attractive willow trees. Unfortunately willows have always preferred to grow in swamps and stream beds, not on artificial hills, so they never did well, making it necessary for Washington to keep replacing them.

In the interest of historical accuracy the Mount Vernon Ladies Association, which now owns and operates Mount Vernon, keeps the gardens as much as possible as they would have looked while Washington was living there. Our guide informed us that the willows had been very pretty when they had been newly planted on those little mounds that spring, but by June they were just as dead as they would have been in the early summer during Washington's lifetime.

Washington's mounds were nothing compared to the ones we found at Poplar Forest, the private retreat Jefferson had constructed between 1805 and 1825 in remote Bedford County where he and his family could escape the uninvited hordes who demanded his hospitality at Monticello. While thousands of visitors still descend upon Monticello, there were very few people on our tour of Poplar Forest, which had been open to the public only since 1986. Those, like us, who had very recently been to Monticello, nodded in delighted recognition when we spotted some of Jefferson's unique architectural trademarks in this quirky little dwelling, whose floor plan is a square within an octagon.

The small mounds at Mount Vernon were intended as garden ornaments. They stand at the end of its "bowling green," inviting the visitor to gaze west. (*Author*)

On either side of the house, two enormous mounds each about a hundred feet in diameter and nearly twelve feet high dominated the grounds. Our guide told us they had been constructed from the dirt excavated from the cellar and the sunken lawn at the rear of the house. Other information published by the site suggested that the mounds might have been the rural equivalent of pavilions constructed at either side of a Renaissance villa.

Although the Poplar Forest mounds dwarfed those at Mount Vernon, evidence suggests that Jefferson had plans for them similar to those of Washington, namely planting them with trees and shrubs. But while the Mount Vernon mounds were meant to be viewed from the mansion, the Poplar Forest mounds were evidently vantage points from which visitors could get a bird's-eye view of the house and formal gardens.

Monticello had no mounds, but then Monticello sits on a hilltop and is surrounded by magnificent hills. From Monticello, Jefferson could admire Montalto, a neighboring mountain rising over four hundred feet above his estate. Our garden tour guide at Monticello explained that Jefferson had various ambitious plans

Thomas Jefferson constructed much more impressive mounds at Poplar Forest. Could they have been inspired by news of the impressive mounds being discovered in the West? (*Author*)

for this mountain, possibly including a waterfall that he could see from his property.

Scholars, tour guides, and site administrators all agree that Virginia gentlemen like Washington and Jefferson who built mounds on their estates were inspired by European examples and European published garden advice. And yet, when it comes to matters of fashion or the decorative arts, one just can't ignore the zeitgeist. The exciting discovery of Mound Builder relics had a huge impact on contemporary Americans. Mount Vernon with its small mounds and Monticello with no mounds were both constructed and landscaped before much was known about the old earthen ruins in the West. Poplar Forest with its huge mounds was taking shape just as genteel Virginia was getting more and more news from the frontier.

3

"Let Us Open the Tombs . . ."

During the final years of the eighteenth century and the first two decades of the nineteenth, it would become so abundantly clear that Jefferson had been mistaken when he wrote the phrase "no such thing existing as an Indian monument" that some authors even ridiculed his error. For example, the traveler Thomas Ashe sneered in an 1808 publication, "I ask those writers . . . when they are again disposed to enlighten the world with their lucubrations, to visit the countries which they profess to delineate; and diligently search for materials there, before they presume to tell us that such have no existence."

As Americans poured into the territory that farsighted men like Washington had long wanted to settle, it became clear that they were entering a vast landscape of ancient ruins. However

most of these Americans were homesteaders who intended to settle down and impose their own footprints on the landscape. More
nineteenth-century farms, market towns, and transportation
infrastructure clearly meant disappearing ruins.

The realization of this simple truth led the scholars of the day
to demand that one learn what one could while it was still possible. In 1796 Benjamin Smith Barton wrote to theologian and scientist Rev. Joseph Priestley, "Let us open the tombs of the ancient
Americans. In these dark abodes, the last asylums of man on this
globe, we may discover materials that will enable us to throw
some light upon the ancient history of the Americans." The same
sentiment led others to attempt to preserve the ancient ruins, if
not in the literal sense, then at least in description and diagram.

But the scholars were also human, so there was of course
another reason for research in the field. Barton added, "If we are
not sufficiently animated by the love of science, let us remember,
that in the tombs of the Mexicans and Peruvians, the Spaniards
have discovered treasures of gold, of silver, and of precious
stones; and that even in the tombs in Florida, valuable pearls are
said to have been found. I think, there can be little doubt that the
opening of the North-American tumuli will reward the labourers
with valuable spoils."

Settlement of the fertile and attractive land that would become
America's Midwest, initially named the Northwest Territory,
began with Great Britain's cession of this region in the peace
treaty that ended the American Revolution. Not long afterward,
the states of Virginia and Connecticut, whose original British
charters granted them land in this area, ceded their interests to
the new United States. By means of a 1784 treaty with the
Iroquois nations, the United States also acquired the claims of
these particular tribes to territory west of Pennsylvania. By 1785
the first land surveys were being conducted on the Ohio frontier.

The Iroquois nations had claimed this countryside by right of
conquest since the mid-seventeenth century, but around the
1730s groups of Shawnee, Delawares, and Wyandots had moved
in and established towns without Iroquois authorization. Since
these tribes had demonstrated their animosity toward American

settlers in both the French and Indian War and the American Revolution, the newly opened territory remained a very dangerous place. Not counting David Zeisberger's Moravian mission, Ohio's first white settlement was a military post established in 1785 and named Fort Harmar, located where the Muskingum River empties into the Ohio.

The Northwest Territory's earliest prospective settlers were a band of stouthearted army veterans who formed the Ohio Company of Associates in 1786. When Congress passed the Ordinance of 1787 (also called the Northwest Ordinance) making the Northwest Territory an official political entity, the Ohio Company of Associates promptly offered to purchase in excess of a million acres.

Founded in Boston, the Ohio Company of Associates was first led by General Rufus Putnam of Massachusetts, a member of the same family that would later produce Frederic Ward Putnam. The company's chief promoter was the spirited lobbyist Manasseh Cutler, physician and pastor of the Congregational Church in Hamilton, Massachusetts. The company's members were New England Yankees, mostly from Massachusetts, who proposed to transplant their legendary industriousness and impeccable morality to the newly opened territory. The first group of settlers named one of the vessels that would carry them down the Ohio River the *Ohio Mayflower*.

Their flotilla arrived at the mouth of the Muskingum in April 1788. On the bank of this river about a mile north of the Ohio, they constructed a stockade they named the Campus Martius to enclose and protect their initial dwellings.

Besides the federal soldiers at Fort Harmar, the Ohio Company members found a number of squatters from western Pennsylvania and Virginia who had built cabins without waiting for congressional sanction. The Yankees described them as lawless "banditti" and "white Indians," but soon came to appreciate their aid in defense of the settlement. They consequently drew up terms on which the squatters might become eligible for tracts of what the Ohio Company termed "donation" lands.

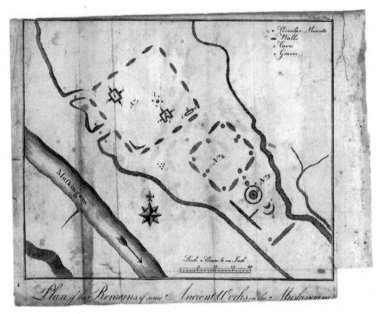

A plan of the earthworks at Marietta drawn by Jonathan Hart and published in *Columbian Magazine* in 1787. The town's grid plan was oriented to preserve the earthworks, including the fifty-acre square called Quadranou, the twenty-seven-acre square called Capitolium, and the mound called Conus.

To keep the squatters in line, the Ohio Company formed and installed a government, so that laws could be made and enforced, and courts could be established. Congress had already appointed the American Revolution veteran general Arthur St. Clair governor of the Northwest Territory, and two of the territory's earliest judges were men who had already explored and written about the area: Samuel Holden Parsons and John Cleves Symmes. Manasseh Cutler had suggested the name Adelphia for their first town, but when the Ohio Company directors met in July 1788, they adopted the name Marietta, ostensibly honoring the French queen Marie Antoinette. The name also constituted a grateful acknowledgment of France's alliance with the United States during the American Revolution.

Its founding fathers wanted to make Marietta a regional commercial center where agricultural products could be shipped to the East, and where products like iron, coal, and glass could be manufactured or processed. Yet while they planned optimistically for the future, they could not ignore the evidence that the location proposed for Marietta had also appealed to other unknown settlers in the indeterminate past. On their elevated plain conveniently near a river junction were the ancient ruins that had generally been interpreted as fortifications by a number of earlier American travelers, including Parsons and Symmes.

Putnam and Cutler did what they could to interpret and preserve Marietta's old ruins. In a 1798 report, Cutler noted that while he was there a number of trees growing on the earthworks were felled. After the annual rings had been counted on the largest of them, Cutler concluded that some of the ancient structures were over four hundred years old. Putnam used his experience in military surveying to draw a map, or what he described as a "plan of the ancient works." When Cutler was back in Massachusetts in 1788, he wrote Putnam, "On my return home I found several letters from different parts of Europe. The most of them request me to send a particular account of the Ancient Works found in North America. These works seem to have engaged the attention of the literati in Europe, and I wish to gratify those with whom I have the honor to correspond, as far as possible. I must beg you to forward to me the surveys of the works at Marietta." Putnam left the map for Cutler's perusal when he visited Boston in 1790.

Because some of the early Marietta settlers were educated Yankees with college degrees, and since the so-called Empire style inspired by the antiquities of Greece and Rome was coming into vogue in the decorative arts at the time that Marietta was being developed, the earthworks of Marietta were soon graced with classical-sounding names. A large square enclosing several platform mounds became Quadranaou, and a smaller square became Capitolium. A tall conical mound was named Conus. What appeared to be a graded, walled ramp between the big square and the river that had proven so handy for American settlers moving things from their flatboats to the elevated plain, became the Via Sacra, meaning Sacred Way.

The frontispiece from *Ancient Monuments* shows Native Americans gazing at the ancient works at Marietta. Also in the picture are the white man's fort and log cabin.

Putnam subsequently oriented the grid plan of modern Marietta to harmonize with its ancient ruins. Marietta's numbered streets that ran parallel to the river, as well as its named streets running perpendicular to the river, were laid out more or less in line with the walls of Capitolium and Quadranaou. The Sacra Via became a main thoroughfare through town. In a 1788 letter to Cutler, Putnam stated, "the situation of the City-plat is the most delightful of any I ever saw, and those traces of ancient walls, mounds, etc., are truly surprising."

The traces remain today, though they're a bit removed from the boutiques, cafes, and restaurants attracting visitors to Marietta's Front Street and Second Street, as well as the community now called Harmar Village across the Muskingum. These two downtowns are linked by a pedestrian bridge that was originally constructed for trains by the B&O Railroad. The local convention and visitors' bureau publishes a guide listing the locations of old historic houses in these neighborhoods built by Marietta's early settlers and their descendants.

The best place to learn how Marietta developed from Putnam's frontier town to its pleasant present state is at the museum named after the Campus Martius which now occupies part of its original site. Visitors can view an early map of Marietta, as well as a diorama showing the relationship of the old stockade and the ancient ruins. They can even tour Rufus Putnam's house, originally incorporated into the Campus Martius fortification, which survived in private hands until it was turned over to the state of Ohio to become an exhibit in this museum. The little dwelling is remarkably elegant considering the time and place it was built. Other fine furnishings on display at the museum illustrate the settlers' ongoing efforts to transplant the refined trappings of the East Coast to their new town in the West.

Elsewhere in the Campus Martius Museum, there's a photo of Marietta taken from 40,000 feet showing the relationship of the modern town with its surviving ruins. It demonstrates that some twenty-two decades after Putnam wrote to Cutler, those traces of mounds continue to be truly surprising.

After orienting ourselves at the Campus Martius Museum, my husband and I began our walking tour of Marietta at Conus, now located in what is called the Mound Cemetery, the final resting place of many of Marietta's founders and early settlers. We approached via shaded Scammel Street, walking through a very nice neighborhood of well-maintained Victorian mansions to the iron fence surrounding the cemetery. We entered through the front gate, which stood invitingly open. A sign and a small field of grave markers adorned with American flags informed us we were in the distinguished company of many American veterans. Another sign identified Conus itself as the burial place of "chieftains."

Conus was covered with trees and other vegetation, but we could make out its shallow surrounding ditch as we walked around to the mossy, uneven stone steps leading to the mound's summit. The top of Conus was a small plateau furnished with benches, where a stone marker in the floor covered a time cap-

sule to be opened in 2076,
which seemed to us like a
promise that the city's current
administrators intended to preserve Conus for the long term.
We paused to admire the view
of the deserted cemetery and
the bluff on the opposite side of
the Muskingum River. Had the
season been winter, we might
have been able to see the river
through the trees.

Conus in Marietta, Ohio. Visitors can
climb the stone steps to the summit of
this thirty-foot mound and view the
Muskingum River in the distance.
(*Author*)

The fairly long walk from
Conus to the Sacra Via was
made interesting by the imposing examples of late nineteenth-
century domestic architecture
that proclaimed just how
wealthy a town Marietta had by
then become. In fact, the man-
sions of Marietta were among its tourist attractions that summer.
Visitors were touring this hillside neighborhood on a little bus fitted out to look like a Victorian trolley. Its clanging bell recalled a
time when real trolleys might have conveyed Marietta's citizens
through town.

Sacra Via, a long and fairly broad public park sloping down to
the river, is furnished with benches and a gazebo. The walls that
once lined it are no longer visible, and a sign explains that the
earth that had formed them was removed by a brick maker in
1843.

On early maps, Sacra Via appeared to have led to a main gateway of Quadranaou, but only about a quarter of this fifty-acre
square was preserved as a public park, so Sacra Via now ends at
Third Street. To one's left a sign identifies the facing open space
as Camp Tupper, the use to which this place was put during the
Civil War. Across a broad stretch of grass, we gazed at what is now
called the Quadranaou mound. Since we happened to be holding

an early map, we could make out its shape. Otherwise, this ancient monument resembles the kind of berm that a real estate developer would place at the edge of a property to block an undesirable view.

Marietta's other surviving mound is even easier to miss. It lies under the public library on Fifth Street, and looks like it was put there on purpose by the architect to give the library a more impressive appearance. We looked for any trace of the old walls of Quadranaou but found no sign of them along Washington Street, which would have been more of less contiguous with Quadranaou's southeastern side.

Early nineteenth-century Americans would be able to take a virtual tour not only of Marietta, but also a number of other sites with ancient ruins in the nation's first comprehensive illustrated study of them titled *Description of the Antiquities Discovered in the State of Ohio and Other Western States* published in 1820. Its author was a pioneer named Caleb Atwater who would come to rival Jefferson for the title of America's first true archaeologist. Born in Massachusetts, Atwater had been a Presbyterian minister before he studied law and moved to Ohio in 1815. As a member of the Ohio state legislature, Atwater promoted Ohio's canal transportation systems and its public schools. Today Atwater's descriptions are the best way of comparing what has survived into the twenty-first century with what the earliest residents had been looking at.

Atwater's publisher was the American Antiquarian Society, which included his book-length study in the first volume of their serial titled *Archaeologia Americana*. The introductory material in the same volume stated that this organization, which had been incorporated in Massachusetts in 1812, had been formed as a national society to promote useful knowledge. Its founders hoped it would become a national repository for artifacts and information that scholars might study in order to interpret the antiquities of the American continent.

Atwater's intentions coincided with those of the American Antiquarian Society in that he wanted to gather all information then available on Mound Builder ruins so that the conclusions set forth by those trying to explain them would be less parochial. He wrote, "It has somehow happened, that one traveler has seen an ancient work, which was once a place of amusement for those who erected it, and he concludes, that none but such were ever found in the whole country. Another in his journey sees a mound of earth with a semicircular pavement on the East side of it; at once he proclaims it to the world as his firm belief, that ALL our ancient works were places of devotion, dedicated to worship of the Sun. A succeeding tourist falls in with an ancient military fortress, and thence concludes that ALL our ancient works were raised for military purposes."

Describing the ruins at Marietta as "some of the most extraordinary ancient works, any where to be found," Atwater acknowledged his own descriptions were enriched by the observations of others, including Putnam's map and an early description by Cutler. He also acknowledged material by fellow antiquarians Thaddeus M. Harris, Dr. Samuel P. Hildreth (who lived in Marietta), and General Edward W. Tupper of the town not far down the Ohio River called Gallipolis.

Though he did not use its classical-sounding name, Atwater described Quadranaou as a big forty-acre square "by some called the town," formed from sixteen separate mounded ridges six to ten feet high, with spaces between them that he interpreted as "gateways." Inside the big square were the structures that later archaeologists would term truncated pyramids or platform mounds, which Atwater described as "elevated squares" with earthen projections that appeared to be ramps or gradual ascents intended to help people climb them.

He described Sacra Via as "covert way" framed with parallel earthen walls twenty-one feet high and precisely 231 feet apart, measuring from the center of one wall to the other. Atwater concluded, "at the time of its construction, it probably reached the river." He compared it to a turnpike road.

He described Capitolium as a smaller square southeast of the big square, enclosing a twenty-acre space, also composed of earthen ridges. It had "gateways" located at each corner and at the center of each of its sides, all of them "defended by circular mounds."

Atwater compared Conus to a "sugarloaf," and described it as 115 feet in diameter and thirty feet high. It was surrounded by a four-foot ditch and connected to Capitolium by a parapet which seemed to lead toward one of the smaller square's gateways. Atwater referred to an 1819 letter from Dr. Hildreth for a description of a pond or reservoir that had been near the big square and remained full of water from the time the town had been settled until "the last winter." Settlers had slowly filled it with refuse and trees that had been felled when the ground was cleared. It had then been drained by the settler whose property it ended up on, who had observed that it had been shaped like an inverted cone and lined with "very fine, ash coloured clay." The proprietor anticipated excavating "several hundred loads of excellent manure" while he continued to explore it.

Atwater concluded, "It is worthy of remark, that the walls and mounds were not thrown up from ditches, but raised by bringing the earth from a distance, or taking it up uniformly from the plain. . . . It has excited some surprize that the tools have not been discovered here, with which these works were constructed."

In his book, Atwater also carefully diagrammed and described the earthworks of his own town of Circleville, the seat of Pickaway County established in 1810, where an ancient perfect circle constructed of earth adjoined an ancient earthen perfect square. Atwater recorded that the Circleville circle, sixty-nine feet in diameter, was actually two concentric earthen circles separated by a deep ditch. The square had no ditch, and its single wall was punctuated by eight regularly spaced gateways at its sides and corners, very similar to the gateways of the Marietta squares. The circle had a single opening communicating only with the square. The Circleville ruins were also similar to those at Marietta in that each gateway in the square had a mound in front of it, which according to Atwater were "intended for the defence of these

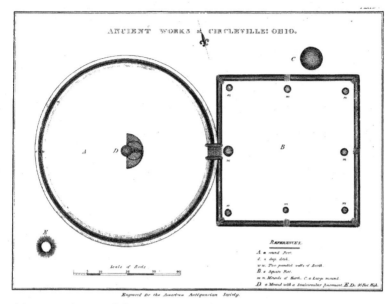

Caleb Atwater's map of the Circleville Work from his *Description of the Antiquities Discovered in the State of Ohio and Other Western States* published in 1820. In Atwater's day, the square was being demolished but the townspeople had preserved the circle by constructing their courthouse inside it. The circle fell to urban development in the mid-nineteenth century.

openings." Atwater recorded that there had once been a mound precisely in the center of the circle that had been hardscaped with a "semicircular pavement on its eastern side."

Like the founding fathers of Marietta, the original developers of Circleville intended to incorporate the ancient ruins into the plan for their town. An early map shows that they built the town's original eight-sided county courthouse at the center of the concentric earthen circles, and named the nearby streets Circle Street and Circle Alley. Atwater noted, "The present town of Circleville covers all the round and the western half of the square fort," but he added that workmen had been demolishing the walls of the square in order to manufacture bricks. Atwater warned that "these fortifications, where the town stands, will entirely disappear in a few years."

Indeed it was not long before the modern residents of Circleville decided that the feature for which their town had been named actually wasted valuable land in desirable downtown locations that could otherwise be profitably developed. In 1837 the state legislature passed an act creating the Circleville Squaring Company. It took a while for all the downtown landowners to agree, but by 1856, Circleville had a conventional grid plan.

The ancient ruins would have an even shorter life in the settlement that would become one of Ohio's most important commercial cities, which got its start as another veterans' colony. In 1787 John Cleves Symmes, while still serving as a judge in New Jersey, petitioned Congress for land between the Great and Little Miami rivers, where he hoped that New Jersey veterans of the American Revolution would settle. The following year a group of men led by Robert Patterson and surveyor Israel Ludlow purchased eight hundred acres in the area and planned a town whose original name combined French, Greek, and Latin word segments to describe its location opposite the mouth of the Licking River: Le-os-anti-ville or Losantiville.

In 1789 General Harmar helped ensure the success of the enterprise by establishing a new federal fort named Fort Washington just across the Ohio River in Kentucky. As governor of the Northwest Territory, Arthur St. Clair organized Hamilton County with the new town as its seat, but changed the town's name to something more compatible with the name of the much admired Washington. Losantiville became Cincinnati, named after the Society of the Cincinnati, an organization whose members were officers who had served Washington in the American Revolution.

By 1790 Cincinnati had a population of about 250, but its growth was impeded by the hostility of local Indians until General Anthony Wayne arrived on the scene in 1793. The forts Wayne built nearby for his Indian campaigns stimulated the economy of the little market town, and it soon had regular riverboat service to Marietta and Pittsburgh. Following Wayne's decisive victory at the Battle of Fallen Timbers and the ensuing Treaty of Greenville, Cincinnati expanded into a regional trading center with mills and warehouses to process and store agricultural products which could be shipped south to growing New Orleans.

Cincinnati folklore has long included a tale that Anthony Wayne drilled his troops while standing on an old Indian mound. However, those who superintended and executed the construction of its original municipal streets were far less interested in historic preservation than the founding fathers of Marietta. Even that mound that should have been famous for its association with the heroic Wayne was leveled by the 1840s.

For information on Cincinnati for his own book, Caleb Atwater relied on material published by Daniel Drake, whom he identified as "an officer of the American Antiquarian Society." Born in New Jersey, Drake had been deposited in Cincinnati by family members then living in Mays Lick, Kentucky, to be educated as a physician by the city's Dr. William Goforth. Drake later studied in Philadelphia and returned to Cincinnati to take over Goforth's practice before becoming a medical school professor in Lexington, Kentucky. Drake had employed his keen powers of observation in researching two publications: *Notices Concerning Cincinnati* published in 1810, and *Natural and Statistical View or Picture of Cincinnati and the Miami Country* published in 1815.

Atwater quoted Drake word for word on several ancient mounds in Cincinnati. North and west of the main part of town near the road to Laurenceberg there had been an elliptical mound with a base circumference of 440 feet and a height of twenty-seven feet, which had been shortened by Wayne to prepare it to serve as a sentinel's post. Drake noted, "It has been penetrated nearly to its centre, and found to consist of loam, gradually passing into soil, with rotten wood . . . a few scattered and decayed human bones, a branch of a deer's horn, and a piece of earthen ware containing [mussel] shells." According to Drake there was a circular mound nearby that was nine feet high and flat at the top that had contained fragments of skeletons and copper beads. Nearly obliterated by the construction of Main Street, another mound had once stood roughly at the intersection of Third and

Main. This mound had been an oval eight feet high and measuring 120 feet by sixty feet, with its diameters oriented to the cardinal points.

Drake included descriptions of other earthworks that early settlers had found while siting Cincinnati which Atwater did not incorporate into his own book. The city had once had an ellipse about 800 feet by 660 feet roughly encircling the block between Vine, Race, Fourth, and Fifth streets. This structure had been built without a ditch and had a gate on its eastern side. Not far outside the ellipse there had been a bank extending south and then east to join the mound at Third and Main. In what were then the northern reaches of the town there had been some low earthen banks forming a very flattened ellipse, 760 feet long with an opening facing more or less southward. Southeast of the ellipse at the center of town was another raised, slightly curving bank that reached from Fourth and Broadway to Fifth and Sycamore. Drake described it as "evidently the segment of a very large circle."

Drake added some information on other mounds and earthworks in the countryside nearby which he called the "Miami Country." Some of these ruins surrounding Cincinnati survived into the twentieth century, including mounds in Newtown and Norwood, probably because they were incorporated, respectively, into an Odd Fellows cemetery and a town park.

You can find some exhibits explaining the civilization of the Mound Builders at the Museum of Natural History and Science in the Cincinnati Museum Center at the city's old Union Terminal. However, you will look in vain for ancient ruins in twenty-first-century Cincinnati. The intersection of Third and Main now borders the highway that carries Interstates 71 and 75 through town. There are many parking lots in this area for folks visiting the city's major sports stadiums. But the closest thing you'll find to an Indian mound is the slight elevation that the pitchers stand on when the Cincinnati Reds play home games at the Great American Ball Park.

By the time Atwater's *Description of Antiquities* was published, early guesses about the purposes of the Midwest's enclosures had developed into a full-fledged scholarly controversy. Manasseh

Cutler ironically observed in a 1789 letter to another minister, "It struck me as rather curious that military gentlemen should contend that they were constructed for religious purposes, and that a clergyman that they were works of defense – opinions so contrary to their professional prejudices."

In 1809 the American Philosophical Society published in the sixth volume of its serial *Transactions of the American Philosophical Society* an 1803 letter on this "fort versus sanctuary" controversy written to Dr. Benjamin Smith Barton by James Madison—not President James Madison but his second cousin, president of the College of William and Mary and the first bishop of the Episcopal Church of Virginia. Based on a visit to the Kanawha River and its countryside, Madison flatly stated, "those works were not fortifications, and never had the smallest relation to military defense." He observed that not only were their walls too low, the spaces enclosed were far too large; how many ancient soldiers would it take to defend an enclosure of fifty acres, or one hundred acres? He added that those structures that had a ditch adjacent to earthen walls often had the ditch inside the structure where it would have been useless for defense. Tall massive mounds had been built too close to walls and located where enemies could easily climb them and fire a "missil weapon" on the defenders. The earthworks had not been constructed in militarily strategic locations, and the length of time it would have taken to build the mounds indicated that adjacent earthworks had also been around for a long time, "not the temporary stations of a retiring or weakened army, but the fixed habitation of a family, and a long line of descendants."

Atwater made no such sweeping judgments, and went so far as to ridicule those who did. He wrote, "Some hasty travellers who have spent an hour or two here, have concluded that the 'forts' at Circleville were not raised for military, but for religious purposes." According to Atwater, some structures were forts, others sanctuaries. He came to the latter conclusion about a forty-acre enclosure in Perry County near Somerset, roughly triangular in shape with a stone mound at its center. "I do not believe this ever to have been a military work, either of defence or offence; but if a military work, it must have been a temporary camp. . . . I should rather suspect this to have been a sacred enclosure, or 'high place,' which was resorted to on some great anniversary." Atwater mused, however, that some ancient earthworks might have been sanctuaries adapted for defense when necessary. He described how one historian recorded that Mexicans (Aztecs) had faced invading Spaniards: "Standing upon their altars and in their temples; upon the tombs of their fathers; defending themselves, their wives, their children, their aged parents, their country, and their gods."

In the years between the publication of Bishop Madison's letter and the appearance of Atwater's book, the American Philosophical Society also published a letter addressed to Thomas Jefferson written by frontier lawyer Henry Marie Brackenridge in 1813. Some points Brackenridge made in the letter he repeated in a chapter of a book published in 1814 titled *Views of Louisiana Together with a Journal of a Voyage up the Missouri River, in 1811*, and they are among the most clearly expressed early interpretations of Mound Builder artifacts.

Politely acknowledging the writings of Jefferson, Barton, and Madison, Brackenridge stated in his book, "I cannot but think their theories [are] founded on a very imperfect acquaintance with these remains: having never themselves visited any but the least considerable." In short, those other theorizers had not seen anything compared to what could be found in the places Brackenridge was familiar with, including St. Genevieve, where he had been sent to school, and the Mississippi and Missouri valleys, where he had traveled. In his 1813 letter to Jefferson, Brackenridge came up with a variation on the fort side of the fort versus sanctuary controversy, writing, "The appearances of fortifications . . . are nothing more than the traces of pallisaded towns or villages." He expanded his argument in his book, explaining that he had himself seen Indian villages surrounded by palisades, and early New England colonists had described Indians defending themselves in forts. He guessed that America's declining number of Indians had stopped building forts and palisades in more recent times when they discovered that these structures could not protect them from the white man's weapons.

In material printed in the first volume of the *Transactions of the Historical and Philosophical Society of Ohio* published in Cincinnati in 1839, and in booklet form following his death, William Henry Harrison weighed in on the fort versus sanctuary controversy based on his own long residence in the Ohio Valley, which had included service as Wayne's aide-de-camp followed by command of Fort Washington. According to General Harrison, the earthworks at Marietta and Cincinnati and those at the mouth of the Great Miami River in a location he knew as Fort Hill "have a military character stamped upon them which can not be mistaken." In contrast, Circleville could not have been a fort. Its square enclosure had too many openings and both the square and circle "were completely commanded by the mound, rendering it an easier matter to take, than defend it."

The Fort Hill of which Harrison spoke is not the current Fort Hill State Memorial, but a hilltop enclosure now called Miami Fort located within Shawnee Lookout Park. The site was first examined by archaeologists in the 1960s and resurveyed in 2009 by the University of Cincinnati Archaeology Field School, whose members tentatively suggested it might turn out to be the largest continuously occupied Native American hilltop site in the United States. Recent research suggests it might have included reservoirs, dams, and raceways to collect water and manage its use.

In addition to the enclosures that were either forts or sanctuaries, there were other earthworks that no one understood, as well as qualities and attributes of the ancient remains that eluded logical explanation. Despite Atwater's cool scholarly objectivity, his *Descriptions of the Antiquities* was also a catalog of mysteries, some still awaiting resolution.

Atwater recorded that the sites of the most extensive earthworks also had what he described as "parallel walls of earth," or walls that sometimes seemed to enclose a space shaped like a very long, flattened oval. Besides the one Drake described in the northern blocks of Cincinnati, Atwater reported that many had been discovered on the Scioto, Ohio, Kanawha, and Big Sandy rivers. They might have been protected roads, or possibly places where people went to watch processions or maybe sporting events, like races, that might have been part of mortuary games, though the ovals usually were not constructed in the shadows of burial mounds.

By the time Atwater published his *Description of Antiquities*, over a thousand ancient wells had been discovered, some more than twenty feet deep. Atwater wondered what the old Mound Builders had been digging for, tentatively proposing that they had been mining rock crystals or stones suitable for arrowheads or spear points. Atwater mentioned that four wells had been discovered in the very bed of Paint Creek by "a person passing over them in a canoe." Each was capped with a stone that had a hole in its middle, apparently for the insertion of a spike that could be used to pry up these lids.

Atwater was not the first scholar to comment on the regularity with which the ancient earthworks had been constructed. The angles of the squares were right angles. When a circle enclosing a mound had a gateway, or a raised platform had a walkway leading up to it, these features were usually on its eastern side, facing the rising sun. "When persons were buried in graves, " Atwater wrote, "these graves were east and west." Atwater would not be the only scholar to posit the question, "Had their authors no knowledge of astronomy?"

Benjamin Smith Barton's exhortation to "open the tombs" in his letter to Joseph Priestley was actually inspired by a collection of artifacts unearthed in Cincinnati in 1794 by Colonel Winthrop Sargent, originally from Massachusetts but then serving as territorial secretary of Ohio. Sargent's communication with Barton and Barton's interpretation of the artifacts were published in the *Transactions of the American Philosophical Society* in 1799. Sargent cited the provenance of the artifacts as a grave about five feet underground near "an extensive artificial mound of earth" which had initially been disturbed by municipal street construction. His descriptions and accompanying drawings showed several elongated cylindrical objects swelling in the middle and grooved at one end composed of stone or some hardened material. Sargent wrote that their surfaces were smooth and regular, "almost as if finished in a turner's lathe." There were disks with holes in their centers, sheets of copper, and a carving decorated with what looked like the head and beak of a bird "not now known in this country." Barton did not speculate too broadly on these finds, except to interpret the markings on a sculpted bone as "hieroglyphicks" and guess that the items had been used for "superstitious purposes." Atwater and Drake both included versions of this list in their own publications.

In the same book in which he ridiculed Jefferson, British traveler Thomas Ashe described his own impromptu attempt to "open the tombs." His book was published in London in 1808 under the lengthy title *Travels in America Performed in 1806 for the Purpose of Exploring the Rivers Alleghany, Monongahela, Ohio, and Mississippi and Ascertaining the Produce and Conditions of their Banks and Vicinity.* Ashe noted that Cincinnati's "principal street leading from the water is cut through [a] barrow, and exposes its strata and remains to every person passing by. Children often amuse themselves in undermining the banks, till large quantities fall down in which they search for, and often find arrow points, beads, and many other curiosities."

His own excavation, which lasted "less than three hours," turned up "my hat full of beads, several arrow points, two stone hatchets, many pieces of pottery, and a flute made of the great bone of the human leg. It is a very curious instrument, with beautifully engraved, or carved figures representing birds, squirrels, and small animals, and perforated holes in the old German Manner." How Ashe disposed of these artifacts he failed to mention. Ashe also recorded, "the dead repose in double horizontal tiers; between each tier are regular layers of sand, flat surfaced stones, gravel and earth. I counted seven tiers, and might have discovered more, but was compelled to desist from the annoyance of the multitude gathering about me." He mentioned that "three out of seven skeletons were in great preservation, and in a progressive state of petrifaction," as opposed to the jumbled and disarticulated bones of the Jefferson mound.

It would be another two decades before local citizens excavated the massive conical Grave Creek Mound that had been astounding settlers and explorers since the late eighteenth century. But when the Grave Creek Mound was finally examined, the dig would be relatively novel in that those who executed it planned and managed to preserve the mound itself.

G rave Creek Mound was located amid much evidence of prior habitation including other mounds and earthworks, as well as patches of ground that appeared to have been deliberately cleared, which early settlers commonly called "Indian old fields." Grave Creek Mound seemed to have been constructed along an ancient path that proceeded from Brownsville, Pennsylvania, across the Ohio River to a place near Zanesville, Ohio. In the journal he kept of his expedition of western exploration, Captain Meriwether Lewis wrote that the Grave Creek Mound was located "on the east bank of the Ohio 12 Miles below Wheeling and about 700 paces from the river." It was near a hamlet of six or seven dwellings then called Elizabethtown, which would later become part of a larger community called Moundsville in present day West Virginia.

Travelers could see that the Grave Creek Mound was big, and different persons estimated its height at various measurements between sixty and one hundred feet. In a journal he kept of a trip made west of the Alleghenies in 1803, Thaddeus Mason Harris reported that by his measurement, the "Big grave" was sixty-seven and a half feet tall. In 1838 road engineers came up with a height measurement of sixty-nine feet.

Like Atwater's description of Conus, early writers also compared its shape to that of a sugarloaf and recorded that it appeared to be part of a grouping of earthworks. If one connected the dots between the Grave Creek Mound, an octagonal enclosure north of it, and two square earthworks on its northeast and northwest, one could draw an elongated diamond. Drawing lines between the Grave Creek Mound and the two square forts alone pretty much made an equilateral triangle.

However, in the years since these structures had been abandoned by their builders, the general area had become very overgrown. In his journal Meriwether Lewis wrote, "the mound is not visible from the river." The first American to claim ownership of

An illustration from *Ancient Monuments* showing the observatory at the summit of the Grave Creek Mound.

the property on which it stood is said to have come across the Grave Creek Mound for the first time while he was out hunting and in the process of chasing down a wounded deer.

That same settler, Joseph Tomlinson, appears to have been unusually conservation minded for his time. Caleb Atwater wrote in his book, "This lofty and venerable tumulus has been so far opened, as to ascertain that it contains many thousands of human skeletons, but no farther. The proprietor of the ground, Mr. Joseph Tomlinson, will not suffer its demolition in the smallest degree. I, for one, do him honour for his sacred regard for these works of antiquity."

In his comprehensive book titled *Moundsville's Mammouth Mound*, the twentieth-century amateur archaeologist Delf Norona, who spent many years studying the mound, referenced local newspapers from the 1830s to reveal growing demands of the community that the contents of the Grave Creek Mound be brought to light. In 1838, one anonymous writer demanded, "Where is the man who could say that our huge Monumental

An illustration from *Ancient Monuments* showing the two burial chambers in Grave Creek Mound. In the nineteenth century, visitors could enter the mound through a tunnel and explore what might have been its lower burial chamber.

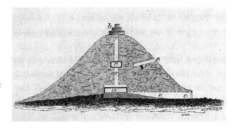

Mound, may not contain relics which will establish it beyond doubt, one of the first wonders of the world!" Perhaps the Grave Creek Mound could serve the Moundsville community by encouraging the fledgling B&O Railroad to choose Moundsville as a station or terminal. In a later paragraph the writer expressed his hope that the Grave Creek Mound "will be a strong inducement for the Baltimore & Ohio Railroad Company to select this spot for crossing the [Ohio] river."

By 1838, Joseph Tomlinson was dead, and his son Jesse allowed his own nephew Abelard Tomlinson to organize an excavation with a man named Thomas Biggs and other amateurs. They decided to tunnel to the center of the mound at ground level, and then sink a shaft from its flat top to meet their tunnel.

They soon unearthed evidence of how the mound had been constructed. It appeared to cover a small natural ridge seven or eight feet high, and it was composed of earth from the surrounding plain which had apparently been carried to the site in baskets or skins. Here and there the antiquarians discovered patches of bluish earth that contained pieces of charcoal and burnt bone.

They discovered a timbered passageway that led to an oval burial vault also lined with logs, which they guessed to be about at the center of the mound. Its roof had been paved with stones apparently from the opposite shore of the Ohio River. Inside were two skeletons, which a Wheeling doctor proclaimed to have been elderly individuals, judging from the condition of their teeth. The excavators also found a number of disk-shaped beads with holes in their centers. The beads had been made from seashells, but at the time they were declared to have been manufactured from the ivory of the tusks of mastodons.

When they believed they had discovered evidence of a second or upper burial vault, the excavators dug a second tunnel to reach it. Its occupant turned out to be the single badly decomposed skeleton of someone who had been interred with a lot more loot, including many "ivory" beads, seashells that might have been strung as a necklace, copper bracelets, and thin rectangles of mica that might have been stitched together to form some sort of garment.

While a few other skeletons were found buried near the top of the mound, it became clear that Atwater's interpretation of the mound as a mass grave was incorrect. There were no thousands of human skeletons buried there.

Several members of the dig team, including Abelard Tomlinson and Thomas Biggs, joined forces to lease the mound in order to transform it into a lucrative tourist attraction. When construction work was finished, visitors could climb a path to the mound's summit where they could take in the view from a three-story observatory, or they could explore the tunnel and enter a dark interior chamber which had been timbered, plastered, and named the "rotunda" by the entrepreneurs. There they could examine by candlelight the various bones and beads that had been discovered inside the mound. Other Native American artifacts found in the local area were later added to the collections of this makeshift museum.

Unfortunately, urban development lagged in Moundsville and few tourists arrived. The rotunda collapsed and the artifacts vanished. By 1860 the mound had a new owner who gave the town a more promising enterprise: a saloon constructed on the mound's flat summit.

If the Grave Creek Mound still gets fewer visitors than it deserves, that may be because it remains to this day difficult to locate. My husband and I approached Moundsville driving south on Route 2, which runs roughly parallel to the Ohio River, where the scenery consisted of the occasional barge and many, many remains of America's steel industry, some continuing to function, others merely developing a sad patina. We turned off on what we thought was the right cross street, but found ourselves in a residential neighborhood with no signs of an ancient pile of dirt.

A guy loading his truck couldn't help us, nor could a group of senior citizens heading out for lunch. The problem may have been compounded by my asking directions to the Grave Creek Mound Archaeological Complex and Delf Norona Museum. Once one of the senior citizens realized we were looking for the "big mound," he explained it was a little farther south, down near the prison.

We located the sinister, turreted stone prison and learned that in the early years of the twentieth century, its wardens also had been responsible for the upkeep of the mound; one of them had constructed a small building at its base where tourists could purchase souvenirs made by prison inmates. This building later functioned as a site museum until it was replaced by the current museum in 1978, which is named for Delf Norona, who also founded the West Virginia Archaeological Society. The site had been placed on the National Register in 1966 and is currently administered by the West Virginia Division of Culture and History. When we arrived on a weekday in August 2007, the complex was being expanded to accommodate the West Virginia Archaeology Center, which opened in the spring of 2008.

Among the exhibits we studied were those illustrating how scholars now think the Grave Creek Mound was built, an effort that took over one hundred years and the cooperation of many participants, something like the construction of a European cathedral. The mound was started over the grave of someone important, then about thirty years later, someone else was buried in the mound, which continued to grow. Finally a ditch was dug around the mound, possibly intended to act as a protective sacred circle. A model illustrated an interpretation of the second burial, with tiny Mound Builder action figures conducting ceremonies on the summit while others carried more dirt to the site.

The Delf Norona Museum was set up so that visitors walked through the interpretive exhibits before exiting outdoors to see the mound. Grave Creek Mound was the first large conical mound that we encountered in our early twenty-first-century travels in the Midwest, and the moment we confronted it I expe-

rienced the same sensation that
would come over me at many other
Mound Builder sites. "I suppose you
want to climb that thing," my husband guessed.

Unlike the steps to the top of
Conus in Marietta, the Grave Creek
Mound had a narrow path that
wound gently around to its summit.
We could see that the grass covering the steep mound had been
mowed recently, and we did not
envy the poor guy whose job that
was. At the top we found a low
stone wall circling an obelisk with
the date 1942 and letters indicating
the four cardinal directions. A
refreshing view of the Ohio River
greeted us on that warm and humid
afternoon, but no sign of a saloon.
Pity.

An obelisk graces the summit of
the sixty-two-foot Grave Creek
Mound where visitors can view
the Ohio River in the distance.
(*Author*)

Despite Benjamin Smith Barton's intriguing lure of "valuable
spoils," and Caleb Atwater's claim that gold and silver objects had
been found in several tumuli (though he himself had never seen
any), the only mineral finds made by early nineteenth-century
antiquarians were artifacts made from copper and mica, which
were hardly precious. Americans were slowly unearthing their
continent's prehistory, but so far, no one was getting rich.

4

The Lost Civilizations

According to Henry Marie Brackenridge the best ancient remains were to be found in a region he named the "American bottom," which included parts of Ohio, Kentucky, Tennessee, and what was then called the Indiana Territory. There the ruins occupied fertile alluvial soil on the Ohio River, the Mississippi, and their tributaries at "the most eligible situations for towns or settlements," as he put it in his book *Views of Louisiana* published in 1814.

Brackenridge was among the first to describe the astounding groups of truncated pyramids at a place called Cahokia. It had been 1811 when Brackenridge crossed the Mississippi River at St. Louis and proceeded through the woods to a plain where he found himself in a field of circular mounds that he compared to enormous haystacks. He climbed one of the largest mounds and took in a view of the Cahokia River bordered by trees and a prairie that stretched to the horizon. Farther along the river he came upon what he described as the "principal mound" of a large group of ruins. Shaped like a parallelogram with an apron step jutting out to the south, it had been adapted for modern use by a nearby community of Trappist monks who had planted a kitchen garden on the apron and sowed wheat on its flat summit. "What a stupendous pile of earth!" Brackenridge wrote.

Brackenridge was among those observers who interpreted the quantity and size of these remains as evidence that their vanished builders had been many in number. He speculated that the Mississippi had once supported as large an ancient population as the Nile or Euphrates. In his book he wrote, "If the city of Philadelphia and its environs, were deserted, there would not be more numerous traces of human existence."

He also imagined that the Mound Builders had been citizens of a relatively despotic empire, similar to those of pre-Columbian Mexico and South America, where individuals had been more or less enslaved by their chieftains. In fact, he speculated that the Mound Builders of the American Bottom might have been some-how in communication with what he called New Spain. In his letter to Jefferson written in 1813 and published in the *Transactions of the American Philosophical Society* in 1818, he contended, "The distance from the large mound on Red River, to the nearest in New Spain, is not so great but that they might be considered as existing in the same country."

Brackenridge compared his astonishment on witnessing Cahokia with that of a traveler contemplating the pyramids of Egypt, but that was the only connection he made between American mounds and the world's other hemisphere. Brackenridge had no particular sympathy for Native Americans, certainly not the local Osage Indians, whom he thought had been treated far too leniently by the former French and Spanish governments of the region. In his book he described how Indians would raid settlers' villages at night, breaking into stables, stealing horses and anything else they could find. However Brackenridge was not willing to deny America's Indians credit for

An early twentieth century photograph of Monks Mound at Cahokia. Henry Marie Brackenridge was among the first to describe this remarkable grouping of mounds forming a pre-Columbian city now located across the Mississippi River from St. Louis, Missouri. (*Library of Congress*)

the ancient ruins of the American Bottom. He wrote, "The American tribes belong to the human race, and . . . men, without any intercourse with each other, will, in innumerable instances, fall upon the same mode of acting . . . . Perhaps the first employment of a numerous population when not engaged in war, would be in heaping up piles of earth, the rudest and most common species of human labor."

He questioned whether ancient colonists from any other shore would have been able to survive "amidst ferocious savages." Even if some brave lost voyagers had stumbled into North America from Europe or Asia and been suffered by the American Indians to live, would they not have been absorbed by the dominant culture, rather than stamping it with marks of their own?

Brackenridge may have had a kindred spirit in Thomas Jefferson, who also endorsed his book, but during the early years of the nineteenth century, their opinion quickly became the contrarian view. The United States had no such thing as a professional archaeologist or anthropologist, but the young nation did have educated people, even among those living on its frontiers. As they explored and diagramed earthworks and opened tombs, all the while trying to reconcile the existence of same with their own understanding of the universe, the local scholars of Mound

Builder country quickly fell in with the initial reactions of the earliest explorers and missionaries: that the ancient ruins of the new world had to have had some connection with the old.

The early nineteenth century was also that time period when Americans were formulating and acting upon what would be called Manifest Destiny, or the idea that the United States had the right and duty to expand throughout continental North America. This entailed the backward Indians getting (or being gotten) out of the way, a feat that was so much easier to justify if the Indians turned out to be not the twilight remnants of a great civilization but rather the ignorant, invading savages who had destroyed one.

A few years following the excavation of the Grave Creek Mound, a small piece of sandstone came to light that would become famous as the Grave Creek Tablet. It has since disappeared, and precisely where, when, and by whom it was discovered remains unclear. Abelard Tomlinson claimed to have found it, but so did others, including Henry Rowe Schoolcraft, a student of Native American legends and folklore, who said he found it lying neglected among other artifacts at the site. Schoolcraft was interested in the tablet because it had on one surface what appeared to be the characters of a written language. Schoolcraft compared them to characters of various Old World alphabets including Greek, Etruscan, Old English, and Phoenician, among others. Other scholars promptly proposed various translations, and for a while the Grave Creek Tablet served as proof set in sandstone that the Mound Builders were an offshoot of civilized life on a different continent.

The question of who the Mound Builders were and where they might have come from was necessarily intertwined with the broader question of how anyone had managed to reach the Western Hemisphere before Columbus. Spaniards establishing colonies in South America were first to grapple with this issue. Initially they questioned whether the natives they encountered were truly rational beings with immortal souls. The pope confirmed that they were indeed human beings, and therefore deserved the rights of men and the benefits of Christianity. This proclamation also made it necessary for the aborigines to have descended somehow from Adam and Eve, since the Bible said nothing about the Lord having created a second first couple in the Western Hemisphere.

The Bible did mention that ten of the twelve tribes of Israel had been lost to history when they were conquered and carried off by the king of Assyria in the eighth century BC. In 1580 the Dominican friar Diego Duran suggested that the American natives had descended from these lost tribes. In 1650 Rabbi Manasseh ben Israel made the theory more popular with his book *The Hope of Israel*, in which he identified Jewish origins for many of the beliefs and even the languages of South American Indians. Protestant clergymen of New England who studied Native American languages in order to preach to the local Indians started hearing Hebrew-sounding words spoken among their intended converts.

But how might the lost tribes have reached the Western Hemisphere? The Jesuit missionary Joseph de Acosta proposed that the old world and the new once had been connected by one or more land bridges over which had migrated flora, fauna, and human beings. His history of the New World was published in Spanish in 1590 and translated into English in 1604. For many readers his argument made it entirely plausible that wandering Jews had slowly made their way across Persia and China, and into America.

In the 1580s, a number of British publications carried the legend of Madog Ab Owain Gwynedd, or the Welsh Prince Madoc, who sailed west c. AD 1170 during a family feud and discovered a new land. He returned to Wales and assembled a party of colonists who took off in ten ships and were never seen again. Recollection of these old stories might have been sparked by the lone British explorer David Ingram, who claimed to have walked two thousand miles through North America where he had encountered one tribe whose language included some Welsh-sounding words. By the eighteenth century, other British explorers were hearing various Indians speaking Welsh.

A more exotic but extremely well reasoned theory of transcontinental migration specific to Mound Builders would arise in nineteenth-century Kentucky. Its author, John D. Clifford, was the scion of a Philadelphia merchant family who had chosen Lexington, Kentucky, as the headquarters for his own attempt at establishing a business empire. He had traveled throughout the state, as well as visiting Ohio and Tennessee, where he had witnessed many Mound Builder remains.

An old legend, currently disputed, held that the word "Kentucky" had meant to the Indians "dark and bloody ground," or a bad place where a lot of people had once died. Kentucky's fertile soil and the game it supported were attractive enough to American traders and explorers who began to visit in the 1750s and established the first permanent settlements in the 1770s. Some of these settlements were known as stations, meaning one or more residences sited and fortified in a way that adapted them for defense in case of Indian attack. Despite the danger, Kentucky's population continued to grow in the late 1770s and through the 1780s, allowing it to quickly evolve from a district of Virginia to the nation's fifteenth state in 1792.

Lexington, Kentucky's largest and most important town, began as a frontier station established in 1779. It quickly grew into an agricultural commercial center, as well as Kentucky's cultural and literary mecca, sometimes called the Athens of the West. The nickname paid tribute to the numerous books in the reading room of Lexington's Athenaeum, as well as its Transylvania University, the first institution of higher learning west of the Allegheny Mountains.

Lexington briefly supported a monthly magazine titled *Western Review and Miscellaneous Magazine*, which might have owed its debut to the faculty of Transylvania University who, like all college professors since, needed somewhere to publish what they had to say. From the fall of 1819 to the spring of 1820, *Western Review* published some highly provocative open letters by John D. Clifford, setting forth his own argument about who the Mound Builders had been and how they had gotten to America.

The letters were undoubtedly read by Caleb Atwater while he was at work on his book, *Description of Antiquities*. Unfortunately the Midwest had too few other intellectual readers to support *Western Review* for very long, so the magazine soon folded, and Clifford's articles were overshadowed by Atwater's more enduring book. Clifford's thoughts have since reached a new audience, thanks to modern scholar Charles Boewe, who edited the articles in a book titled *John D. Clifford's Indian Antiquities* published in 2000.

Possibly because it was an important pillar of his larger argument, Clifford took the sanctuary side in the fort versus sanctuary controversy in his first letter published in 1819. Rather than even use the word "fort," Clifford called the earthworks "circumvallatory earthen walls." He wrote, "I am induced to believe that most of the circumvallations were erected for open temples or places of worship, and that the tumuli, when adjoining and outside the same, are the graves of human [sacrificial] victims."

A telltale clue was the fact that while the old earthen walls often were built near springs or courses of water, they rarely enclosed them. "Nor could the inhabitants procure drink without exposure in all cases to the missle weapons of their enemies," he wrote.

Clifford's proposed sanctuaries included the ancient ruins of Circleville, where he differed with local resident Caleb Atwater. Clifford wrote, "If the square circumvallation had been intended for defense, seven wide entrances would never have been made in the manner mentioned, nor would the low circular mounds placed rather on one side have afforded any means of defense. They seem to have been erected for the purpose of placing theron statues of the Janitor Gods [not the gods of good housekeeping, but gods such as Janus who was the Roman spirit of archways and doorways]."

Clifford used his next several letters to argue his case on who had constructed the circumvallations and tumuli. In his second letter he made clear whom he thought the builders were not. He wrote, "The manners and customs of our present North American Indians are so totally incompatible with the characteristics displayed in these laborious constructions, that we cannot suppose their ancestors concerned in the formation of them. . . . They possess few of the civilized arts, such as the ancient relics display, whilst their mode of burial and religious rites are totally different."

According to Clifford, the Mound Builders had been genuine Indians, that is to say Hindus from India, or something close enough. In his fourth letter he wrote, "In asserting our aborigines to be of Hindu descent I do not perhaps totally contradict those authorities which make them a Tartar race." He went on to quote other scholars who concluded that the Hindus had descended from the Tartars or were in some way linked with them.

Yet Russia, Siberia, and the subcontinent were rather far away from Ohio and Kentucky, so how did the Mound Builders get here? In his fourth letter Clifford answered, "The Hindus however afford us still better proof that they possessed the art of navigation in the most remote times." Centuries earlier they had sailed to lands as distant as Java and Japan. Clifford went on, "As Japan and the adjacent islands are on the route to the American coast I see no cause to doubt their having visited it in earlier times."

Clifford laid out the evidence for his argument in letters three, four, and five. Hindu temples were surrounded by walls, and were generally situated on watercourses, or had tanks of water outside so that worshippers could purify themselves prior to entry. Mound Builder burial customs were similar to those of India in that corpses sometimes showed evidence of having been burnt. Clifford mentioned that conch shells of the species Murex had been discovered in Kentucky, usually by settlers clearing out springs located near ancient earthworks. Many of these shells were rare and curious, in that they had reversed spirals, placing their mouths on the left, rather than the right hand side. Clifford's research told him "that a shell of this description was consecrated by the Hindus to their god Mahadeva." Didn't these shells suggest that they had been brought by ancient Mound Builders from Asia to be used at American springs for ritual cleansing?

Clifford's strongest evidence was a clay vessel that had been given to him by a physician in Nashville. In his fifth letter Clifford described it simply as "a flagon, formed into the shape of three distinct and hollow heads joined to the central neck of the vessel by short thick tubes leading from each respective occiput." Each of its faces, he observed, was decorated with paint suggesting Hindu caste marks. He had to assume the vessel was intended for some sort of religious ritual, since its unusual shape made it highly impractical for drinking or any other domestic purpose. Clifford concluded, "If my

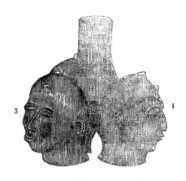

A sketch of the Triune Idol. John D. Clifford and Caleb Atwater both thought its shape suggested Hindu deities.

conjecture is reasonable and the place where the Flagon was found is strong confirmation thereof, we have almost direct proof of the identity of religion between the Hindus and our aborigines."

Clifford's letters certainly made an impression on Caleb Atwater, who reached many of the same conclusions in his book. He concurred that Hindus and southern Tartars well acquainted with the useful arts had made their way to America long ago. Atwater included an engraving of Clifford's three-headed clay pot drawn by a Miss Sarah Clifford of Lexington. Naming it the Triune Idol, Atwater asked his readers, "Does it not represent the three chief gods of India, Brahma, Vishnoo, and Siva?" He also mentioned the seashells found near Lexington which were considered sacred to the god Mahadeva in India, and the fact that ancient earthworks were invariably located on or near streams, just like the temples and sacred places of India.

Actually the Triune Idol was neither as ancient nor as rare as Atwater and Clifford supposed. Clay pots shaped like human heads were made by Indians living somewhat farther south until around the seventeenth century.

Tennessee had not been a state very long before its citizens organized to preserve and record its own ancient history. Settlers had been moving into the area since the 1770s, and before Tennessee was admitted to the Union in 1796, those dwelling in its eastern portion resided in a short-lived American state called Franklin. By 1820 concerned Tennessee gentlemen were meeting in Nashville to form an antiquarian society whose members included Caleb Atwater and John Haywood, a lawyer and justice of the state's supreme court, who served as the society's president. Haywood had lived in Tennessee since 1807. In 1823 he published a collection of anecdotes from various sources about Tennessee's long-ago inhabitants which he titled *The Natural and Aboriginal History of Tennessee*.

Like Atwater's work, the value of Haywood's book to modern archaeologists remains in its detailed descriptions of what Tennessee's ancient ruins looked like nearly two hundred years ago. For example, Haywood described the ancient remains at a place he called Bledsoe's Lick, now the town of Castalian Springs, which he reported had been lately examined by a man named Ralph Earl, an artist who managed the Nashville Museum. There a low wall enclosed about sixteen acres of land with a raised platform thirteen to fifteen feet high just east of a somewhat higher mound to which it once might have been connected with a stairway.

Haywood described a complex of mounds now known as Mound Bottom on the Harpeth River. He observed that its mounds appeared to be grouped in threes and were situated near the remains of an artificial well or tank which he speculated might have held water "for sacred uses."

Haywood described an enclosure surrounded by a wall of undressed stones piled up and covered with earth, which has come to be called the Stone Fort. A farmer attempting to cultivate ground inside it had plowed up "a stone very beautifully carved and ornamented, much superior to any known art of the Indians."

Haywood did not omit the now famous Pinson Mound Group, a complex including the highest mound in the state of Tennessee.

Haywood reported that in his day it was eighty-seven feet high, circular at its base, but rising to a platform that was a fifty-foot square.

Haywood was first to describe the symbols painted on bluffs high above some of Tennessee's rivers. Many appeared to represent the sun and moon, but others seemed to be part of some alphabet distinct from the Roman characters familiar to speakers of English. Typically these symbols were painted so high above the river bank that several nineteenth-century ladders placed end-to-end could not have reached them, and settlers could study them closely only by climbing trees. No one could figure out how the aborigines had managed to paint them without growing wings, or what they had used for paint, because the symbols did not seem to have faded since settlers first discovered them.

According to Haywood the painted rocks were frequently found near enclosures with mounds, or caves where skulls had been unearthed. He assumed that "the paintings are supposed to have represented the deities whom the people adored." Today archaeologists call these symbols petroglyphs, pictographs, or rock art. They have been discovered throughout North America, but few professional archaeologists specialize in their study, nor has anyone yet come up with an explanation much better than Haywood's.

Haywood quoted Clifford in speculating that the Triune Idol, which actually had been discovered within the boundaries of Tennessee, had been a sacred vessel, and he joined the Clifford and Atwater chorus in supposing that the local Mound Builders had Hindu connections. But Haywood's olden Tennessee had also been quite the scene of racial diversity. Human remains discovered in a fairly good state of preservation in a Tennessee cave led Haywood to believe that some aborigines had auburn hair and fair complexions. Tiny skeletons suggested that Tennessee had been home to a race of pygmies. Larger skeletons implied that "gigantic men of the North" may have had a hand in wiping out the more civilized Tennessee dwellers.

Haywood was also convinced that ancient Romans had journeyed to Nashville and Fayetteville because in his day ancient

Roman coins had started turning up here and there. The first had been found in 1818 when workers were digging a foundation for a Nashville home. In 1819 workers found a second coin while excavating a cellar for a home in Fayetteville located not far from some ruins thought to be an ancient fort. A third coin was found in a gully about two and a half miles away. In 1823 two other coins were discovered in the junk left behind by a Fayetteville resident who had moved away. These coins dated from the first to the beginning of the fourth centuries AD and led Haywood to conclude that those residing in Tennessee during that period had had some intercourse with the ancient Roman Empire. Since the Romans had obtained silk from faraway China, was it so difficult to believe that their coins somehow had been carried to China and Japan, then across the ocean with seafaring Hindus?

Atwater knew about other Roman coins said to have been discovered in a cave near Nashville but thought such anomalies had been deliberately planted by modern folks with a sense of humor who wanted to amaze and confound the gullible antiquarians exploring ancient American ruins. Atwater wrote, "That some persons have purposely lost coins, medals, etc., in caves which they knew were about to be explored, or deposited them in tunnels, which they knew were about to be opened, is a well known fact which occurred at several places in this western country."

Atwater was probably right. The man who left two coins behind in his Fayetteville house was named Mr. Colter. After he moved to Alabama in 1823, no more Roman coins were discovered in the ancient ruins of Tennessee.

In 1824 U.S. senator Humphrey Marshall of Kentucky published an expanded edition of his 1812 history of that state whose shortened title remained *The History of Kentucky*. A Kentucky resident for over thirty years, Marshall told his readers that the book was intended to preserve information about Kentucky's pioneers that might otherwise go to the grave with the folks who still remembered it. He also included a fast-paced introductory essay on the prehistory of Kentucky, and indeed the entire ancient world, by one C. S. Rafinesque, who identified himself in his byline as a "professor in Transylvania University, member of the

Kentucky Institute, and 15 other scientific or literary societies in the United States and in Europe."

Born near Constantinople, Constantine Samuel Rafinesque as a young man in 1802 came to Philadelphia, where he served as apprentice in the Clifford family merchant business, and no doubt first became acquainted with John D. Clifford. After about two years Rafinesque returned to Europe to spend a decade in Sicily working for the U.S. consul in Palermo, later operating as a merchant, and beginning to indulge his lifelong avocation as a student of natural history.

The naturalist and scholar Constantine Samuel Rafinesque (1783–1840) was inspired by the ancient monuments of Chillicothe to study Mound Builder ruins and write about ancient history. *(Library of Congress)*

Upon returning to America, Rafinesque contracted with a Pittsburgh bookseller to research and draw a new map of the Ohio River. Rafinesque set out in 1818 via flatboat down the Ohio, through Marietta and Cincinnati, making his way to Louisville and eventually the river's mouth. In his autobiographical book known by its shortened title *A Life of Travels*, Rafinesque wrote that on his return east, he stopped in Lexington where his old friend Clifford encouraged him to take a faculty position at Transylvania University. Needing to return to Philadelphia to wrap up his business dealings there, Rafinesque traveled through Ohio on foot by way of Chillicothe, Lancaster, Zanesville, and Steubenville. He wrote, "It was near Chillicothe that I saw the first great monuments and pyramids or altars, of the ancient nations of N. America; they struck me with astonishment and induced me to study them."

While he remained a friend of Clifford until the man's death in 1820, Rafinesque apparently harbored a great deal of animosity for Atwater which he blatantly expressed in his review of Atwater's book which appeared in *Western Review and Miscellaneous*

Magazine in 1820. Rafinesque's main criticism was that Atwater had left too much out: "We beg leave to suggest that his labours are not yet complete, that we have reason to believe his descriptions have been sometimes incorrect, and that there are yet a number of monuments he has failed to describe." Rafinesque also (unfairly) criticized Atwater for appropriating material from Clifford and others without attribution. Following a host of other criticisms, including that of Atwater's grammar, Rafinesque concluded his review with the faint praise that Atwater's work was "an excellent supplement to the previous labors, in the same field."

Rafinesque had been traveling and documenting his own observations on ancient ruins and he continued his criticism of Atwater in a two-part article published in the *Cincinnati Literary Gazette* in 1824. He enumerated the sites described by Atwater, plus those site descriptions Atwater had lifted from Drake (twenty-nine in all), then went on to list over forty other sites that "appear to have escaped the notice of Drake and Atwater."

Rafinesque ended his second article with the prediction that America's ancient Mound Builder ruins would someday command the same respect as the antiquities of Egypt, possibly when someone wrote a definitive history of ancient America, which was precisely what Rafinesque was planning to squeeze into his introductory essay to Marshall's *History of Kentucky*.

Titled "Ancient Annals of Kentucky," Rafinesque's essay began in an Eden whose "Adamites" and "Antediluvians" probably never made it to the Bluegrass State, unlike the descendants of Noah who were said to have evolved into various empires, including the Atlantes of northern Africa who came to dominate the greater Mediterranean area. "It was during the splendor of this empire, that America was discovered," Rafinesque wrote, by bold sailors who navigated from the islands of the Atlantic to the West Indies and thence to America, which they named Atala, and where they proceeded to settle down and spread out.

These Atalans built a great western Atlantic empire beyond the Alleghenies with its metropolis located somewhere on the Ohio River. Rafinesque wrote that they "lived in towns; built houses of wood, clay and rough stones. They worshipped the sun and moon as emblems of the Deity, and built them circular temples. They knew geometry, architecture, astronomy, glyphic signs, or writing, the use of metals, agriculture, &c." They also stayed in touch with contacts overseas: "An intercourse was kept up more or less regularly between all the primitive nations and empires from the Ganges to the Mississippi."

Then disaster struck. The simultaneous eruptions of volcanoes plus earthquakes sank "the Atlantic land," and inundated the east coast of America. In Europe they thought that the entire Western Hemisphere had been destroyed, while the folks in America's interior became separated and divided into many states and nations, including one that Rafinesque called the Talegans of Kentucky, Illinois, Ohio, and Virginia, later known as the Talegawes or Alleghanys.

A people that Rafinesque named the Iztacans next reached America from the west via "the peninsula of Alasca," establishing a number of states in the new world, including the Natchez empire. Although they caused the Talegans to retreat north of the Ohio River, they "borrowed many customs from them."

They were unfortunately followed by the Oghuzians, who also arrived over the Bering Strait via Siberia and proceeded to wage war over their more civilized predecessors, expelling them from the lands that they inhabited. These people became the ancestors of America's historic Indian tribes.

At the end of his essay, Rafinesque appended a list of "Authors and Works consulted," including both classical and contemporary authors. He unaccountably left out Plato's Dialogues, probably the source for the material in his essay that sounds like the tale of the destruction of Atlantis. The *Oxford English Dictionary* defines the Oghuz peoples as Turks who spread south and west from Central Asia in the eleventh century, eventually settling in Anatolia. The word "Iztacan" fails to appear in any major English language dictionary or encyclopedia. Of course, one could change a few letters of that word and come up with Aztecan, and there's a place called Iztacalco in Mexico. The Prussian explorer and naturalist Alexander von Humbolt, who had published an account of his recent travels in Central and South America, had mentioned a mountain in Mexico called Iztaccihuatl. As a naturalist himself, Rafinesque was an old hand in classifying and describing new species of plants and animals; could he possibly have applied these skills and simply made up the names for some of the nations and tribes that populate his ancient Annals?

Rafinesque died in Philadelphia in 1840 and his mortal remains lay buried in a modest grave until 1924, when they were exhumed and transported to Transylvania University in Kentucky. In a 1987 article in *Pennsylvania Magazine*, Charles Boewe questioned whether Rafinesque's fans had managed to dig up the right body from the cemetery, where interments had been vertically stacked to save space. The man who chronicled so many lost civilizations might have become lost himself en route back to Lexington.

Whoever is buried in Rafinesque's Lexington tomb, he or she has a very nice resting place, but not one that visitors can see without making arrangements through Transylvania University's Public Relations Office. Rafinesque's tomb is in the school's main building, which is called Old Morrison, behind a locked, unmarked door. The hidden room is decorated to resemble a tiny cemetery with a brick wall and an iron gate, where vintage lamps provide moderate lighting and much mournful atmosphere. Rafinesque's stone sarcophagus lies beside the tomb of another faculty member identified as Professor Bonfils.

Naturally, where there's a mysterious campus tomb, there's some campus lore. Rafinesque left his post cursing the college and its president who had dismissed him, not for being a poor teacher but for spending too much time off campus pursuing activities that were literally extracurricular. Not long after Rafinesque's departure, the college's main building burned and the college president died shortly after resigning. Legend still has it that every seven years Rafinesque's curse causes "something" to happen at Transylvania University. In 1969 there was another fire in Old Morrison which, significantly, spared its tomb room.

The students show proper respect. The university celebrates Rafinesque Week, and four lucky students are selected annually to spend a night behind closed doors with Professors Rafinesque and Bonfils.

Needless to say, the same Midwestern scholars who were speculating about where the Mound Builders had come from were also offering ideas on what had happened to them and where they ended up. Atwater cited architectural evidence that they had migrated south into Mexico: "Our ancient works continue all the way into Mexico, increasing indeed in size, number and grandeur, but preserving the same forms, and appear to have been put to the same uses."

Clifford speculated that the Toltecs, or predecessors of the Aztecs, had migrated from the north, their histories failing to mention this fact because "They did not choose to record what is esteemed the disgrace of proud and warlike nations." As confirmation for his theory that the Mound Builders had become the Aztecs, he mentioned the work of John Heckewelder published by the American Philosophical Society in 1819. The Rev. John Heckewelder was an eighteenth-century Moravian missionary who had spent much time traveling with and safeguarding Christianized Indians on their journeys between Bethlehem, Pennsylvania, and Detroit. Upon retiring in Bethlehem in the early nineteenth century, Heckewelder worked with members of the American Philosophical Society to record what he had learned from the Indians under the title *History, Manners, and Customs of the Indian Nations*.

Heckewelder noted that the traditions of the Lenape or Delaware Indians held that their ancestors had once lived in the distant west of the American continent. Migrating eastward they had come to a river called Namaesi Sipu (sounds rather like "Mississippi") where they met up with other Indians called the Mengwe (or Iroquois) who were also seeking desirable real estate farther east. They discovered that the land east of the river was home to a powerful nation called the Talligeu or Talligewi, or Alligewi, who had constructed many large towns on the banks of rivers. The Lenape thought they had secured safe passage through

Alligewi territory, but they were set upon by Allegewi who became alarmed at just how many Lenape were crossing the river. The Lenape then joined forces with the Mengwe and declared war, causing the Allegewi to try to protect themselves by erecting fortifications. After many battles the Allegewi acknowledged what seemed inevitable and fled down the Mississippi. The visitors divided the spoils: the Mengwe occupied land around the Great Lakes, while the Lenape went farther south, eventually to the Susquehanna Valley and Chesapeake Bay. To John D. Clifford, this certainly sounded like a history of the Mound Builders told from their conquerors' point of view.

Although he misspelled his name, Rafinesque mentioned Heckewelder as one of the authors consulted for his introductory essay in *History of Kentucky*. There he identified the Lenaps as one of the Oghuzian nations, specifying their original western home as the Multnomah and Oregon rivers. Following their war with what he named the Talegans while en route to their historical lands in Pennsylvania and Maryland, he noted that they "became partly civilized by the prisoners and slaves that they made."

Before his death Rafinesque had time to publish only a portion of the more comprehensive effort he was planning: a multi-volume work on the prehistory of North and South America titled *The American Nations or, Outlines of their General History, Ancient and Modern*. Possibly to refute some criticism he had received since *History of Kentucky* had appeared in print, this new work contained references to a primary source tending to confirm some of his earlier assertions. Rafinesque claimed that an Indiana doctor had received from a Lenape patient a history of the Lenape nation recorded in pictographs on a bundle of painted sticks. Rafinesque translated the pictographs into a creation myth and a tale of wandering during which the Lenape drove the Talega or agricultural nations from their homes in the general area of Ohio and Indiana.

Although Rafinesque claimed that he had somehow lost the original painted sticks, his English translation of this text called the Walam Olum was generally accepted as an accurate account through most of the nineteenth century. Only in the middle of the twentieth century did archaeologists become suspicious. Now generally believed to be a hoax, Rafinesque's Walam Olum lives on to tarnish his significant achievements as an early botanist and naturalist.

In his discourse on the aborigines of the Ohio Valley originally published in 1838, William Henry Harrison—soon to be elected the ninth president of the United States—agreed that the Mound Builders of the Ohio Valley had fled south to become the Aztecs of Mexico, and military man that he was, Harrison provided the most dramatic account of their defeat at the hands of savages. "No people," he wrote, "in any stage of civilization, would willingly have abandoned such a country, endeared to them as it must have been, by long residence and the labor they bestowed upon it, unless, like the descendents of Abraham, they had fled from the face of a tyrant, and the oppressions of unfeeling taskmasters." Harrison speculated that the forts constructed by the agricultural Mound Builders showed that they had faced assailants for many years whom he guessed were "those who still depend upon the chase for food, or who have advanced still further, and draw their subsistence from flocks and herds of their own rearing." Although safe behind their walls, the Mound Builders "might behold, from their summits, the devastation of their ripened fields."

Harrison went on to envision the ancient Mound Builders retreating from their enemies until finally driven "to make a last effort for the country of their birth, the ashes of their ancestors, and the altars of their gods." That valiant last stand, he speculated, had taken place at the fortress he had examined at the confluence of the Great Miami and Ohio rivers, probably an earthen enclosure on an elevation located in what is now called Shawnee Lookout Park. He described it as a "citadel, more elevated than the Acropolis of Athens, although easier of access, as it is not like the latter, a solid rock, but on three sides as nearly perpendicular as could be, to be composed of earth."

In 1833, a man who made his living crafting saddles and harnesses, but pursued a sideline of writing pamphlets about famous Americans, penned his own version of the theory of non-Native American origins for Mound Builder remains. Josiah Priest suggested on his title page that his conclusions were based on "travels, authentic sources, and the researches of antiquarian societies," but he really borrowed heavily from, and embellished greatly upon, earlier scholarly works to come up with a synthesis of accepted knowledge, or to put it less politely, a tabloid version of pretty much everything that had so far been proposed. Titled *American Antiquities and Discoveries in the West*, his subtitle betrayed the author's agenda: *Being an Exhibition of the Evidence that an Ancient Population of Partially Civilized Nations, Differing Entirely from Those of the Present Indians, Peopled America, Many Centuries Before its Discovery by Columbus.*

In his preface Priest asserted, "Along the different eras of time, different races of men, as Polynesians, Malays, Australians, Phoenicians, Egyptians, Greeks, Romans, Israelites, Tartars, Scandinavians, Danes, Norwegians, Welch [sic], and Scotch, have colonized different parts of the continent." He also repeated the popular sentiment that the Indians whom contemporary Americans knew had not been the people who built the mounds, but rather those who ran off the Mound Builders: "so the Chippewas and Iroquois prostrated the populous settlements on both banks of the Ohio."

Priest interpreted the ancient ruins at Marietta as a fort, and one that so strongly resembled descriptions of Roman military earthworks "that even the Romans may have built it." Rome had once been mistress of the known world, and Roman vessels had sailed clear around Britain. Surely it was possible they had ventured a little farther west. As supporting evidence he mentioned that a Roman coin had been found on a riverbank in Missouri.

Even Priest had to acknowledge that Romans capable of minting coins had also been a literate people who had left behind many documentary sources, none of which mentioned they had discovered America. Priest blamed the "Goths and Vandals, who overran the Roman empire, in which the discoveries, both of countries and the histories of antiquity, were destroyed."

Some of the earliest settlers of Lexington, Kentucky, had discovered what Priest called a catacomb, its entrance sealed with stones. When they entered it they found themselves in a spacious room with niches built into its walls, each occupied by a mummy as well preserved as the Egyptian variety. Priest inquired, "Why not allow the authors of the antiquated works about Lexington, together with the immense catacomb, to have been, indeed, an Egyptian colony?" The Egyptians had engaged in some maritime commerce, and if they hadn't purposely attempted a transatlantic crossing, could not a vessel or two have been driven to the American continent by a freak storm?

Priest noted that in several American locations Indians were heard to have been speaking in Welsh. On the Triune Idol, Priest went with the prevailing opinion that immigrant Hindus had fashioned it for religious purposes.

Sensationalist though he was, Priest got very lucky. Despite or perhaps because of all his fanciful claims, Josiah Priest's book became a big best seller that was read by many more Americans than any scholarly work published before it. Over 22,000 copies were sold.

Finally Benjamin Barton Smith's prediction had come true. "Valuable spoils" had at last been dredged out of the Mound Builder tombs.

5

Mormons and the Mounds

The various lost civilizations theories put forth by America's scholars and writers of pop history between the beginning and the middle of the nineteenth century happened to coincide with the literary movement called Romanticism. Romantic poets and novelists developed a fascination for the occult, the exotic, the obscure, and that which seemed remote in place or time, as they produced works in which emotion triumphed over reason, and sentiment over intellect. In America, Edgar Allan Poe became the master of the macabre. James Fenimore Cooper brought romance to the frontier and its vanishing native population. It was inevitable that other authors who wrote fiction intentionally would take on the remote and mysterious Mound Builders, while one young zealot who published something very different would be accused of plagiarizing one of their works.

In his 1832 poem, "The Prairies," William Cullen Bryant's "disciplined and populous race" of ancient agricultural Mound Builders falls prey to "roaming hunter tribes, warlike and fierce." Nor would it be long until their ruins, still visible to solitary wanderers like himself, would succumb to the "advancing multitude / which soon shall fill these deserts."

In 1839, Cornelius Mathews wrote a novel in which he populated the prairies with a race of ancient heroes living in cities furnished with mounds and towers of granite and marble. Its title, *Behemoth: A Legend of the Mound-Builders*, referred to a giant mastodon capable of defeating entire armies, which appears on the scene to wreck havoc and destruction on Mound Builder civilization. In this man-against-nature tale, chief Bokulla leads a small brave band of men who manage to contain the creature by walling up the entrance to the canyon where it lives. There the monster impotently rages and rampages until it dies.

Daniel Thompson followed in 1864 with *Centeola; or, Maid of the Mounds*. Heroine Centeola of the Tribe of Feathered Serpents of the Empire of Azatlan is the adopted daughter of an old sage. Centeola is herself a seer who happens to believe in a single benevolent God. En route to the Azatlan Imperial City, she meets hero Tulozin, a noble from another tribe, who falls in love with her. Centeola's mission in the city is to persuade the Imperial Powers That Be to halt their practice of human sacrifice. Time is short, for rough and savage hordes are preparing to move in on Azatlan from the north.

The stone walls of the Imperial City form a parallelogram surrounding a sacred enclosure which houses the pyramid of Mixitli, god of war, plus the temples of other gods. Centeola rides a white horse, and as she approaches the city she sees for the first time the domesticated mastodons that move heavy loads for the Azatlan people.

Centeola fails to stop the sacrifice of nineteen virgins and nearly becomes a victim herself, even though she is dramatically revealed to be the long-lost daughter of the aging Azatlan king. She and her entourage are saved by brave Tulozin and the providential intervention of two stampeding mastodons followed by a massive earthquake that causes the sinful Imperial City to vanish into a black chasm.

Centeola and Tulozin marry and bravely try to fight off the northern savages for a number of years. Eventually the Azatlan people migrate to "the genial climate of the palm trees" where they found the Aztec Empire. The author offers no explanation why the Aztecs later reinstated the practice of human sacrifice.

In the same period a young man named Joseph Smith produced a work today known as the Book of Mormon. Published in 1830, it tells the tale of several groups of Hebrew refugees who come to America in biblical times where they establish great civilizations and adopt Christianity through the direct intervention of Jesus. Some Americans accepted the Book of Mormon as holy scripture that had been divinely revealed to an honest young man seeking true faith and salvation. Detractors regarded it as something Joseph Smith either made up or copied. A theory came into circulation that Smith had plagiarized the Book of Mormon from an unpublished historical romance novel about Mound Builders, and the so-called Spaulding Theory about the origin of Mormonism was born.

For a well-researched and dispassionate history of the Book of Mormon and the Mormon faith, I turned to Hubert Howe Bancroft, still considered a worthy historian of the American West, whose works published in the late nineteenth century remain valuable sources of information for modern historians and anthropologists. Bancroft begins his *History of Utah* in the wilds of western New York during the early nineteenth century, a time and place that he wrote would nurture "the germ of a new theocracy, destined in its development to accomplish the first settlement of Utah."

Born in Vermont in 1805, Joseph Smith moved with his family to New York, first taking up residence in Palmyra, Wayne County, then Manchester, Ontario County. One day in the spring of 1820, Smith was reading his Bible when he came across the passage, "If any of you lack wisdom, let him ask of God." Smith did just that, upon his knees out in the woods. Thick darkness fell and a pillar of light descended upon him. In the sky, Smith saw God the

Father and His Son, of whom Smith inquired which religion he should join. He was told to join none at all, for they were all abomination in the eyes of the Lord. Needless to say, no one believed the youthful farm boy when he told them about the vision.

On September 21, 1823, a figure appeared to Joseph Smith. It was robed in white and it levitated near his bedside. Introducing himself as Moroni, a messenger of God, this apparition told Smith of a book engraved on golden plates bearing an account of the early inhabitants of the American continent, and two stones called the Urim and Thummin that would be required to translate the story into English.

Having also received knowledge that these artifacts would be found buried nearby in a hill called Cumorah, Joseph visited the site the following day and promptly located them in a stone vault. Smith was prevented from removing them at that time by the reappearance of Moroni, who told him to leave them be for now but to return to the same spot at the same time each year for the following four years.

In his footnotes, Bancroft quotes sources explaining that these thin golden plates were engraved on both sides with Egyptian characters. The plates were fastened together at one edge with three rings, rather like a three-ring binder. Bancroft explains that the Urim and Thummim were transparent crystals "set in the rims of a bow" like the lenses in a pair of glasses, but a pair of glasses far too big to fit the human face.

To make a long story short, Smith began his translation of the text on the plates in 1827 with the assistance of two believers who served as his scribes. In 1830 a New York printer produced a first edition of his translation. Moroni took back the original plates, but not before Smith had shown them to several disciples who would be able to swear they had really existed.

In the ensuing years, Smith attracted both devout followers and hostile mobs. In 1844, Smith was shot while in an Illinois jail. His followers tried to start settlements in the Midwest, then set their sights on the sparsely settled West where they became the neighbors of Indian tribes, mainly the Ute peoples.

The publication of the Book of Mormon was swiftly followed by the appearance of anti-Mormon literature. In 1834 a tract appeared with the misspelled title *Mormonism Unvailed*, its author and publisher identified as Eber D. Howe of Painesville, Ohio. Its introduction clearly reflected the animosity with which some greeted this new faith. The author called it "the depths of folly, degradation and superstition, to which human nature can be carried." The parents of young Joseph Smith he described in his first chapter as "lazy, indolent, ignorant and superstitions – having a firm belief in ghosts and witches; the telling of fortunes; pretending to believe the earth was filled with hidden treasures, buried there by [Captain] Kid or the Spaniards."

The purpose of *Mormonism Unvailed* was to lay out the theory that Joseph Smith, being too ignorant to come up with his own material, had plagiarized the Book of Mormon from an unpublished novel written by the Rev. Solomon Spaulding, a Dartmouth graduate and evangelical clergyman who had lived in New York and later moved to Ohio, where he was inspired by the local ruins to become an amateur archaeologist. Spaulding had conveniently died in 1816, and was therefore not around to compare his own manuscript, titled *Manuscript Found*, with Smith's Book of Mormon.

Howe quoted Spaulding's brother John and his widow Martha, both of whom recalled Spaulding reading to them from the drafts of his novel. Both contended that the prophets named Nephi and Lehi in the Book of Mormon had made their debut as fictional characters in *Manuscript Found*. Both maintained that Spaulding's book was based on his own theory that Native Americans were the descendants of lost tribes of Jews who had journeyed to the Western Hemisphere in ancient times. Howe included a statement by Spaulding's one-time business partner, who also recalled that Spaulding had read parts of his work in progress to him. In his statement, this witness wrote, "I well recollect telling Mr. Spaulding, that the so frequent use of the words 'And it came to pass,' 'Now it came to pass,' rendered it ridiculous." The witness concluded, "I never heard any more from him or his writings, till I saw them in the Book of Mormon."

For his theory to be credible, Howe needed to explain how Joseph Smith might have gotten hold of a copy of *Manuscript Found*. Howe suggested that Spaulding had sent it to a publisher where it remained in limbo until after Spaulding's death because author and publisher could not come to terms on the publication contract. One of the publisher's employees was supposed to have conveyed the manuscript to Smith and connived with him to use it to invent a new and possibly lucrative religion.

Buried in the extremely interesting footnotes of Bancroft's *History of Utah*, I found references to two nineteenth-century publications suggesting that the real mastermind of the Spaulding theory was a man named Doctor Philastus Hurlbut. Rex C. Reeve, Jr., the author of an introductory essay in a 1996 edition of *Manuscript Found*, researched these sources thoroughly and had much more to reveal about this shady and shadowy character.

It seems that Doctor Hurlbut (Doctor was not a title but his first name) had joined the Church of Jesus Christ of the Latter Day Saints and become an elder of the Mormon faith. However, his colleagues kicked him out for the sins of pride and debauchery, causing Hurlbut to turn against the church and preach against its adherents. He soon met up with acquaintances of Spaulding from whom he learned of *Manuscript Found*. Fellow anti-Mormons advised Hurlbut to sell the concept for the book that would be titled *Mormonism Unvailed* to Howe so that it could be published as the work of a man with a much better reputation than Hurlbut's.

Hurlbut and Howe both had seen Spaulding's *Manuscript Found*, yet neither published it, which would seem the logical thing to do had the drafted manuscript really been as damning as they claimed. Instead Howe deliberately kept it under wraps. *Mormonism Unvailed* also contains some language toward the end of the text that would seem to be offered as an explanation, just in case anyone else ever found and read *Manuscript Found*. Hurlbut and/or Howe mentioned that a manuscript written in Spaulding's handwriting had been discovered in a trunk and shown to several of the witnesses whose statements appeared in *Mormonism Unvailed*. According to the authors, these witnesses explained that

that particular manuscript was an early draft of the novel and not the one they had been talking about in their statements.

Manuscript Found was written by Spaulding in Conneaut, Ohio, sometime between 1808 and 1812. It was finally published by the Mormons themselves in 1885. It had been transferred with other documents to a man named L. L. Rice who purchased the newspaper Howe had published. Apparently unaware of what he had in his possession and its implications, Rice hung onto it for over forty years until he donated it to the archives of Oberlin College in Ohio where it still remains. If there were any other drafts of *Manuscript Found* written by Spaulding they have yet to surface. Proponents of the Spaulding theory can still be found, but their arguments are considerably weakened now that anyone can read and compare *Manuscript Found* with the Book of Mormon.

Spaulding employed a device well known and loved by authors of historical fiction when he claimed that his novel was based on a genuine old document which he literally had unearthed. In *Manuscript Found*, the manuscript in question was supposed to have been written on twenty-eight rolls of parchment that had long remained hidden in an artificial cave covered by a flat stone on top of an Ohio mound. Spaulding was able to understand it because it was "written in eligant [*sic*] hand with Roman Letters & in the Latin Language."

The tale on the parchment rolls supposedly began with the story of Fabius and other Christian Romans who were blown off course during an ocean voyage to Britain. After a five-day storm, they found themselves on the shore of a land populated by savages who wore skins and lived in wigwams, from whom they were able to purchase land and good will by trading cloth and knives.

Since the group of castaways included several young women (both "ladies of rank" and "bucksom Lasses"), the Romans decided that the decent thing to do while they were stranded in the wilderness would be to marry one another. Although the women's movement was a long way off, Spaulding allowed each female character to choose which man she wanted for her husband.

Yet the Romans remained uneasy living among the local aborigines with their odd hair styles and their painted faces who went around half naked in the summertime. Fabius begins Chapter IV with the lament, "Gracious God! how deplorable our situation! are we doomed to dwell among the hords [sic] of savages — & be deprived of all social intercourse with friends & the civilized world? & what will be the situation of our ofspring [sic]?"

In an attempt to get back to the enlightened Roman Empire of Constantine, the castaways decided to do what Columbus and other explorers would later attempt, namely go east by traveling west. They never make it back to Europe, but they do discover the land of the fairer-skinned Ohons (later spelled Ohions) who weave cloth, grow crops, domesticate horses and "Mammoons" (mammoths? mastodons?), forge iron and lead, and craft pottery. The Ohions also build large forts with earthen ramparts and canals or trenches. They have a written language, though "the works of the learned are not very voluminous."

No sooner do the Ohions appear in *Manuscript Found* than the Roman Christians turn into what modern television scriptwriters call a dropped story line. They vanish from the novel, as Spaulding turns to the history of the Ohion Empire.

In Spaulding's ancient Ohio, there are two nations: the Sciotans and the Kentucks, who live on either side of the Ohio River in relative peace. Somewhat like the Greeks and Trojans, they go to war over a woman. The lovely Sciotan princess Lamesa elopes with the handsome Kentuck prince Elseon rather than go through with the loveless marriage that has been arranged for her. Sciotan honor depends on her return to the fold. The war proceeds for many pages and gives Spaulding a chance to explain the Ohio mounds as resting places for the chiefs who fell in battle.

That work of scripture or literature commonly called the Book of Mormon consists of fifteen books, of which the Book of Mormon is only one. It also includes several books of Nephi, as well as individual books of Jacob, Enos, Jarom, Omni, Mosiah, Alma, Helaman, Ether, and Moroni, each of them divided into chapters. The reason they are collectively titled the Book of Mormon lies in the subtitle of this work, which defines it as "an account written by the hand of Mormon, upon plates taken from the plates of Nephi." I looked at three editions: one published in

1830, one published in 1920, and an online version that I found at the official web site of the Church of Jesus Christ of the Latter Day Saints.

The 1830 edition had notes on its title page saying it had been printed for the author, Joseph Smith, Junior, in Palmyra, New York. Joseph Smith began with a preface explaining some of the problems that he was already enduring at the hands of "evil designing persons" who were out to "destroy me, and also the work." Like the later editions, this one included two paragraphs known as the Testimony of Three Witnesses and the Testimony of Eight Witnesses: the people Smith had permitted to see the plates and the engravings on them. Other markings on the volume indicated it once had been part of the library of the Union Theological Seminary, an interdenominational institution founded in 1836. As if the seminary wanted to be certain to take no sides, pasted into the volume were two newspaper clippings dating from the 1880s promoting the Spaulding theory.

The 1920 edition had a more biblical look in that the text on each page was printed in two columns, and each page had a header identifying its book and chapter. It included a handy guide to the pronunciation of names and identified Joseph Smith as the translator of the material, not "author and proprietor," as he had been named in the 1830 edition.

I did a lot of clicking around on the official web site of the Church of Jesus Christ of the Latter Day Saints before I found it, but I was able to locate an electronic copy of the Book of Mormon, together with editions of the Old and New Testaments. The site described the Book of Mormon as "Another Testament of Jesus Christ." The book's introduction attested to its validity, inviting the public to read it, ponder its message, and then "ask God, the Eternal Father, in the name of Christ if the book is true." One's reply would come through the Holy Ghost.

According to the Book of Mormon, the earliest refugees to come to the New World from the Old were the Jaredites who departed the Near East around the time that the Tower of Babel was constructed. However their story appears rather late in the Book of Mormon text, and is told by Moroni based on twenty-four golden plates that comprise the Book of Ether, a prophet descended from Jared. Arriving in the promised land following a fierce storm, the Jaredites till the earth, build cities, and multiply until their civilization dissolves into internecine war. Ether observes a mighty battle and the death of millions at the hill named Cumorah in New York, then known as Ramah to the Jaredites.

The remainder of the Book of Mormon deals with Israelites and their descendants escaping Jerusalem just before its destruction by Nebuchadnezzar. Their leader is Lehi, and they also arrive in the Western Hemisphere following a perilous ocean voyage. Over the course of hundreds of years and hundreds of pages of text, they also prosper and multiply, but divide into two nations called the Nephites (after Lehi's son Nephi) and the Lamanites (after another more recalcitrant son of Lehi called Laman). According to Bancroft's analysis of the Book of Mormon, "The former [Nephites] advanced in civilization, but the Lamanites lapsed into barbarism, and were the immediate progenitors of the American aboriginals." The Nephites were blessed by visits from angels and the resurrected Christ Himself. The Nephites and even the Lamanites for a time adopted Christianity. But once the Nephites begin backsliding the Lord allows their civilization to fall to the Lamanites. Following another devastating battle at Cumorah, Nephite prophet Mormon survives to write the history of ancient America on golden plates. He gives them to his son Moroni who deposits them at Cumorah.

I admit I did not read the entire Book of Mormon. I skimmed through the chapters of the various books hunting for descriptions of the material culture of the Jaredites, Nephites, and Lamanites. I learned that these peoples worked metals, domesticated animals, wove cloth, and built structures where they conducted religious ceremonies, as well as other buildings of timber and cement.

What I did not find were any descriptions of the construction or use of any earthen circles, squares, or ellipses, walled pathways, or mounds shaped like haystacks or sugarloaves. It almost seemed as if Mormon, Moroni, Nephi, and everybody else in the

Book of Mormon had never seen any genuine Mound Builder structures. As it happens, Joseph Smith had yet to visit the Midwest during the years when he was translating the Book of Mormon, though the Mormons would set up shop in Ohio shortly after its publication.

I also failed to find much similarity at all between *Manuscript Found* and the Book of Mormon. *Manuscript Found* is about Christian Romans and a fictional race of Ohions; it has nothing to do with lost tribes of Jews. There's no Nephi or Lehi in *Manuscript Found*. Variations on the phrase "it came to pass," so common in the Book of Mormon, never appear in *Manuscript Found*.

In fact, any similarities between the two works are limited to generalities that might well be coincidental or arising from the influence of the Zeitgeist on both writers. Both works deal with people coming from the Eastern Hemisphere to the Western Hemisphere. Both include descriptions of great and desperate battles, and both deal with the twilight of advanced but flawed and doomed civilizations. Those who made charges of plagiarism in their signed statements for *Mormonism Unvailed* were either mistaken or lying. The Book of Mormon may have appeared at a time when Americans were fascinated with Mound Builders, but it certainly was not plagiarized from a novel about them.

Fact or fiction, the Book of Mormon is accepted as gospel by about six million Americans who practice what is by no means an easy faith. But if you're looking for a rollicking good read and insight into what nineteenth-century Americans were imagining about Mound Builders in the era of Romanticism, just skip the Book of Mormon and read Daniel Thompson's *Centeola* instead.

6

That Old-Time Religion

Toward the middle of the nineteenth century the earlier fort versus sanctuary controversy would evolve into a nationwide effort to measure, map, and describe the Midwestern ruins in an effort to categorize and classify them. The idea was to replace wild speculation with objective conclusion based on a substantial body of data. Professor Constantine Samuel Rafinesque could well have made a claim to having initiated this effort. In an open letter published in *Western Review and Miscellaneous Magazine* in December 1819, titled "On a Remarkable Ancient Monument Near Lexington," he listed many of the kinds and shapes of ruins that had already been located, urging that they be classified into five categories: temples, fortifications, towns, mounds, and "miscellaneous monuments." He wrote, "Under this view of the subject, we shall enlarge our ideas on the capacity and ability of the former inhabitants of this soil, and all our researches will tend to illustrate their acquirements and their civil history." Just a few years following Rafinesque's death his call would be answered by a team of master classifiers who would organize the Midwestern ruins under almost those exact headings.

In 1848, Americans were able to purchase a book titled *Ancient Monuments of the Mississippi Valley: Comprising the Results of Extensive Original Surveys and Explorations* by Ephraim George Squier and Edwin Hamilton Davis. The book was praised for its execution as well as its scope. While earlier studies had been geographically parochial, Squier and Davis attempted a nationwide survey, though they naturally failed to include much of the distant West where reports of new finds were just beginning to come in. Rafinesque might have appreciated a last-minute change in their title from *Aboriginal Monuments* to the broader *Ancient Monuments*, a term he himself had frequently used.

In their preface, Squier and Davis used the Latin term "de novo" to describe their project as a whole. They explained that they had started by discarding all preconceived notions and they had proceeded "as if nothing had been known or said concerning the remains to which attention was directed." The trouble with earlier compilations, they explained, was that data had been "mixed up with the crudest speculations and the wildest conjectures. Even when this was not the case, the fact that the original observations were made in a disconnected and casual manner, served still further to confuse the mind of the student and render generalization impossible."

Edwin Hamilton Davis was born in Ohio in 1811 and studied medicine at Cincinnati Medical College before setting up his practice in Chillicothe. While still a student, Davis began exploring Ohio's ancient ruins. As American settlers enlarged Ohio's towns and provided the young state with transportation infrastructure, Davis watched while many antiquities were obliterated. He began collecting Mound Builder artifacts and corresponding with other interested scholars. After *Ancient Monuments* was published, he moved to New York City where he taught medicine and continued in private practice.

Ephraim George Squier was born in New York in 1821 and tried his hand at various endeavors while he developed his talents as a writer and editor. He met Davis in the 1840s while he was in Ohio working for the *Scioto Gazette*. When their project was finished, Squier wrote a second monograph on New York antiquities, and later managed to get himself appointed as charge d'affaires to Guatemala, where part of the attraction must have been the opportunity to study the antiquities of Central America. In middle age he succumbed to mental illness and was committed to a New York insane asylum.

Compiling and publishing a comprehensive study of ancient ruins to be found in a huge and loosely defined geographical area was a rather expensive undertaking for a doctor and a journalist. Squier, the more ambitious member of the team, traveled east to drum up financial support. Fortunately he was able to locate a newly founded and well-funded institution in Washington, DC, which planned to publish a series of scholarly monographs for which his and Davis's study could conceivably be suitable.

In 1829, wealthy British scientist James Smithson died and left over $500,000 to the United States on the condition that a nephew of his died without issue. Following the nephew's death in 1835, the cash was shipped to America, a country Smithson had never visited, where his will had stipulated it be used to found an institution for "the increase and diffusion of knowledge among men." After Congress finally accepted the bequest in 1846, the Smithsonian Institution was organized, and physicist Joseph Henry became its first secretary.

Henry probably realized that he was risking the fledgling Smithsonian's reputation by publishing a book on American archaeology as volume number one of what was intended to be a prestigious series called Contributions to Knowledge. The field of archaeology had yet to mature as a scholarly or scientific discipline, and thus far, all its practitioners were amateurs, including prospective authors Squier and Davis. However, their topic would definitely appeal to the general public, and Henry also probably realized that the well-heeled Smithsonian Institution was perhaps the only organization in America which could afford to publish a volume with the number of expensive illustrations that Squier and Davis proposed. Henry took the gamble, but assumed enough editorial control to ensure that Squier and Davis would make good on their plan to avoid speculation so that the book could indeed be called a contribution to knowledge.

Squier conducted most of the surveys and excavations and did most of the actual writing, while Davis the collector analyzed the recovered artifacts and provided most of the cash that the partners would invest. As the effort neared completion, Davis got wind of what he interpreted as a plot by Squier to take full credit for the book. By the time copies were in print, Squier and Davis were no longer on speaking terms. Henry had to step in to keep the peace and assure Squier that sharing credit was the professional thing to do, even if Squier thought he had done most of the work. Henry encouraged Squier to look forward to all the future opportunities that the book's publication would bring him.

Squier and Davis did a lot of their own digging, particularly among the fascinating remains of Ross County, Ohio, which were practically in their backyards. On the subject of their methods they wrote, "Care was exercised to note down, on the spot, every fact which it was thought might be of value, in the solution of the problems of the origin and purposes of the remains under notice; and particular attention was bestowed in observing the dependencies of the position, structure, and contents of the various works in respect to each other and the general features of the country. Indeed, no exertion was spared to ensure entire accuracy, and the compass, line, and rule were alone relied upon, in all matters where an approximate estimate might lead to erroneous conclusions."

Since Squier and Davis could not be everywhere, they relied on field agents such as John Locke, James McBride, and in particular Charles Whittlesey of Cleveland, who submitted plans and descriptions of many remains in northern Ohio. In print they commented that Whittlesey's "archaeological researches have been both extensive and accurate." They also incorporated information published by Rafinesque, whose papers they borrowed from a man named Brantz Mayer who had acquired them after Rafinesque's death. In their text, Squier and Davis informed readers they had double checked Rafinesque's "accuracy in all essential particulars."

Squier drew most of the maps in *Ancient Monuments*, and they were the best that the American public had so far seen. Besides illustrating the topography on which the ruins had been constructed, Squier's maps often had cross-section or elevation diagrams, as well as arrows to indicate which way was north. Over the years, the major criticism these maps have drawn is that they make the ruins look too perfect by not indicating where they had been eroded or otherwise degraded.

It was Charles Whittlesey who presented Squier and Davis with a previously unpublished map of Marietta, which they described in a footnote as having been drawn in 1837 "from a careful survey of these works." This was the map that showed how the grid plan of the modern town had been designed to incorporate and preserve the ancient ruins. It showed all the mounds and enclosures, the position and scale of the graded way (or Sacra Via) from the town to the river, and the relative size of the old stockade built by the pioneers. Squier and Davis preserved the old map by printing it as a full-page illustration in *Ancient Monuments*.

Squier and Davis also managed to correct some of Caleb Atwater's misinterpretations. Atwater's description of stones covering wells submerged in the bed of Paint Creek makes them sound to the modern reader like manhole covers, and naturally raises a lot of questions about how they might have been constructed and used. Squier and Davis contended that these were "natural productions," actually a natural range of "septaria," or stone nodules that were frequently found wedged into local slate formations.

Squier and Davis's major contribution to American archaeology was to classify the ruins according to what they speculated had been the Mound Builders' purpose for them. They separated earthworks from mounds, then further divided the earthworks into Enclosures for Defense versus Sacred and Miscellaneous

Enclosures. They divided the mounds into Sacrificial (or Altar) Mounds, Sepulchral Mounds, Temple Mounds, and Observation Mounds, adding a category comparable to Rafinesque's "Miscellaneous Monuments" for mounds that were "entirely inexplicable" as they put it, naming these particular mounds "Anomalous Mounds."

Squier and Davis noted their observations regarding the relationships between mounds and enclosures. Altar mounds were usually in or near enclosures, while burial mounds were isolated or appeared in groups far from the enclosures. The regularly shaped temple mounds, so named by Squier and Davis because they assumed they were "in some way connected with the superstitions of the builders," were usually inside, but sometimes just outside, the enclosures.

Both the mounds and the enclosures were constructed from either earth or stone, whatever was easiest to come by at the spots where they were built. However there were also mounds composed of clay that evidently had been moved some distance. Squier and Davis guessed, "The object of this may perhaps be found in the fact that mounds composed of such materials better resist the action of the elements, and preserve their form."

Their research showed that altar mounds were constructed of alternating layers, or strata, of dirt, sand, pebbles, or mixtures thereof. At their cores, one found an altar of clay or stone that showed signs of having been subjected to fire. Altar mounds tended to be the best sources of relics including pipes, pottery, spear-heads, and other artifacts, sometimes mixed with bone fragments.

Burial mounds could be cone-shaped, elliptical, or pear-shaped, from six to eighty feet high. They were generally raised over a single skeleton laid out full length in a burial chamber of stone or timber. Sometimes a layer of charcoal implied that this individual's funeral rites had involved something being burned, perhaps as a sacrifice.

According to Squier and Davis, the Grave Creek Mound, one of the largest in the Ohio Valley, deserved "more than a passing notice." They included an engraving depicting the mound being admired by sightseers, which also illustrated the tunneled entrance to the crypt and the observatory at the summit. Squier and Davis noted that of all the many sepulchral mounds they had studied, Grave Creek was the only one so far with two ancient burials. It was also the only mound in which a tablet had been discovered possibly inscribed with a written message, but Squier and Davis were dubious about its authenticity. They wrote, "Until it [i.e., the tablet] is better authenticated, it should be entirely excluded from a place among the antiquities of our country."

Burial mounds were often found in a group, with smaller mounds arranged around larger ones. Squier and Davis thought the large mounds were the graves of great chiefs which had been surrounded by the graves of other members of their distinguished families. As for Grave Creek, they wrote, "It is possible that, instead of building an additional mound, a supplementary chamber was constructed upon a mound already raised." Squier and Davis concluded that not every Mound Builder had merited his or her own mound, and that much of the ancient population had probably been interred with little ceremony on the banks of rivers in ground that since had been plowed up by modern farmers.

The flat-topped mounds that Squier and Davis called terrace or temple mounds, they described as the "sites of temples or of other structures which have passed away, or as 'high places' for the performance of certain ceremonies." They observed that some of the burial mounds had come to resemble altar mounds when a collapsing crypt had created a flat top or indentation. Some of these temple mounds were to be found in Marietta, Newark, Portsmouth, and Chillicothe in Ohio, but one encountered more and more of them as one traveled south. There were remarkable ones in Kentucky and Tennessee, and certainly the most remarkable of all was the one Brackenridge had located in Cahokia, Illinois.

Squier and Davis made their contribution to the still raging fort versus sanctuary controversy by publishing their opinion that some of the earthen enclosures indeed had been forts. These were the ones that had been constructed in strategic or commanding positions. To those who argued that they seemed to have all too many openings, Squier and Davis suggested that some of the openings might once have been filled with bastions constructed out of more perishable materials. The forts also probably once had crowning palisades of wooden stakes, watchtowers, and reservoirs to hold water in case of a lengthy siege.

Squier and Davis also observed that most of the military works were located in northern Ohio, where they appeared to form a line of defense against the advance of enemies who might have been moving south from Lake Erie. They quoted Whittlesey's observation that the structures in the north seemed typical of what one always found on a nation's frontier. Squier and Davis added that in western river valleys such as the Scioto Valley between Columbus and Chillicothe, mounds had been built on certain tall hilltops and spaced in such a way as to suggest that they could be used for observation and signal fires that could spread news in a hurry of impending invasion to those dwelling farther south.

Yet there were other enclosures, geometrically regular squares and circles, that the Mound Builders had constructed on broad river bottoms where the terrain was fairly flat. Squier and Davis wrote, "The structure not less than the form and position of a large number of the Earthworks of the West, and especially of the Scioto valley, render it clear that they were erected for other than defensive purposes."

Some of the nonmilitary circles there were fairly small ones "with a nearly uniform diameter of two hundred and fifty or three hundred feet." They had a single opening or gateway, usually but not always facing east, and if they had ditches, the ditches were usually inside the circle. Smaller circles, ranging from thirty to fifty feet in diameter with no opening, were assumed by Squier and Davis to be the foundations for lodges or buildings. The largest circles were those connected to squares or other geometrical shapes, which could enclose a space as large as fifty acres. Such circles were usually fairly low, about three to seven feet in height, and the few that had ditches also had them inside their walls.

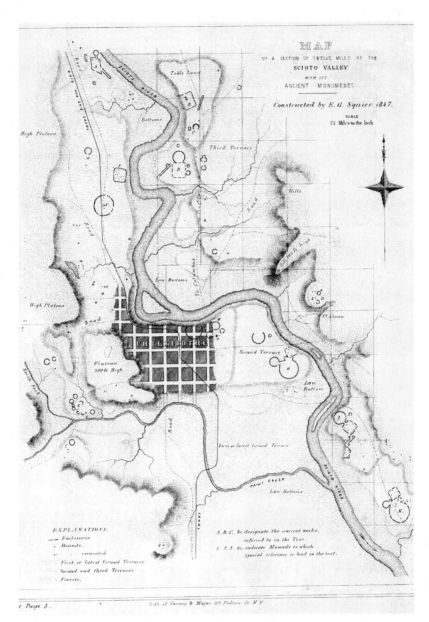

The map of the Scioto Valley surrounding Chillicothe, which appeared in *Ancient Monuments*. The grid plan of the mid-nineteenth-century city lies between the Scioto River and Paint Creek. The Ohio and Erie Canal runs more or less parallel to the river right through town.

Regarding the connecting squares, or sometimes octagons, Squier and Davis repeated observations already on record that they had gates at the corners and middles of their walls where small mounds were located. Squier and Davis remarked that several of them "are exact squares, each measuring one thousand and eighty feet wide,——a coincidence which could not possibly be accidental, and which must possess some significance. It certainly establishes the existence of some standard of measurement among the ancient people, if not the possession of some means of determining angles." These large enclosures, Squier and Davis concluded, were too large to be temples themselves, but rather cordoned off some sacred area where shrines, altars, or temples had been located and religious rites performed.

What others had described as roads or avenues, Squier and Davis named graded ways, or parallels, referring to the earthen embankments that defined them. That these were meant to facilitate transportation seemed obvious, but Squier and Davis did not venture much of a guess as to how, when, or why the Mound Builders had used them. "The most remarkable one," according to Squier and Davis, was the graded way south of Piketon in Pike County, Ohio. Over a thousand feet long and over two hundred feet wide, with flanking embankments over thirty feet high, it ascended about seventeen feet from one river terrace to the next. Its grade was so easy that the builders of the Chillicothe and Portsmouth Turnpike had constructed their modern road right through it. Squier and Davis included an engraving showing a stagecoach passing between its embankments and commented, "Indeed, hundreds pass along without suspecting that they are in the midst of one of the most interesting monuments which the country affords."

The Great Serpent of Adams County, Ohio, Squier and Davis classified among "sacred enclosures," while most of the nation's other effigy mounds appeared in a chapter titled "monuments of the North-west." These, constructed in the shapes of animals, birds, reptiles, or humans, were generally found closer to the Great Lakes in Michigan, Iowa, or Missouri, and especially in Wisconsin. Most were located on level prairies between

Milwaukee on Lake Michigan and the shore of the Mississippi River at Prairie du Chien, along a natural path which Indians of the historic era had used as a warpath, and the United States Army had adapted as a military road. Squier and Davis admitted that little yet was known about the effigy mounds but suggested that they must have had a symbolic or superstitious meaning. They cited them as evidence that the earthworks of what was then America's Northwest were distinctly different in character than those of the Ohio Valley or the southern states.

A significant portion of *Ancient Monuments* dealt with the artifacts that were the fruits of Squier and Davis's extensive excavations, which they classified by raw material and supposed function. They contradicted the overheated assumptions of earlier antiquarians who had found European objects in burial mounds. Squier and Davis suggested that these had been deposited fairly recently by modern Indians who considered the mounds good places to dig graves for their own dead whom they interred with prized possessions, often objects acquired from Europeans.

According to Squier and Davis, the Mound Builders had been skilled craftsmen, though they did not employ the most advanced techniques. They had probably not discovered the potter's wheel or the technique of glazing their pottery. The Mound Builders had hammered implements and ornaments from copper but "without the intervention of fire." They used stone, as well as animal bones and horns, to make knives, axes, and pestles, as well as spearheads and arrow points. They fashioned the same materials into a surprising number of beads as well as gorgets, amulets, and what Squier and Davis identified as "pendants," or objects resembling architects' plumb bobs. The Mound Builders also cut thin sheets of silvery and opaque mica into scrolls, disks, and other shapes, often pierced with a tiny hole suggesting that they might have been attached to garments.

"The mound-builders were inveterate smokers," Squier and Davis wrote, adding that their pipes constituted "a singularly interesting class of remains." The bowl where they placed tobacco, or whatever they were smoking, was often carved in the shape of some animal and usually located in the middle of the pipe's stem, rather than at the pipe's end. Squier and Davis described pipe bowls carved into eagles, heron, owls, ducks, and one that looked to them like a toucan. They added engravings to illustrate the ones they considered the most artistic and beautiful, including a tufted heron bending over to capture a fish.

They had high praise for the artistic skill that the Mound Builders exhibited in their other stone sculptures, which included animals such as beavers, otters, wildcats, and again, a lot of birds. They wrote, "Many of these exhibit a close observance of nature and a minute attention to details, such as we could only expect to find among a people considered advanced in the minor arts." Modern-day Indians could not match them, even though the Indians of Squier and Davis's own time had been exposed to European art and superior carving tools.

Among the artifacts rarely found were sculptures of the human head and sculpted tablets. Squier and Davis disagreed with some of their predecessors that any of the designs on these tablets constituted an example of written language, firmly stating that the Mound Builders had left no evidence whatsoever that they had developed an alphabet or a system of hieroglyphics. According to Squier and Davis, they also left nothing behind that might have been intended as a pagan idol or object of worship.

The relics were generally in better shape than the skeletal remains, which Squier and Davis described as decayed and prone to disintegrate at the touch. The authors spent much time looking for an intact Mound Builder skull and finally found one in a mound in the Scioto Valley near Chillicothe, but even that was missing its lower jaw. They warned that much of what one might find exhibited and labeled as Mound Builder crania were probably the skulls of modern Indians who had been buried near the surfaces of ancient mounds.

Like Rafinesque before him, Ephraim Squier claimed that greater Chillicothe had inspired him to study American antiquities, and the map he and Davis included in their book clearly shows why. Squier and Davis drafted a twelve-mile section of the Scioto Valley showing the grid plan of Chillicothe wedged between the Scioto River and Paint Creek, and literally surrounded by mounds, earthen circles, squares, and enclosures of other geometrical shapes. In their description, Squier and Davis noted that greater Chillicothe "possesses a deserved celebrity for its beauty, unexampled fertility, and great number, size, and variety of its ancient remains. Situated in the middle of southern Ohio, and possessing a mild and salubrious climate, this seems to have been one of the centers of ancient population."

The town of Chillicothe was established in the 1790s despite resistance from the Shawnee who considered the region their own. Many of its earliest settlers were Revolutionary War veterans from Virginia, and many of its better dwellings resembled Virginia mansions. When Ohio became a state in 1803 Chillicothe was its first capital, and a Virginia gentleman named Edward Tiffin the first governor. For a time Chillicothe was the most genteel town in the Old Northwest, where many famous personages were welcomed at the estate of Ohio's senator and later governor Thomas Worthington, whose 1807 mansion was designed by no less an architect than Benjamin Henry Latrobe, best known today as designer of the U.S. Capitol and many other public buildings.

However, Chillicothe's growth was necessarily impeded until its farmers obtained better transportation for agricultural products than via the Ohio River to the Mississippi and distant New Orleans, or east to Wheeling, West Virginia (then still part of Virginia) and thence farther east via the not so convenient National Road. In 1825 work began on the Ohio & Erie Canal intended to link the Ohio River with Lake Erie. When the 308-mile system was fully operating in 1832, Chillicothe became a port town, and the docks on its Water Street were soon teeming with the rigs of farmers and the flat-bottomed boats of canal men. Its population grew rapidly in the 1820s and the 1830s, as did a new industry for the town: boat construction.

In the last paragraph of their preface, Squier and Davis observed that the time available for a complete examination of ancient ruins was growing short. They might have been thinking of booming Chillicothe when they mentioned the constant encroachments of agriculture and the "leveling hand of public improvement" threatening to obliterate the ancient monuments that they had so carefully diagrammed in and around Chillicothe.

When my husband and I visited Chillicothe to see what was left of any ancient monuments, we discovered that Squier and Davis were still on hand to guide us. The National Park Service has united five remaining sites under the aegis of the Hopewell Culture National Historical Park, but as the sites are not contiguous, the ranger who greeted us at the main visitor center handed us printed material indicating their locations which was illustrated by Squier and Davis's maps of each site.

According to Squier and Davis, perhaps the most remarkable site in the entire Scioto Valley was one bearing the name Mound City thanks to the large number of mounds contained within its low and nearly square walls. The owner of the property on which it stood had permitted them to investigate thoroughly, and Squier and Davis consequently excavated almost all of them. Squier and Davis unearthed human remains, some showing signs of cremation, many shards of broken pottery, copper disks, sheets of opaque mica, shell and pearl beads, plus a treasure trove of about two hundred finely crafted pipes. Squier and Davis concluded that "the principal [mounds were] found to contain altars and other remains, which put it beyond question that they were places of sacrifice, or of superstitious origin."

Across the river at Hopeton Works, Squier and Davis found not mounds but a square-and-circle earthwork complex with several supplemental circles and two parallel walls that led from one corner of the square toward but not quite to the Scioto River. Squier and Davis observed that the path thus formed was wide enough "to admit the passage of a coach." As depicted on their map of the Scioto Valley, the path seems to lead in the general direction of Mound City.

My husband and I were the first visitors of the day in 2007 when we arrived at Mound City where a slight mist was still hanging over the mounds. We were first to enter its enclosure, and soon we were out of sight of the visitor center among the turf-covered mounds, where the site's profound silence made our footsteps seem curiously loud on the grass. The mounds at this

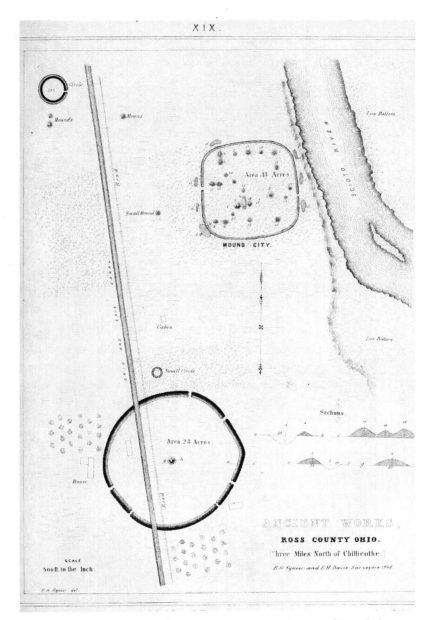

Mound City, north of Chillicothe, in *Ancient Monuments*. Squier and Davis's diagram was used in the reconstruction of the site following its use as a World War I cantonment.

site are not the highest one can find, but the sheer number of them and the size of the surrounding enclosure makes this park perhaps the best place to get a sense of the scale of the civilization that constructed them. Mound City indeed. The site is now surrounded by a belt of woodland that has been allowed to resume its natural state, isolating the place and permitting visitors to experience some of the same amazement that nineteenth-century settlers would have felt.

We exited the enclosure on its far side near a bluff overlooking the river, where a path led us to a small deck. As we leaned on its railing, peering through the foliage at the water below us and listening to a recorded interpretative message about Hopeton Works across the Scioto, I realized that this was the only place in Chillicothe where I had a sense of being in close proximity to a wide and significant body of water. Hopeton Works itself we did not see; it was closed to the public except for specific days during the summer when visitors could take guided walks.

There's some question about exactly how much of the original Mound City we saw, since a good deal of the acreage that Squier and Davis studied was incorporated into a World War I cantonment called Camp Sherman for the training of military doughboys. Camp Sherman nearly quadrupled the population of Chillicothe and added a temporary city of about two thousand buildings to the area, including many barracks, a hospital, and a short line railroad. Local archaeologists and civic leaders were sometimes successful in getting the United States Army to construct buildings without razing the mounds of Mound City, but Camp Sherman needed its own water and sewer lines, so the site endured a different kind of excavation.

After the war ended in 1918, Mound City would never be the same. The Ohio State Archaeological and Historical Society began investigating what was left of some of the mounds in 1920 and 1921. In 1923 President Warren G. Harding signed a proclamation to make Mound City a national monument. By 1925 funding became available to clear the site of Camp Sherman debris, which was followed by the reconstruction of the mounds and enclosure walls using Squier and Davis's map as a blueprint. In the 1930s the

The mounds of Mound City, now part of the Hopewell Culture National Historical Park. Visitors can wander among the reconstructed mounds in this thirteen-acre space enclosed by walls three- to four-feet high. (*Author*)

Works Progress Administration added improvements to the site including a picnic shelter, parking lot, and boat landing. They also added soil to improve the appearance of the mounds, often without consulting Squier and Davis's maps. By the 1940s Mound City was a place where people went to enjoy themselves, families sitting on the mounds to consume their picnic lunches and organizing games of softball and horseshoes among them.

The National Park Service has worked long and hard to turn the primary public use of Mound City from recreation to interpretation, and to make the place look like it did when Squier and Davis arrived. In the 1960s nearly all the reconstructed mounds were reexcavated to ensure they stood on original locations. Recent efforts have been made to restore the turf. Features that appeared on the Squier and Davis map but long since had disappeared from Mound City are reappearing. In 1998 test excavations for the relocation of a trail turned up evidence of a long-lost pit. Since 2009 archaeologists from the Midwest Archaeological

Center have been studying the enclosure wall and the surface within not occupied by mounds.

Once Squier and Davis had left the scene, the Hopeton Works on the Scioto's opposite shore continued being plowed by farmers using equipment that was increasingly efficient for agriculture but destructive to ancient monuments. In the 1980s and 1990s a sand and gravel vendor acquired some acreage and began quarrying operations. Congress authorized the National Park Service to purchase part of the Hopeton Works in 1980, but it took until 1992 for the entire site to become part of the Hopewell Culture National Historical Park. The first archaeological investigation since Squier and Davis's was initiated in 1994, and today work continues on what is now called the Hopeton Earthworks Project.

Five miles south of Chillicothe on a bluff overlooking the east bank of the Scioto, Squier and Davis mapped a monument they called the High Bank Works. It consisted primarily of an irregular octagon joined to a circle by a short neck, plus supplemental circles. Squier and Davis wrote, "The coincidences, in the dimensions, between this and the 'Hopeton Works,' will be at once observed," but they added little more about it. At that time the walls of the octagon and circle were respectively twelve and five feet high, but by the end of the century they were succumbing to local farmers who had also cut a lane through the structure's neck so they could more easily move their wagons through the area. High Bank Works joined the Hopewell Culture National Historical Park in 1992, and archaeologists soon began using geophysical surveys and limited excavations to study it. It was closed to the public when we visited, but National Park Service literature told us that this site is one of only two known complexes containing an octagon, also mentioning that it is at the moment one of the least understood sites.

On the north fork of Paint Creek, on the estate of a man they identified as W. C. Clark, Squier and Davis mapped the site they called Clark's Work, which they included in their chapter titled "Works of Defence" with some qualifications. Clark's Work included an enclosure roughly shaped like a rectangle with one

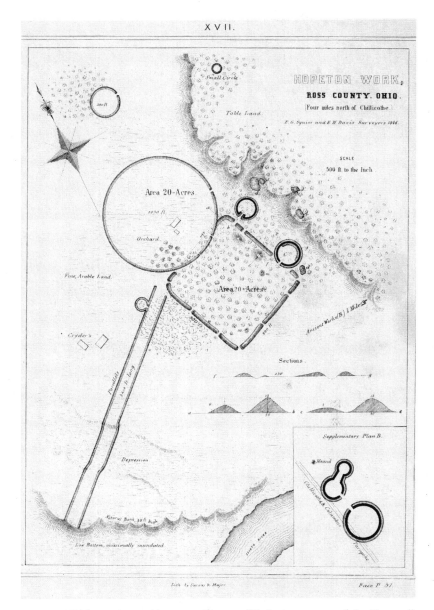

Hopeton Works, in *Ancient Monuments*. Hopeton Works is now part of the Hopewell Culture National Historical Park and the scene of current research called the Hopeton Earthworks Project.

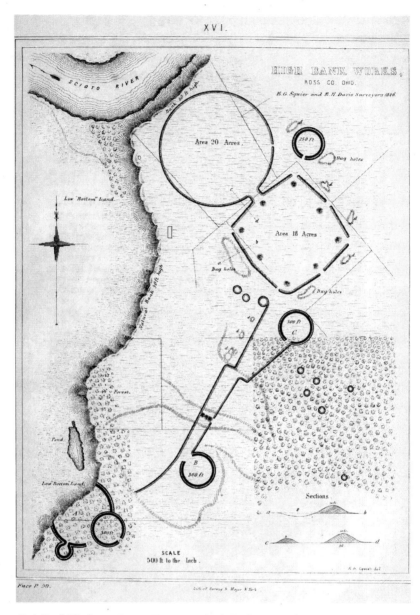

High Bank Works, in *Ancient Monuments*. High Bank is one of two sites with a circle-octagon earthwork complex. The other is in Newark, Ohio. A road might have connected these sites in pre-Columbian times.

rounded corner, adjoining a square. Inside the rectangle they found a circle and a second earthwork shaped like the letter D enclosing seven mounds including three large conjoined ones. Squier and Davis wrote, "The minor works which [Clark's Work] encloses, or which are in combination with it, are manifestly of a different character, probably religious in their design and would seem to point to the conclusion, that this was a fortified town, rather than a defensive work of the last resort."

The map they drew showed that the road between Chillicothe and Frankfort had been built right through the parallelogram and part of the D-shaped structure. Over the years the road became a railroad right of way, and subsequently part of the Tri-County Triangle Trail now popular with bikers, runners, and in-line skaters. The site itself remained overgrown and minimally accessible to visitors until a sort of detour trail was constructed, allowing hikers to climb to an observation point from which they could view the remaining embankments.

Squier and Davis mined the mounds of Clark's Work for artifacts, as did other archaeologists in the 1890s and 1920s. After the site, which had long since been renamed the Hopewell Mound Group, became part of the Hopewell Culture National Historical Park in 1992, modern archaeologists began investigating the previously unexplored spaces surrounding the mounds. Using minimally invasive techniques they have recently discovered evidence of one previously unknown mound and earthwork. Researchers hope to learn more about exactly how the site was constructed.

In the pages following their general map of the Scioto Valley, Squier and Davis included a map of a six-mile section of the valley of the main branch of Paint Creek. It showed the many bends of the creek with its tributary runs, as well as the Milford and Chillicothe Turnpike running through the center of tiny Bourneville. It also included much clearer and finer depictions of the same monuments Atwater had included in his map of the same area.

The monument that both Squier and Davis and Atwater labeled "A" consisted of a circle and a square both opening off an enclosure that was neither circle nor square, but something in between. Roughly in the center of this oddly shaped structure, Squier and Davis identified the largest single elliptical mound in the valley, standing nearly thirty feet high, plus some smaller con-joined mounds to its east. They noted that the circle had nearly succumbed to the plow, while the square was often inundated when freshets forced creek water through a dry channel that had formed through it. However the big mound and the deep pits that surrounded the entire monument were serious enough impedi-ments to agriculture and the elements to save at least some of the site long enough to become the Seip Mound State Memorial. Some surrounding land with remnants of earthworks more recently became part of the Hopewell Culture National Historical Park.

My husband and I turned off busy Route 50 into the memori-al's small parking area, then visited a kiosk with a diagram of the original tripartite earthen enclosure and information about what later excavation of its large mounds revealed. Archaeologists later restored what is now called the Seip Mound, which rises at the end of a dirt path through a grassy field. We walked the path, observing a brick farmhouse on our left, which also appeared to have occupied this site for a long time. Before we got to the mound we stopped to read a sign saying that analysis done in 1971 had identified the location of a prehistoric house that contained many pieces of mica, prompting archaeologists to speculate it had been home to a craftsman, though today's archaeologists dispute this claim.

Since there were no signs warning us not to, we climbed the Seip Mound. I had heard that one can see part of the surrounding circle and some remaining mounds from the Seip Mound sum-mit. It was pretty dry in the summer of 2007 when we visited, and all we could see around us were fields that had turned very brown and the grounds of what appeared to be a nearby school.

One thing we noticed while visiting all the various compo-nents of the Hopewell Culture National Historical Park was that we were always driving out of town. Chillicothe long ago expand-ed beyond the few square blocks that Squier and Davis indicated on their map of the Scioto Valley, in the process swallowing up

The Seip Mound, now located in Seip Mound State Memorial, was once the central mound in a complex of geometric earthworks. Surrounding land has been acquired by Hopewell Culture National Historical Park. (*Author*)

much of the remains of what they had described as a center of ancient population.

We also had a difficult time finding much remaining of the Chillicothe of Squier and Davis's day. The busy Ohio & Erie Canal they diagrammed running roughly diagonally through town had vanished, though it was still remembered in the name of the Old Canal Smokehouse, a modern restaurant located on what was once one of the canal's banks, where we enjoyed a very filling meal of smoked barbeque. The old downtown had become repopulated with boutiques, but most residents did their main shopping in Chillicothe's second downtown, in the big box stores and chain restaurants of the strip malls lining Bridge Street north of the Scioto River. The young clerk at our hotel suggested we drive over there so as not to miss Chillicothe's brand-new seafood restaurant—Red Lobster.

When I took Squier and Davis's map of the Scioto Valley and compared it side by side with the map we had obtained from the Chillicothe Convention and Visitors Bureau, I realized that one ancient earthwork complex they had failed to name but described as "much reduced, although distinctly traceable" had been very likely directly beneath the hotel where we were staying.

The sense I had of the old ruins being swallowed up was nowhere more evident than when we went to visit the Story

The Story Mound stands nearly twenty-feet high on about an acre of land now surrounded by suburban development and separated from visitors by a chain link fence. (*Author*)

Mound, which was not part of the Hopewell Culture National Historical Park. We drove through a residential neighborhood looking for this site, which we found not far from an elementary school surrounded by small houses that looked like they had been part of a post–World War II subdivision. We found the Story Mound protected by a chain link fence and identified by a sign as an "archaeological preserve" off-limits to trespassing. It looked so incongruous in its current surroundings that I felt sorry for it.

Following the wealth of evidence that Squier and Davis had set before their readers, the section of their book titled "Concluding Observations" occupied very few pages, nor were there a lot of original or unequivocal conclusions to be found elsewhere in the text. But Squier and Davis had never been in the business of drawing conclusions, which they made clear in that chapter's first sentence: "With the facts presented in the foregoing chapters before him, the reader will be able to deduce his own conclusions, as to the probable character and condition of the ancient population of the Mississippi Valley."

They did propose that the numerous agricultural and religiously devout Mound Builders had been "essentially homogenous in customs, habits, religion and government," based on "the great uniformity which the ancient remains display." The question remained whether the Mound Builders were "at one time diffused over the entire [Mississippi] valley, or that [they] migrated slowly from one portion of it to the other."

The Mound Builders had certainly had "a connection more or less intimate" with "the semi-civilized nations which formerly had their seats among the sierras of Mexico, upon the plains of Central America and Peru." Mound Builder artifacts were made of materials from places as far distant as the Alleghenies, the Great Lakes, and the Gulf of Mexico, causing Squier and Davis to speculate that "this fact seems seriously to conflict with the hypothesis of a migration, either northward or southward."

Mound Builder remains were old, but it was impossible to say exactly how old, and they had not been built by American Indians. In making this last conclusion Squier and Davis pulled their punch by quoting another "eminent archaeologist," Albert Gallatin (better known as America's fourth secretary of the Treasury), who had observed about the Grave Creek Mound: "It indicates not only a dense agricultural population, but also a state of society essentially different from that of the modern race of Indians north of the tropic."

Many of the same conclusions appeared more forcefully stated in a 1872 book titled *Ancient America, In Notes on American Archaeology*. Its author, John Denison Baldwin, was a New England journalist who had worked at the Hartford newspaper *Charter Oak*, and Boston's *Daily Commonwealth*, before becoming proprietor of the *Worcester Spy*. Baldwin was the unabashed and self-proclaimed popularizer of Squier and Davis's *Ancient Monuments*. His book was based on articles he had written for the *Worcester Spy* which were in turn based on Squier and Davis's material, which Baldwin declared "must be regarded as the highest authority." His book was to be a summary of theirs, more accessible to general readers including those who could not afford the original, which had gone on sale for the not inconsequential price of ten dollars.

Although Baldwin contended that the Mound Builders had indeed migrated from the South because "the remains indicate that their most populous and advanced communities were at the South," he agreed with Squier and Davis about the different types of mounds and earthworks, their indeterminate albeit great antiquity, and the concept that they were evidence of a united people organized as a nation with a central government. He certainly agreed that American Indians had not constructed the ancient remains: "It is absurd to suppose a relationship, or a connection of any kind, between the original barbarism of these Indians and the civilization of the Mound-Builders." Baldwin backed up this assertion with the same quote from Albert Gallatin, and he invented a differentiating and descriptive phrase which he used repeatedly in his book to describe the Native Americans familiar to his own contemporaries: "wild Indians."

Somewhat different classifications and interpretations of Mound Builder ruins appeared in an 1858 book titled *Traditions of De-coo-dah and Antiquarian Researches* by William Pidgeon, the same antiquarian who had initiated excavations at the Serpent Mound. This work remains intriguing largely because Pidgeon insisted that he had the inside story on Mound Builders which he had learned from the Indians themselves.

Of all the authors who had thus far published Mound Builder information, Pidgeon was among the most well traveled. He had already visited South America when he moved to the Miami Valley in Ohio in 1829. Between 1837 and 1839 "business pursuits" took him into the upper Mississippi Valley. In 1840 he traveled from St. Louis to Galena, Illinois, by steamboat, later visiting Dubuque in Iowa, as well as the Wisconsin Territory where he got to know the local Indians and decided to explore farther west. "Having provided myself with a rifle, tomahawk, and blanket," he wrote, "I crossed the Mississippi nine miles below the Indian boundary-line."

Pidgeon had a special relationship with an Indian descended from the Elk nation whose name, De-coo-dah, meant mockingbird. De-coo-dah shared Pidgeon's wanderlust, having migrated from one Indian nation to the other since his infancy. They got friendly when Pidgeon offered him food and shelter during two severe winters, resulting in his adoption as De-coo-dah's son. As such De-coo-dah entrusted him with the Indians' ancient traditions, including the secrets of the Mound Builders. "Treasure them then," De-coo-dah admonished him, "in your paper-book, and keep them as the dying gift of De-coo-dah."

Among the information Pidgeon published in his paper book was the interpretation that conical mounds or tumuli marked the spot where a great warrior had fallen. Their purpose was to "protect his ashes and to preserve the memory of his name and exploits."

Pidgeon revealed that those effigy mounds shaped like birds or beasts that were frequently found in Wisconsin were "national monuments," or the totems of a particular nation. They were raised as tribes migrated, and if they appeared to be a combination of two different creatures, then they were meant to memorialize the union of two nations.

The large circles of the Mound Builders were "national circles" where the various tribes and bands of a particular nation gathered each year and pitched their tents to feast, bond with one another, and agree upon who would be hunting where during the ensuing year. Pidgeon quoted De-coo-dah's observation that the white man had been entirely wrong in ever supposing that the circles had anything to do with war. "The traditions of my fathers," Pidgeon quoted De-coo-dah, "show them to have been only the scenes of mirth and festivity." The mounds within circles were "towers" for the use of a nation's king, its war chiefs, its prophet, and other dignitaries. According to tradition, the other enclosures "of great extent, varying in form and relative connection" marked the sites of ancient cities and sanctuaries.

When Pidgeon presented De-coo-dah with a diagram of the ancient ruins at Circleville, De-coo-dah recognized it immediately as a place he had known in his youth as "Sci-o-tee," and he was less than pleased to learn that an American town now occupied the site. In fact, his hand moved to the handle of his knife as he inquired, "Do the bones of my fathers rest in peace?" De-coo-dah subsequently explained that the Circleville circle had marked the geographical center of the territories of four united nations and was the nations' annual gathering place where many weddings had been celebrated.

Pidgeon claimed to have personally excavated quite a few ancient ruins, and he included an account of what he unearthed in a mound some miles south of the road between Cumberland and Wheeling. Pidgeon started digging straight down from the center of the top of the mound, while an old white man and his two sons assisted him by opening what amounted to a drift mine from the side. It was Pidgeon who discovered a smooth flat stone covering a burial vault which held a decayed skeleton. Pidgeon suggested resealing the grave, but discovered that the old man was holding a grudge when it came to what he perceived as the body of a Native American. He claimed that the deceased was "a d—d Indian, and he would never show them any quarter, dead or alive," because his own parents had suffered greatly at Native American hands. The old man picked up a big rock and hurled it, "crushing the little mass of bone to dust."

In Pidgeon's book De-coo-dah is not amused to hear about Pidgeon's pot hunting activities and asks Pidgeon to stop disturbing the remains of his people's dead. Pidgeon wrote, "I took up my spade, and deliberately threw it into the lake; and he then immediately became cheerful, and we smoked together the pipe of friendship."

Pidgeon was well aware of the publication of *Ancient Monuments*, and here and there in his own book he referred readers to the superior illustrations of Squier and Davis. Comparing a few of Squier and Davis's site descriptions with Pidgeon's description and interpretation of the same site can make for interesting reading.

For example the Newark Works, a group of structures covering about two square miles in Licking County near where the Raccoon Branch (or North Branch) joins the South Branch of the Licking River, Squier and Davis had described a "very extensive and complicated series of works." This included a circle-octagon and circle-square earthwork linked by a broad avenue defined by parallel walls of earth. The Ohio & Erie Canal ran right through the eastern riverside earthworks complex, and a little town called Lockport had displaced a truncated pyramid and several mounds.

Squier and Davis commented, "The ancient lines can now be traced only at intervals, among gardens and outhouses. At the period when the original survey, upon which this plan is constructed, was made, which is twelve years ago, the lines could all be made out. A few years hence, the residents upon the spot will be compelled to resort to this map, to ascertain the character of the works which occupied the very ground upon which they stand."

Squier and Davis described a singular feature in the center of the circle near the square where there were four mounds more or less joined together to form a shape that Squier and Davis compared to a bird with outstretched wings. They noted a resemblance to the effigy mounds of Wisconsin, and also observed that the bird's head pointed directly to the entrance to the circle.

Squier and Davis observed that the small circle at Newark was the same size as the one at Hopeton, as well as the one attached to the octagon at High Bank. Squier and Davis wrote, "It is not to be supposed that these numerous coincidences are the result of accident."

Although Squier and Davis avoided conjecture, Pidgeon claimed to know exactly what these Newark earthworks had been used for. He called Newark the "Prophet's Metropolis," or an ancient seminary complete with residences for priests, holy circles, a festival square, and secluded avenues, no doubt for the kind of contemplative strolling that medieval monks were supposed to enjoy.

Located on a natural terrace overlooking the Little Miami River was a ruin known to Atwater as the Ancient Fortification, whose moniker had been abbreviated to Fort Ancient by the time Squier and Davis published their book. Its very extensive walls followed the lines of the hilltop on which it had been constructed, enclosing about one hundred acres, with two irregularly shaped forts joined by a narrow isthmus. Atwater was not the first, nor would he be the last, to observe that with a stretch of the imagination, the shapes of the two joined forts could resemble the continents of North and South America.

Material in the books by Atwater and by Squier and Davis con-

sistently reported that its walls were pierced by many openings
located at irregular intervals. Atwater counted fifty-eight; *Ancient
Monuments* depicted over seventy. However in *Ancient Monuments*
the openings were interpreted not as gateways, but gaps that had
once held wooden blockhouses that had since rotted away. John
Locke, who wrote the description of Fort Ancient that Squier and
Davis published, observed, "Under a military system, such as we
feel warranted in ascribing to the people by whom this work was
constructed, it must have been impregnable."

Although Pidgeon also referred to this structure as Fort
Ancient in his own book, he had some doubts whether those
defending themselves against merely primitive weapons really
had required such a stronghold. He blamed its numerous openings on the wear and tear of Mother Nature over time. Pidgeon
thought the walls of Fort Ancient had once been continuous and
lined with a deep interior ditch. Pidgeon even offered another
name for the irregular ruin but was apparently hesitant to reveal
his source. "Tradition," he wrote, "assigns to this remarkable work
the name of MOON CITY. . . . Ancient Americans are tradition-
ally represented to have worshipped the moon, and, moreover, to
have regarded it as the elysium or place of refuge for the departed
spirits of obedient females, where they might indulge at their ease
the passion of curiosity, in a ceaseless journey about the world."

Despite the amount of information that Pidgeon obtained
from Native American sources, most notably his friend De-coo-
dah, Pidgeon just could not let go of the old notion "that the present Indian, and the ancient mound-builder were of distinct
national origin." In his introduction he had repeated many canards
then in circulation about Roman military camps in the Mississippi
Valley, Egyptian mummies in Kentucky, and the ancient Roman
and Persian coins found along American riverbanks. But to
Pidgeon the mounds and earthworks themselves were the ultimate evidence of foreign influence because they "indicate[d]
enterprise and energy among the mound-builders that would
compare favorably with the present advancement of internal
improvement, and show a national character for energy unknown
in the annals of savage nations."

So how did Pidgeon explain all De-coo-dah claimed to know about the ancient Mound Builders? Pidgeon suggested that perhaps there had been two ancient peoples originating from two continents other than the Americas. After spending years at war, they were weak enough to fall prey to intruding hordes of Asiatic origin and become assimilated into the savage ways and wandering habits of their conquerors. Thereafter the old mystic Mound Builder lore was passed down only to special individuals like De-coo-dah, while most of the Indians of the historic era had long since ceased to know anything about the ancient ruins.

By the time America was recovering from its Civil War, more Mound Builder data was available to more people, but unless one personally knew an Indian sage, there was little new being interpreted about Mound Builders. That would be left to the next generation of American scholars, who would be setting forth their theories in what amounted to a new scholarly world, after shocking theories made by European scholars had had time to sink into the American mind. Until then, Americans were taking seriously biblical injunctions like the one in Deuteronomy 4:2: "Ye shall not add unto the Word which I command you, neither shall ye diminish aught from it." Anyone who contradicted the knowledge contained in the Old and New Testaments of the Bible, or tried to add anything to them, was in for trouble. Just ask the Mormons.

7

Fall of the Empire

In the earlier years of the nineteenth century, the Danish archaeologist Christian Jurgensen Thomsen at the Copenhagen Museum succeeded in imposing some order on European prehistory by organizing ancient tools according to the material from which they had been crafted. In 1836 he suggested that humans had passed through three ages of technological development, naming them the Stone Age, the Bronze Age, and the Iron Age. In a book published in 1865 titled *Pre-historic Times*, British anthropologist Sir John Lubbock created a fourth age by dividing the Stone Age into old and new periods named the Paleolithic and the Neolithic. Those participating in and growing wealthy from the nineteenth century's Industrial Revolution seemed to welcome the notion that their modern technologies were the culmination of the steady development of humans' problem-solving abilities.

Meanwhile, European geologists were revolutionizing their own science by applying the principles of stratigraphy to determine the relative age of fossils by how many strata, or layers of rock, they had lain beneath. A three-volume work by the Scot Charles Lyell titled *Principles of Geology* first published in 1832–33, which popularized this concept and made clear the great antiquity of the earth, would become a classic in its field. In England and France around the middle of the nineteenth century, the discovery of man-made stone tools in certain geological strata associated with extinct fauna suggested that they had been crafted much earlier than 4004 BC, the date established for God's creation of the universe in the chronology published by Anglo-Irish prelate James Ussher and long accepted by Christians worldwide.

In 1856 in the Neander Valley near Dusseldorf, quarry workers unearthed parts of a skeleton that looked to some like they had belonged to a weirdly deformed human, while other scholars speculated that this "Neanderthal Man" might have been a member of some archaic ancestor race that had since disappeared from the earth. This and other evidence led Charles Darwin to write his famous books *On the Origin of Species* (1859) and *The Descent of Man* (1871). Darwin proposed that humans had had a very lengthy history on earth, nor were they necessarily a finished product, but rather an evolving species.

In America, in the decades that followed, archaeology continued its own evolution from an avocation into a scholarly profession. Universities began to offer course programs, and full-time positions opened up in major museums. The European discoveries and the consequential intellectual departure from literal interpretation of religious teaching gave the new professionals much to ponder about prehistoric America, leading to an era when many known remains would be restudied and reclassified, and new interpretations proposed.

The Smithsonian Institution began the process when its secretary Joseph Henry commissioned Samuel F. Haven to write *Archaeology of the United States,* which was published in 1856 by the Smithsonian in volume eight of its Contributions to Knowledge series. The subtitle of Haven's book was *Sketches,*

Historical and Biographical, of the Progress of Information and Opinion Respecting Vestiges of Antiquity in the United States. Scholars have called this the first synthesis of North American archaeology. The text was largely Haven's opinion on literally everything that had been published on the subject so far. What qualified Haven to write such a book was a remarkable command of the contemporary canon acquired during almost twenty years with the American Antiquarian Society, plus the historical research he had begun not long after his graduation from Amherst.

Haven acknowledged the yeoman's work accomplished by Caleb Atwater: "Considering the difficulties that were to be surmounted in tracing lines often buried in forests, and otherwise obscured by time, before repeated observations had assisted the judgment, the surveys are more accurate than could reasonably be anticipated." While he declared Atwater guilty of some "premature speculation" at a time when "almost every writer on the subject . . . had been engaged in determining by what foreign people the mounds and fortifications might have been raised," Haven concluded that at least Atwater had not organized his facts to suit a pet theory. Haven also revealed he was aware that Atwater's interpretation of the possible Hindu origin of the Triune Idol owed much to the articles of John D. Clifford.

Haven gracefully let Atwater off the hook for the "remarkable instances of fanciful deduction" that went to press in the few years following his own publication. Haven observed that John Haywood in his *Natural and Aboriginal History of Tennessee* had described the prehistoric residents of his state "with a particularity that could hardly be surpassed in a history of a living and familiar people." Haven contended that Constantine Rafinesque in his *Ancient History, or Annals of Kentucky* had presented "the succession of peoples and empires, with a lavish profusion of names and pedigrees, and an air of intimate acquaintance with their civil and religious customs, and the motives and results of military operations, which seems to imply the possession of an insight the reverse of prophetic, but equally supernatural." Haven pronounced Josiah Priest's *American Antiquities and Discoveries in the West* as "a sort of curiosity shop of archaeological fragments, whose materials are gathered without the exercise of much discrimination, and disposed without much system of classification, and apparently without inquiry into their authenticity."

Samuel F. Haven had known about the work of Squier and Davis back when their project was young. While Squier was traveling in the East fundraising and hunting for a publisher he had called at the American Antiquarian Society and pled his case before Haven.

Haven reported Squier and Davis's methods of classification but declined much analysis of their work, possibly because he disagreed with one of their key conclusions.

Samuel F. Haven (1806–1881), the long-time librarian at the American Antiquarian Society, wrote the first synthesis of North American archaeology in his 1856 book, *Archaeology of the United States*.

While Haven could not rule out the possibility that some ancient casual voyagers had inadvertently arrived in America, he thought that most of the Western Hemisphere's aborigines had arrived via the natural route provided by the Aleutian Islands. Moreover they had done so at a time prior to the development of Chinese, Japanese, or Mongolian cultures, when most of the world's population were "mere wanderers, without arts, and with no religious faith save the primitive oriental worship of the sun."

While he refrained from offering much speculation in his own conclusion, it was clear that Haven thought that the same wanderers had slowly spread out and left the remains that his predecessors had studied. As evidence he mentioned that early Spanish and French explorers and missionaries "observed no want of harmony between the social condition of the natives and whatever works of art came to their notice." Native Americans of his own day were producing artwork of comparable quality to that excavated in the Midwestern mounds. Lewis and Clark had reported seeing occupied or recently deserted Indian villages surrounded by earthen embankments, sometimes in the shape of a circle. Finally, although the science of philology was admittedly young, Europeans needing to communicate with the Indians had been compiling vocabularies since the 1500s, and these had yet to yield any definite associations with any languages of the Old World; instead Native American languages tended to resemble each other.

Haven did point out the inconsistency between the ruins' silent testimony that a large population had once resided in an area that Europeans had found relatively vacant. He left his readers to ponder whether the earlier occupants had just packed up and moved, or whether they might have been decimated by plague or war. As Haven put it, "What mighty cause of destruction anticipated by a few centuries the mission of the whites it is not easy to conjecture."

Despite his dry wit and persuasive arguments Haven failed to revolutionize popular perception of the Mound Builders. His publication was essentially a monograph available to a relatively small number of scholars. In the latter half of the twentieth century, Haven's publication was rediscovered by other historiographers, and he probably enjoyed a larger circulation then than he had had in his own lifetime.

Henry W. Henshaw took up the task of Mound Builder reevaluation in a monograph in a Smithsonian Report published in 1880-1881. In his work titled *Animal Carvings from Mounds of the Mississippi Valley*, Henshaw took a fresh look at the artifacts that had been unearthed at various sites with the objective of determining whether they were really so far superior in craftsmanship from anything that American Indians had been known to create.

Henshaw was no archaeologist, nor had he ever excavated any Mound Builder ruins. He was a naturalist who had spent several years studying birds of the United States. He had been inspired to study Mound Builder animal carvings when he discovered that Squier and Davis had probably misidentified some species of birds and animals whose images had been carved by Mound Builders and reproduced in their book.

One of the arguments for a geographically extensive Mound Builder empire, or at least evidence of widespread trade and communication, had been the presence in the mounds of sculptures that looked like manatees, which lived no farther north than the rivers of Florida. Squier and Davis reported that in their time seven of these had been found. Henshaw observed that if these were to be considered evidence of trade or contact with the Deep South, why had no archaeologist unearthed such an item in the Deep South itself? Henshaw examined the "manatee" carvings and saw otters, animals which would have been very familiar to Mound Builders in the Midwest.

Squier and Davis had identified three bird sculptures as the even more exotic tropical toucan. Henshaw considered these representations "totally dissimilar from each other, and not only not resembling the toucan, but conveying no conceivable hint of that very marked bird."

Summing up the zoological knowledge of Squier and Davis, Henshaw wrote, "of forty-five of the animal carvings, including a few of clay, which are figured in Squier and Davis's work, eleven are left unnamed by the authors as not being recognizable; nineteen are identified correctly, in a general way, as of a wolf, heron, toad, etc; sixteen are demonstrably wrongly identified, leaving but five of which the species is correctly given."

In Henshaw's opinion, Squier and Davis had generally overrated the artistic skills of the Mound Builders. Henshaw regarded the Mound Builder animal carvings as having been executed "with a skill considerably above the general average of attainments in art of our Indian tribes, but not above the best efforts of individual tribes."

Henshaw extended his criticism to what Squier and Davis had termed effigy mounds. In his opinion, none of them looked enough like a specific animal to be identified as such. Henshaw wrote, "There are many examples among the animal shapes that possess peculiarities affording no hint of animals living or extinct, but which are strongly suggestive of the play of mythologic fancy or of conventional methods of representing totemic ideas."

A case in point was Ohio's so-called Alligator Mound (see page 239). Squier and Davis had captioned their diagram "The Alligator" because that's what the locals called this mound, but

Henshaw contended it could have been meant to represent any long-tailed animal except an alligator, because its tail was clearly curled.

Secretary Joseph Henry had long been interested in expanding research sponsored by the Smithsonian Institution into the field of ethnology, or the study of people and races, which together with archaeology formed the broader social science of anthropology, or the study of human origins, development, and history. The Smithsonian had already published one study on kinship by Lewis Henry Morgan, who had been studying kinship systems among Native American tribes from the 1840s. In 1877 the work that would win Morgan the title of Father of American Anthropology appeared: *Ancient Society*. Morgan's theory of social evolution took humankind through the major stages of savagery, barbarism, and finally civilization, comparable to Thomsen's three ages of technological development.

In 1878 the secretary of the interior received a petition to research and study North American Indians from Major John Wesley Powell, a follower of Morgan. Born in 1834 in New York State not far from the town of Palmyra, Powell moved west with his family, finally settling in Wheaton, Illinois. Like other scholars before him, Powell was inspired by the ancient ruins in the area surrounding Chillicothe where he had unearthed various artifacts as a young man. Following study at Wesleyan and Oberlin colleges, Powell enlisted in the Union army. He lost his lower right arm in the Battle of Shiloh but returned to military service, eventually earning the rank of major. Powell became a professor of geology at Illinois Wesleyan University where his summer field trips evolved into the feat that brought him national fame. In 1869 the major led an expedition through the Grand Canyon on the Colorado River. Powell subsequently became director of the United States Geographical and Geological Survey of the Rocky Mountain Region.

Powell had become interested in the Indians residing in the areas he had explored. At the nation's Centennial Exposition in

Philadelphia in 1876, where the Smithsonian teamed up with the nation's Bureau of Indian Affairs, Powell had mounted an exhibit of the objects he had collected illustrating the crafts of America's Ute and Paiute Indians. In Powell's opinion, Americans needed to understand the institutions, customs, philosophy, and religion of the Indians if the nation was ever to solve what folks had come to call the "Indian problem."

In 1879 Congress passed a bill resulting in the creation of the Smithsonian Institution's Bureau of Ethnology. Having been named its first director, Powell began organizing his agency to study every aspect of Indian life including languages, religious practices, and decorative arts. Powell could not afford a large staff but he sought out specialists who could work part-time as field investigators.

Powell's agency lacked sufficient funding to hire archaeologists too, but when it came time for the House of Representatives to renew his agency's appropriation in 1881, a congressman from Ohio inserted an amendment appropriating five thousand dollars to "be expended in continuing archaeological investigation relating to mound-builders and prehistoric mounds." Powell placed in charge of his new division a former critic named Wills de Haas, who had been calling for the bureau's mission to be enlarged. When de Haas resigned within a year, Powell replaced him with a man named Cyrus Thomas, a former minister who had worked with the United States Geographical and Geological Survey and then resided in the southern tip of Illinois where the river port named Cairo had earned for its metropolitan area the nickname of Little Egypt.

It was 1886 before the Smithsonian published Powell's report on his bureau's progress during the fiscal year 1882–1883. Powell used the phrase "a limited amount of work" to describe the bureau's archaeological efforts, explaining that the Bureau of Ethnology had been organized by him while conducting explorations and surveys in the Colorado River valley with no plans to undertake archaeological excavations in the Midwest. But now that Powell's mission had been expanded, he proposed that his bureau would conduct a "thorough investigation" of the mounds and earthworks "with a view to determining the purposes for which they were used, and the grade of culture of their authors, and the relations existing between the builders and the tribes inhabiting the country on the advent of European civilization to this continent." In other words, Powell proposed to answer once and for all the question of whether the Mound Builders were Indians.

Once Powell had broadly defined the project, Cyrus Thomas made plans to answer the question through four avenues of research. He proposed to classify the old ruins according to their external form and shape. Then his team would investigate the way in which each different kind of structure had been built. They would then develop a system of regional archaeological districts, or figure out which types of structures were generally found where. Finally they would collect and examine objects from the various ruins that would further aid in classifying the mounds and defining the archaeological districts.

Cyrus Thomas began his work on United States antiquities east of the Rockies in 1882 with a small division of field agents whose activities he directed from his office in Washington, DC. While it would have been ideal for the agents to survey and diagram all existing mounds first, then proceed to excavate them, the need for speed and efficiency inspired Thomas to rotate the field agents between northern sites in the warm weather and southern sites in the winter. They excavated monuments as soon as they had been surveyed.

Thomas's agents even managed to discover what amounted to virgin Mound Builder territory. Bishop James Madison had written about Mound Builder ruins in West Virginia's Kanawha River valley, but nary a word or diagram had appeared in the works of Atwater or Squier and Davis. This may have been because through much of the nineteenth century this area remained remote and exceedingly undeveloped. In the mid-1850s Charleston, West Virginia, boasted a population of fifteen hundred, which had risen only to four thousand by 1870. The general area was loaded with valuable coal, but getting enough to market had been extremely difficult until the Chesapeake and Ohio Railroad brought train service to Charleston in the 1870s. Shortly thereafter the Kanawha and New River valleys became home to many thriving mining operations.

After one of Thomas's agents named P. W. Norris explored the Kanawha River Valley in 1883 and 1884, Thomas was able to report that it contained one of the most extensive and remarkable groups of ancient works in the nation. Mounds in the Kanawha Valley ranged from a few inches to forty feet in height, and the area had all sorts of enclosures including circles, parallel lines, and elevated ways. To Thomas they seemed very similar to the ruins of Ohio's Scioto Valley, and they suggested a relationship between their ancient builders.

Cyrus Thomas (1825–1910), an entomologist and professor of natural science, definitively identified the Mound Builders as Native Americans.

P. W. Norris and the Smithsonian Institution subsequently excavated one of West Virginia's larger mounds known as the Criel Mound, which stood thirty-three feet high in South Charleston, West Virginia. In prior years the citizens of South Charleston had built a racecourse around it and leveled its summit to serve as a judges' stand. As the excavators tunneled down from the top of the mound they found various human remains, finally arriving at a burial vault at a depth of over thirty feet. Inside they found a body covered with bark and surrounded by ten other individuals arranged in two semicircles around it. The decedents had been buried with lance heads, arrowheads, shells, and beads. Norris concluded that these eleven persons had been buried at the same time, possibly following death in battle.

My husband and I located the Criel Mound in 2008 in a neighborhood that has come to be known as Staunton Park south of the Kanawha in South Charleston. We saw that the mound had been embellished with a stone wall and archway which seemed to define it as a gateway to this industrial district. A sign acknowledged the mound's racecourse heritage and described one of the skeletons that Norris unearthed here as "a powerful giant of nearly 7 feet." Twin spiral staircases led to the mound's summit. A number of local businesses had taken names acknowledging its imposing presence, including HeathN's Bar and Grill and the Mound Antique Mall.

On nearby D Street in the former art deco LaBelle Theatre we visited a small museum which was the self-identified interpretive center for the Criel Mound, but we got little new information thanks to what had to be the nation's most rigid interpretation of NAGPRA. In what would have been the old theatre's lobby there was one glass case housing a collection of arrowheads as well as pipes and other items labeled as Mound Builder reproductions. The label explained that the city of South Charleston had a strict policy prohibiting the exploitation of human remains which it extended to include items buried with the deceased. Apparently for a time it had also been extended to images of items buried with the deceased. A staffer led us to a small exhibition of photographs of what the Smithsonian archaeologists had found in various local mounds. These included blades and implements made of stone, and jewelry and beads fashioned out of shells and coal. The staffer commented, "We took these photos down for a while, but then we decided it was safe to put them back up."

Cyrus Thomas placed great importance on field notes, or data recorded on site in memorandum books. For mounds and earthworks the field notes included forms, character, dimensions, and the nature and dimensions of their strata. In the case of artifacts and remains, the field notes recorded their exact positions in the structures in which they had been found.

Recovered items were also assigned field numbers and packed for shipment to Major Powell at the Washington, DC, office of the Bureau of Ethnology. In a report published in 1887, Thomas commented, "The specimens procured by the field assistants in person constitute by far the most valuable portion of the collection, since the particulars regarding their discovery and surroundings are known. Among them will be found not only nearly every variety as to material, form, and ornamentation hitherto obtained in that

Once a judging stand for the race track that circled it, the Criel Mound, originally thirty-three feet high, now stands in Staunton Park, serving as a gateway to industrial South Charleston in West Virginia. (*Author*)

part of the United States east of the Rocky Mountains, but also a considerable number of new and interesting kinds." The collection of over four thousand items included a great deal of pottery, even some specimens that were complete and unbroken. There were stone tools of every imaginable kind, including pipes, axes, spear points, and agricultural implements. There were ornaments made of shell, bone, and copper, as well as specimens for what Thomas called the bureau's "craniological collection."

The field agents also managed to unearth quite a few items that clearly had not been locally manufactured. These included silver jewelry and crucifixes, copper hawk bells, iron implements, glass beads, and brass kettles. One silver bracelet discovered in a Wisconsin mound was stamped with the word "Montreal." A silver plate found in a mound group in northern Mississippi was stamped with a Spanish coat of arms. Many of these items were clearly grave goods deposited with decedents who had been buried in mounds that had been constructed long before. However, the positions in which others had been found led Thomas to conclude that they had been deposited with those mounds' original interments.

By 1894 Cyrus Thomas had supervised a sufficient number of surveys and studies to publish his conclusions in his masterwork titled *Report on the Mound Explorations of the Bureau of Ethnology* which appeared in the bureau's Twelfth Annual Report. It had been preceded by *Catalog of Prehistoric Works East of the Rocky Mountains*, which was basically a list of known ruins by county within each state, including a bibliography of earlier publications in which the ruin had been described. *Report on the Mound Explorations* came to be regarded as the third great analysis of Mound Builder remains of the nineteenth century, and it made Thomas yet one more candidate for the title Father of American Archaeology.

Thomas began by differentiating his Mound Builder study from earlier works, Squier and Davis's *Ancient Monuments* being the most significant. According to Thomas, these authors had started out with a practical classification system by dividing their monuments into constructions of earth versus stone, but then they had gone much too far by classifying them by what they had supposed to be their uses. Thomas wrote in his introduction, "There is not a particle of evidence that any inclosure [*sic*] was formed for religious or 'sacred' uses, or that any mound was built for 'sacrificial' purposes in any true or legitimate sense of the term." Squier and Davis had used those adjectives because the associated enclosures and mounds had contained structures they assumed to be altars. Thomas commented, "If they are in error in this respect their whole theory falls to the ground and the use of these terms is unwarranted and misleading."

Thomas also disputed many of Squier and Davis's measurements, which he stated had been recorded in imprecise round numbers. In many cases Squier and Davis had failed to note whether they were measuring from the inside, outside, or middle of earthen walls that could be fairly thick. In general, Squier and Davis's measurements had made the ruins seem more regular and well engineered than Thomas's field agents had found them to be nearly fifty years later. For example, Hopeton Works had one fairly square right angle, but two other corners were far less regular than they appeared in *Ancient Monuments*, and two of its sides were curved, not to mention that the circle at Hopeton Works was really more of an ellipse. Recent remapping of Hopeton Works using much more sophisticated and accurate instruments confirmed Thomas's assessment.

Thomas reclassified the ruins in more general terms. He divided the mounds into conical tumuli, elongate or wall mounds, pyramidal mounds, and effigy mounds. The earthworks he separated into "inclosures"; walls and embankments; excavations; canals and ditches; and pits and caches. Other ruins addressed in his study included graves and cemeteries; garden beds; refuse heaps; house sites and hut rings; and cairns.

Thomas lamented that to date very little had been done to define the archaeological districts or sections of the Western Hemisphere. He noted that in general there was a Mexican and Central American section, a South American section extending south from Costa Rica, a Pueblo section, and a California or Pacific Slopes section, in addition to the Mound Builder section it had been his task to study, whose precise boundaries had yet to be defined. Within the Mound Builder area where ancient works were chiefly found along watercourses or near lakes, there appeared to be three distinct districts. Besides the concentration of geometrical works in and around Ohio, there was a Dakotan district whose distinguishing characteristics were its effigy mounds and long narrow earthen embankments. There was also a southern district with flat-topped mounds apparently intended to elevate dwellings and other edifices.

Thomas himself had first arrived at the bureau carrying the baggage of belief in a separate superior Mound Builder race, but exposure to Powell plus his own work in the field had convinced him otherwise. By 1887 he had been willing to state in an interim Smithsonian Bulletin titled *Work in Mound Exploration of the Bureau of Ethnology*, "The links discovered directly connecting the Indians and mound builders are so numerous and well established that there should be no longer any hesitancy in accepting the theory that the two are one and the same people."

In his various publications by the Smithsonian between 1887 and 1894, Thomas convincingly laid out his evidence and his arguments in more detail. In general he demonstrated that the ancient ruins were less sophisticated than they had been portrayed, while the Indians were probably more so. Moreover he established continuity between prehistoric and postcontact America, banishing the lost civilization theories forever to the realm of fiction.

Whenever and wherever Europeans had advanced into regions where mounds and earthworks had been discovered, they had encountered no one but American Indians. In fact, early Europeans had discovered primarily in the South that American Indians were still constructing mounds and earthworks. Elsewhere they came across Indian villages surrounded with palisades, sometimes braced up by earthen embankments. Thomas proposed that if the wooden portions of such constructions were burned or simply left to rot, they would leave behind the same sort of "earthworks" so plentiful in Ohio.

The mounds and earthworks implied that their builders necessarily had to remain in the same place for some time. Europeans had long maligned Indians as restless, roving nomads who spurned a settled lifestyle because they depended on hunting and gathering for their food. However when the earliest Europeans had arrived in North America, they observed that most Indian tribes had what Europeans called a fixed seat, or a region they generally called home, and that in these places indeed they had practiced agriculture, though not in the same way or on the same scale as Europeans.

In the past much had been made of the perceived precision of geometrical earthworks, which implied that their builders had developed units and instruments of measure. In his *Report on the Mound Explorations*, Thomas reported that as a general rule, "The figures [i.e., earthworks] are more or less irregular, and indicate nothing higher in art than an Indian could form with his eye and by pacing. Circles and squares are simple figures known to all savage tribes and easily formed; hence the fact that a few, and a very few, approach mathematical accuracy is not sufficient to counterbalance the vast amount of evidence on the other side."

Materials removed from burial mounds showed that the mortuary customs of the ancient Mound Builders bore striking similarities to the burial customs of modern Indians. That the Indians continued to dig new graves in old mounds showed that they understood the original purpose of these ruins. Corpses buried at the heart of old mounds were often contained in cists (a primitive tomb or vault) made from flat stone slabs. As late as the mid-nineteenth century, there had been Ohio old-timers who could point out relatively recent Indian burials in similar stone cists, though these had not been covered with massive earthen mounds.

Never mind that the modern Indians disclaimed knowledge of the old earthworks and mounds. Europeans had found them generally to be vague when it came to passing down their own history, frequently forgetting or omitting events that Europeans thought they should have considered important. For example, tribes living in the American South didn't seem to recall De Soto's expedition among them when French explorers visiting the same territory asked about this a little over a century later.

Having presented his case that the Mound Builders were the ancestors of modern Indians, Thomas got more specific and identified them as the ancestors of contemporary Cherokees, a point on which today's scholars disagree. His theory was that these aborigines had moved from Ohio to the Carolinas and Tennessee where they continued to construct mounds, though on a much smaller scale. Thomas further proposed that their route of migration had taken them through West Virginia where they had resided long enough to leave behind the ancient works his field agents had studied near the city of Charleston. Thomas added that the name for the Mound Builders in Delaware tradition as recorded by earlier historians was Tallegewi, which sounded to him a lot like Chellakee, an alternate pronunciation for Cherokee.

Thomas also stated his conclusions about whom the Mound Builders were not likely to be related to. Even though the Midwest was home to some truncated pyramidal mounds, some with ramps or roadways leading to their flat tops, absent from the Midwestern mounds was "any evidence in them of architectural knowledge and skill approaching that exhibited by the ruins of Mexico and Central America, or even equaling that exhibited by the Pueblo Indians." The architects of Mexico, Central America, and points south built in stone; the best masonry produced by Mound Builders consisted of cists or vaults, cairns, and rude walls made from cobblestones and undressed blocks. If the Mound Builders had come from Mexico or Central or South America, it seemed odd that they would have suddenly abandoned stone construction. If they had migrated in the opposite direction, it was equally peculiar that they became such proficient masons without leaving any evidence of the evolution and development of this skill.

Once the powers that be at the Smithsonian had reasonably resolved the problem of who the Mound Builders were, its scholars would engage with others over the question of when the Mound Builders had built their structures and crafted their artifacts, which was related to the larger question of the age of humans in America. Once European paleontologists had discovered *Homo neanderthalensis*, their American counterparts started searching for fossils of other hominids, or humans who differed physically from modern man. No one found any, therefore scientists concluded humans must have arrived after they became fully physically evolved but while each remained what Haven had called a "mere wanderer." Haven himself had declined to venture a guess in terms of how many years ago that might have been.

In 1877 a physician named Charles C. Abbott began excavating gravel deposits on his farm near Trenton, New Jersey, and discovered what appeared to be the remains of an ancient campsite which he proclaimed to be twenty or thirty thousand years old. Frederic Ward Putnam, who had studied the Serpent Mound and was then curator of the Peabody Museum of Archaeology and Ethnology at Harvard University, studied the Trenton gravel artifacts, and while he deferred to geologists to date the gravel deposit, he declared that the objects found in the gravel deposit would be the same age. Putnam proposed the artifacts were evidence that humans had reached Trenton by the end of the Ice Age when the region had become habitable. A Paleolithic stone tool found in a gravel deposit by Charles L. Metz of Madisonville,

Ohio, convinced him that humankind had reached Ohio around the same time. In an 1890 article titled "Prehistoric Remains in the Ohio Valley" published in *The Century Magazine* as a sort of introduction to his Serpent Mound article, Putnam wrote, "These were found under the same conditions, and in the same gravels of the same geological age, as those previously discovered in the Delaware Valley by Dr. C. C. Abbott."

In the same article Putnam mentioned a date considerably less than twenty or thirty thousand years. He noted that archaeologists had classified the American skulls they had been digging up into two categories: long and narrow or dolichocephalic, versus short and broad or brachycephalic. That the peoples known as American Indians had achieved what Putnam called "a certain uniformity in the physical characteristics, and an amalgamation of myths, customs, and arts," seemed to require a fairly lengthy period for successive waves of immigrants with different types of skulls from northern and then southern and central Asia to sufficiently mingle. Putnam wrote, "First of all we must remember that this valley was inhabited by man at a period so remote as only to be approximately stated in years; but that at least ten times ten centuries have passed away since the implements of stone, fashioned by this early man, were lost and covered by the overwash of the glacial gravels as the great ice sheet melted in its retreat to the north, and the rivers cut their way through the gravel it had deposited along its southern border." And within that ten-thousand-year window he placed the different peoples who had created Mound Builder ruins at different times.

Around the same time period Major Powell and other Smithsonian scholars at the Bureau of American Ethnology were beginning to argue the case that man had not been residing in the Western Hemisphere anywhere near as long. They soon managed to create the general consensus that America had nothing to rival the Paleolithic finds of Europe.

W. H. Holmes had been trained as an artist but moved into geology and subsequently archaeology and the Bureau of Ethnology where he would later succeed Major Powell as chief. When he examined the rude implements that had been discovered in the Trenton gravels, they looked to him like the sort of thing modern Indian craftsmen discarded as imperfectly made, so maybe their crude state meant not that they were ancient, but that they were factory rejects of a sort. It has been more recently agreed that the Trenton gravel finds were not Paleolithic.

In 1907 the Smithsonian's Bureau of Ethnology published a work by the Czech anthropologist Ales Hrdlicka titled *Skeletal Remains Suggesting or Attributed to Early Man in North America*. The work was a very technical debunking of the notion that man had arrived in America prior to the geologic Pleistocene period, also then known as the Glacial Period. Hrdlicka examined various human remains from different geographical areas and confidently concluded, "If early man did exist in North America, convincing proof of the fact from the standpoint of physical anthropology still remains to be produced." When it came to Mound Builder skulls, Hrdlicka concluded that what others had suggested were primitive characteristics were either deformities or consistent with the skeletons of modern Indians. According to Hrdlicka everything that humans had constructed or crafted in America had been done within a span of three or four thousand years.

Hrdlicka went on to debunk many other frauds in his career. While he did help to professionalize the field of archaeology, he was so dogmatic an ideologue that few other scholars were willing to stand up to him with a contrary opinion. It would be a long time before anyone argued that humans had been living in America for more than around three or four thousand years.

So by the beginning of the twentieth century, the Mound Builders turned out to be Indians building structures and practicing crafts that had not been so sophisticated after all. There was no far-flung civilization and certainly no central government. The Mound Builders weren't even all that old. The great Ancient Imaginary Empire of Mound Builders had fallen.

8

The Hopewell
Culture of Death

Having popularized the Serpent Mound in an 1890 article in a widely read general audience magazine, Frederic Ward Putnam took on the project of popularizing the science of anthropology the following year when he was appointed "Chief of Department M, Ethnology and Archaeology" for the 1893 World's Columbian Exposition to be held in Chicago. Originally planned to commemorate the four hundredth anniversary of Christopher Columbus's arrival in the new world, the opening of this huge fair was delayed one year due to the complexity of its execution, and Putnam's problems were no less vexing than those of any other of its department heads. Putnam planned to fill an entire building with exhibits illustrating the lives of humans who had dwelt in North, Central, and South America from its earliest inhabitants on. After the fair was over Putnam reported that never had so much material been assembled in one place, and Putnam intended that much of it remain in Chicago. Indeed, his department's exhibits became the nucleus for the anthropology department at the Field Museum of Natural History.

Of course, Putnam had not been working alone; he had directed nearly a hundred field assistants on various collecting expeditions. As his field assistant in Ohio, Putnam chose Warren K. Moorehead, a recent student of prehistoric anthropology at the Smithsonian Institution, who established teams at various Mound Builder sites, including one that Squier and Davis had named Clark's Work and proclaimed "one of the largest and most interesting in the Scioto Valley." Between September 1891 and January 1892, Moorehead's crew of laborers excavated with shovels and scrapers, one Civil War veteran carefully working with a hand trowel. Moorehead described his experiences in two publications: *Primitive Man in Ohio*, a book published in 1892, and a 1922 monograph for the Anthropological Series published by Chicago's Field Museum of Natural History.

Like Squier and Davis before him, Moorehead illustrated this site located on the north fork of Paint Creek outside Chillicothe as an earthwork shaped more or less like a rectangle enclosing an area of about 111 acres adjoining a sixteen-acre square. Inside the rectangle were a circular enclosure and a second enclosure which Moorehead described as semicircular, but which others have described as D-shaped. Inside the D-shaped enclosure were seven mounds, the three largest seemingly joined together in a row.

Squier and Davis had classified Clark's Work as a work of defense, but described it as "a fortified town, rather than a defensive work of the last resort." Moorehead agreed that the entire site had been a fortified town, but expressed doubt that its low and insubstantial walls would have offered much protection from a determined party of warriors. Moorehead found what he interpreted as indications of habitation throughout the rectangle, and the words "village site" appeared on the plan in his 1892 book where they were most numerous.

Squier and Davis had already examined most of the mounds at the site and carried off hundreds of artifacts. In the ensuing years the general area had been continuously cultivated, while local pottery hunters had performed their own impromptu explorations by sinking shafts through its other mounds, but Moorehead was gratified to discover that neither Squier and Davis nor anyone else since had come close to exhausting the site. In the largest mound at the site, which was thirty-three feet high, Moorehead located 150 burials accompanied by a profusion of artifacts. Many were made of copper and included figures or effigies as well as tools and breastplates. Other burial artifacts were fashioned from mica, bone, and stone. Moorehead was sufficiently impressed with a headdress ornamented with what appeared to be a set of antlers made of copper-covered wood to use its image as the frontispiece for his 1892 book.

Squier and Davis had located a cache of flint disks and predicted that the site held more. Moorehead's men began to discover them buried in bunches or pockets separated by layers of sand. Eventually they gathered over seven thousand light blue disks made of flint which he thought had been extracted from a source two miles northwest of the site. Moorehead piled them up outside the tent that served as his quarters and took a photograph for his book. He commented, "We think the mound to have been a place of storage, where the natives living within the enclosure kept material to be subsequently worked into implements." In a corner of an exhibit called *Following in Ancient Footsteps* at the museum of the Ohio History Center in Columbus, which interprets recent as well as historical discoveries, when we visited in 2013 we saw a small mound of this sort of flint disks displayed with an excavation photo. The exhibit identifies the disks on display as Indiana flint.

Though the two men worked independently, Moorehead and Putnam both concluded that Ohio had been home to two distinct groups of primitive humans. There were those who had resided in large villages, as well as a seemingly more advanced culture who had built the earthworks and mounds. Moorehead renamed

Clark's Work Hopewell, in honor of its current owner, Captain M. C. Hopewell, and within a few more years another scholar would apply the name Hopewell to all sites that shared similar features and artifacts, making it what archaeologists call the "type site" for an entire culture.

However, Moorehead was not about to bring back the concept of an ancient empire. Using the terminology of Lewis Henry Morgan, he was careful to note that those people who had constructed sites like Hopewell did not really constitute a civilization. He wrote, "Nothing more than the upper status of savagery was attained by any race or tribe living within the limits of the present state of Ohio." Despite the ruins and artifacts they left behind, the Hopewell people never developed a written language, built sophisticated permanent dwellings, or discovered that the plentiful local coal could be used for more than making ornaments. Moorehead ended his 1892 book with the comment, "Where [the Hopewell] lived and enjoyed savage pleasures, indulged in barbaric pursuits and semi-religious festivals, the Shawnee Indian afterward erected towns and villages. Close upon his heels followed the white settlers. Then was instituted a real civilization in the Ohio Valley."

In the first decade of the twentieth century an archaeologist named William Corless Mills, who had collected Indian artifacts as a boy and initially pursued a career in pharmacy, would examine mounds at two other Hopewell sites and publish his groundbreaking conclusion about the meaning and purpose of the Hopewell mounds, and how the Hopewell people had constructed them. Mills had been the curator of archaeology at the Ohio State Archaeological and Historical Society since 1898 and would later serve as the society's director from 1921 until his death in 1928. In an article Mills wrote about his excavation of the Edwin Harness Mound he reported, "On the 14th day of August, 1903, I commenced the final explorations of the mound, by exposing to view from time to time as the work progressed, the entire site of the mound, recording and photographing the burials and other important features of the mound." In 1909 Mills would also study the Seip Mound and publish those results as well.

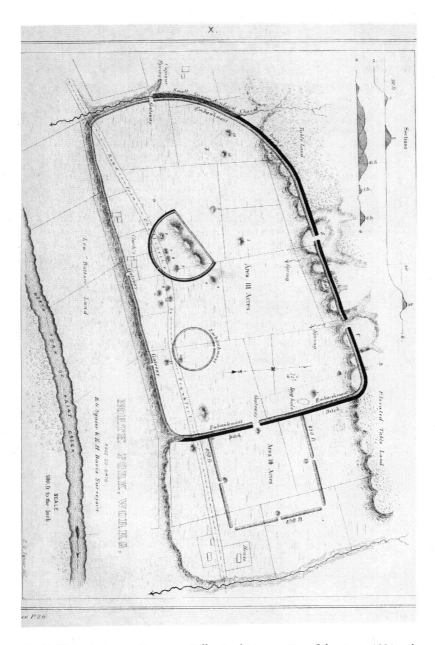

Clark's Work, in *Ancient Monuments*. Following his excavation of the site in 1891 and 1892, Warren K. Moorehead renamed it Hopewell. It became the "type site" for all sites where similar features and artifacts were found.

Like the Hopewell site's mounds, both the Harness and Seip mounds were located in earthwork groups that included other mounds erected in and around the earthworks. The two sites were not very far apart. The Harness group was located in Liberty Township in Ross County about eight miles south of Chillicothe on the east bank of the Scioto River. The Seip group lay in the valley of Paint Creek in Ross County's Paxton Township off a road connecting Bourneville and Bainbridge. Both sites were named for their property owners, who were farmers. In both cases the tracks of local railroads ran nearby.

Squier and Davis had examined the Edwin Harness Mound in 1846, classifying it as an anomalous mound that had served as both an altar and burial mound. In 1885 Frederic Ward Putnam had further explored the mound by building a sloping trench that stretched through about a third of it. He located a dozen burial chambers and removed some human remains and grave goods. In 1896 Warren K. Moorehead had taken up where Putnam left off, employing a tunneling method and locating yet more interments and grave goods. When Mills began his own work he was able to locate one of the shafts that Squier and Davis had sunk through the mound, but he disagreed with their conclusion that what they had found at its bottom had ever been an altar. "The object of the mound was purely mortuary," he wrote, in fact calling the entire structure a "charnel house" where the dead were sheltered and prepared for burial prior to being placed in their graves.

Mills's exploration at both Seip and Harness showed that such charnel houses were constructed on a cleared site where a roughly circular edifice was erected by sinking wooden posts upright in the ground with openings left for entrances. The Seip Mound had had three distinct circular enclosures. Inside these palisaded spaces were several fireplaces where cremations were conducted, the deceased's remains then being removed to burial places in the same structure. When the charnel house began to get crowded, the entire structure was set on fire, and a mound erected over it as a monument to the dead. At the Seip Mound, Mills found what seemed to be a stairway constructed of flat stones, no doubt to make it easier for the mound builders to reach the rising summit bearing heavy loads of earth.

Upon examining the burials, Mills concluded that once their human remains were deposited in their graves together with curious implements and ornaments, everything would be covered with grass and twigs and set on fire, before being covered over with clay. Mills reported five uncremated bodies buried at various heights in the Seip Mound rather than at floor level of the charnel house. He concluded that these were not intrusive burials but rather members of the "same culture," since some were accompanied with grave goods similar to those of the deceased buried below. He thought that three of them might have died while the mound was under construction, while the other two had been brought to the mound following death and burial elsewhere, since their bodies had been dismembered and placed in a single grave.

The Harness and Seip mounds yielded up literally thousands of examples of grave offerings. The best preserved were items fashioned from copper, including large rectangular plates and finely crafted spool-shaped earrings formed from two small copper disks connected by a short rod, evidently made to be worn in pierced ears. There were pendants and beads made from seashells about half an inch long and drilled through for stringing. Roughly two decades later, the Seip Mound would be the scene of the discovery of what was reported as the "great pearl burial": literally thousands of pearls in a single sepulcher which held the remains of four adults and two infants. Both Seip and Harness contained potsherds and shreds of crudely woven fabric similar to what American pioneers had called homespun. Seip had shreds of tanned leather resembling soft chamois. The remains of what had obviously been garments had apparently survived because they had been in contact with grave offerings made of copper. Implements and ornaments made from bone tended to succumb to funerary fires, but Mills recovered pendants made from polished animal teeth. Both mounds also yielded ornaments made from human jaws. Scattered around the graves and throughout the mound were animal bone digging tools, presumably lost or discarded during mound construction.

Besides the shell beads that had obviously originated on some faraway beach, Mills found other materials at Harness from equally distant points of origin. There was mica from North Carolina, lead ore from northern Illinois, and obsidian from Yellowstone. Mills wrote, "The finding of so much material of this sort, whose source of supply was so far from the site of the mound, indicates that the prehistoric inhabitants of this section had an inter-tribal trade, for it certainly would have been impossible for the Ohio tribes to visit those distant points mentioned."

After excavating the Edwin Harness Mound, Mills was permitted to examine another small mound nearby in a field in front of the house of a Mr. Robert Harness. Within he found twenty-eight burials. Twenty-seven of them were uncremated and had been placed at or near the base of the mound accompanied by a few flint knives and arrowheads. The twenty-eighth interment, which had been cremated, Mills concluded was intrusive to this particular mound. Mills described the builders of the Seip Mound and the Edwin Harness Mound as members of the Hopewell Culture, which he called the "highest culture of aboriginal man in Ohio." The builders of the less sophisticated Robert Harness Mound he identified as members of the Fort Ancient Culture. And if the twenty-eighth Hopewell-like cremated burial was intrusive to this Fort Ancient mound, Mills arrived at the obvious conclusion: "The people of the Fort Ancient culture were the first to occupy the surrounding territory, and consequently the Hopewell culture occupied this territory at a later period."

In 1913 Mills hired as assistant Henry Clyde Shetrone, who had been born in Fairfield County, Ohio, in 1876. Shetrone had no formal training in archaeology; he was a newspaper reporter who had been writing about Mills's finds. Shetrone would later take Mills's place as curator of archaeology when Mills became director of the Ohio State Archaeological and Historical Society, and when Mills died in 1928 Shetrone became the director, a position he held until his retirement in 1947. Shetrone wrote for the society's quarterly journal, and his background in journalism made him especially well qualified to write *The Mound-Builders*, published in 1930, which synthesized the available knowledge at that time in terms that laymen would enthusiastically read. His book has since been reprinted as a classic.

Mills and Shetrone collaborated in excavating Scioto County's Tremper Mound, so named because it was located on the estate of Senator William D. Tremper. Located within an elliptically shaped earthwork, the Tremper Mound had an irregular shape that had caused Squier and Davis to classify it as an effigy mound. Some folks said it looked like a tapir, others like an elephant. Tremper's sons had done some digging into the top of the mound but thus far no one had explored it down to its base. The Tremper Mound was essentially a virgin mound.

William Corless Mills (1860–1928), right, and Henry Clyde Shetrone (1876–1954) at the Mound City excavation. Their research conduced in 1921 and 1922 corrected many assumptions made by Squier and Davis in *Ancient Monuments*. (*Ohio Historical Society*)

In July 1915, Mills and Shetrone began excavating down to the mound's floor whose central portion had been covered with several inches of fine sand. As they had expected, they discovered that Tremper had been a place of cremation and burial. In his published report Mills changed the language he used to describe such a place from "charnel house" to "sacred place," while Shetrone in his 1930 book compared the site to a modern church and its adjoining churchyard. Today some professionals refer to such structures as big houses, or spirit houses.

The surviving holes in which the upright posts of its walls had been placed suggested that the original structure had been an oval enclosure to which "chapel-like" annexes had been made. That the placement of these annexes suggested the head and legs of some animal had been purely coincidental. There were several crematories in the main oval section and the additions on the eastern side, and each compartment was also furnished with basin-shaped, clay-lined fireplaces showing evidence of wood fires being burned over long periods of time, suggesting they had been constructed to accommodate sacred or ceremonial fires. The floor of one addition on the north side was strewn with animal bones and broken pottery plus mica flakes, suggesting a place where people ate meals and crafted mica.

The Tremper Mound contained several large repositories of human ashes and a large cache of grave goods. Unlike the final resting places within other Hopewell mounds, the Tremper Mound Builders seemed to have buried the remains of their dead in large communal graves, while also depositing grave goods not with the individual deceased, but in a central location. This was a more efficient use of space as far as the burials were concerned, but an open repository of finely crafted objects might be a temptation for thieves. The Tremper Mound Builders seemed to have addressed this problem by intentionally breaking or otherwise destroying the grave offerings. A second cache of objects found two and a half feet above Tremper's floor had been deposited in perfect condition, likely because they were placed on site after the structure had been set on fire and while its covering mound was being built.

Mills and Shetrone also found some individual burials at Tremper. There were two cremated interments in the area with the cache of grave goods and two more in graves below the mound's floor, one of which had been walled like a vault with thin slabs of sandstone.

Among the artifacts recovered from Tremper were spool-shaped earrings made of copper as well as pipestone ear ornaments shaped like napkin rings that seemed to have been used to stretch holes in a Mound Builder's earlobes. There were pieces of mica ornaments and boat-shaped objects carved from stone. But Tremper's most fascinating artifacts were its platform pipes, many of them with bowls carved into the shapes of animals positioned so that they faced the smoker. Once Shetrone finished joining their broken pieces back together, the degree of sophistication that the pipes exhibited seemed to place the Tremper Mound Builders at the apex of Hopewell Culture. A pipe with a sitting dog carved as though baying at the moon suggested that the Tremper builders had domesticated the dog. The eyes of a bird known as a Carolina paroquet had been represented with inserted pearls, and the bird had been carved with its head tilted charmingly to one side. Similar animal effigy pipes discovered by Squier and Davis at Mound City had been sold to a museum in England, but Mills and Shetrone compared the Tremper pipes with illustrations in *Ancient Monuments* and con-

Tremper Mound cremation site. The Tremper Mound, excavated by William Corless Mills and Henry Clyde Shetrone in 1915, contained several crematories, repositories of human bones, and collections of grave goods.

cluded that the builders of Mound City and the Tremper Mound had been somehow related. Perhaps the Mound City builders had migrated down the Scioto Valley to relocate near Tremper.

Tremper also yielded some intrusive burials consisting of skeletons interred about a foot beneath the top of the mound. These appeared to be burials of members of the Fort Ancient Culture, which tended to contradict the evidence of the Robert Harness Mound that the Fort Ancient Culture had preceded the Hopewell Culture. The 1916 exploration of a Fort Ancient site called the Feurt Mounds and Village, located just across the Scioto River from Tremper where Hopewell-like objects had been discovered, led Shetrone to conclude in a 1920 article and his 1930 book that the Hopewellian builders of the Tremper Mound had lived at the same time as the Fort Ancient people.

Following their very rewarding work at Tremper, Mills and Shetrone moved to Mound City, a site that might have seemed far less promising in their day. By the time World War I was over and the soldiers had marched out of Camp Sherman, at least half of Mound City's mounds had been more or less obliterated. The earth that had composed these mounds had been recycled as fill for grading projects, and any related artifacts irretrievably scattered. However when Mills and Shetrone excavated in 1920 and 1921 they found sufficient remains to confirm their earlier notions and dispel a number of assertions made by Squier and Davis. They reported that the Mound City mounds had been burial mounds, not altar mounds. None of the basin-like structures at ground level had been altars for human sacrifice, but rather the same sort of crematories that had been unearthed at Tremper.

In the mound they referred to as Number 8, where Squier and Davis had found over two hundred effigy pipes, they found a burial just an inch or two below the surface of the earth. Inside the grave they found the cremated remains of a single individual together with copper artifacts that had been intentionally destroyed, causing them to conclude that the custom of "killing" grave offerings was not limited to Tremper.

It had taken the intervention of the Ohio State Archaeological and Historical Society to save Mound Number 7 from being reduced to landfill, and as a result, what Mills and Shetrone called Mound City's nucleus not only had been left standing, it had been relatively undisturbed. Beneath number 7 Mills and Shetrone located Mound City's finest and largest crematory basin, and judging by its evidence of repair work, they proposed that it had been long and intensively used. Upon examining the floor of number 7 they discovered evidence of disturbed earth, which led to the discovery that number 7 had a "basement" with a clay floor and another crematory basin which evidently also had been used for a long time.

From a log-lined vault in Mound Number 9, Mills and Shetrone recovered an object that would lead to a great deal of speculation about the social and dietary customs of Hopewellians: a wooden artifact covered with copper and shaped like a death-cap mushroom at the business end of what might have been a wand or baton used by a Hopewell priest.

Squier and Davis left no record of having done any exploration of Mound Number 13. Since this mound was only three feet high, the army had constructed a barracks on top of it and graded away what was left. Mills and Shetrone discovered twenty burials and a

Tremper effigy pipes featuring carved squirrels, beavers, porcupines, raccoons, bears, turtles, and otters. Their similarities to pipes discovered at Mound City suggested that the builders of these two sites had been related. (*Ohio History Connection*)

crematory basin in number 13, including one grave lined with sheets of mica, resulting in number 13 being renamed the Mica Grave Mound. In another section they found evidence of clothing and other objects but no burials, inferring that this section of number 13 might have served as a shrine.

Among the remaining artifacts that Mills and Shetrone recovered from Mound City were a few more pipes similar to those Squier and Davis had found, and a number of copper plates formed into various shapes including stylized eagles in flight. There were headdresses made of copper, or copper combined with other materials like woven fabric, hinting they might have been further decorated with other perishable materials such as feathers. Mound Number 13 had examples of copper deer antlers that might have been attached to some sort of skin or fabric head covering. Ten thousand beads of various kinds might have been strung into necklaces or attached to other pieces of clothing.

Mills and Shetrone had not been hopeful about finding intrusive burials in the Mound City mounds that had survived Camp Sherman, but they did locate thirteen uncremated intrusive burials accompanied by harpoons, flint arrow points, and other implements fashioned from deer antlers, which seemed like evidence that yet another culture had at some point occupied the middle and lower Scioto Valley.

In a 1922 article published by Chicago's Field Museum of Natural History, Warren K. Moorehead attempted to date the Hopewell Culture, but could do so only in a relative way. He guessed that all Ross County's Hopewell sites had been simultaneously inhabited, and he placed the site called Hopewell at about AD 1400–1500, adding that it must have been abandoned before 1550, certainly by the time the area had been explored by Europeans, or surely they would have recorded making a visit.

The issue of dating the Hopewell Culture was related to the question of when humans had arrived in the Western Hemisphere, and ever since the didactic anthropologist Ales Hrdlicka had proclaimed that humans had arrived not more than three thousand years before, any scholar who suggested otherwise was committing professional suicide. But in 1927, in an article titled "The Antiquity of Man in America" published by the American Museum of Natural History, Jesse Dade Figgins boldly proposed that the prevailing wisdom was all wrong. Figgins, born in Maryland in 1867, had started his professional life as an ornithologist. At the time his article appeared, he was director of the Colorado Museum of Natural History where he was best known as the talented artist who painted backgrounds for the museum's stuffed and mounted specimens.

Figgins had been drawn into the field of archaeology in 1926 when museum field workers, excavating the skeleton of a bison that had been extinct for eight or ten thousand years, found a man-made stone weapon point. Figgins traveled to Folsom, New Mexico, the site of this find, together with other experts to supervise further excavation, realizing that the find implied that this long extinct animal might have been brought down by a contemporary human hunter. A similar find had been made in Texas in 1923 but critics had dismissed the point as intrusive. Calling the Folsom find an "anticipated surprise," Figgins continued the work until other points were found beneath or embedded in the dead bison's rib cage. Figgins invited experts from the American Museum of Natural History and the Smithsonian Institution to come to New Mexico to see the evidence in situ for themselves. Discovery of similar "Folsom points" in similar settings elsewhere in America soon followed, and led to a new interpretation with which even Hrdlicka had to agree. Humans had lived on this continent when extinct bison roamed the landscape, and they had had the wits, the tools, and the guts to provide themselves with a tasty steak dinner.

Not long afterward in 1932 in Clovis, New Mexico, archaeologists confirmed that a different sort of weapon point had been unearthed in the rib cage of a wooly mammoth. The elaborate Clovis point differed from the Folsom point in that it was longer and designed to fit a weapon like a spear that a hunter could thrust into the vital organs of some very big game. The shorter Folsom points may have been designed to fit a weapon like a spear thrower and therefore worked better on smaller game like bison and deer. Clovis points tended to be discovered underneath layers of earth in which Folsom points had been found, indicating that the Clovis hunters had predated the Folsom hunters.

All this led archaeologists to believe through most of the twentieth century that after 12,000 BC, North America's earliest inhabitants, hunters called Paleoindians, migrated out of Alaska toward the continental United States. Either before or not long after they started moving south they invented the Clovis point. These points, which are characterized by technologically difficult fluting, have not been found in Asia. Some scholars have argued that Clovis points made their users so successful they contributed to a phenomenon called Pleistocene overkill, though other factors, primarily climate change, also contributed to the extinction of North America's megafauna around this time. Over the years Clovis points have been found in all forty-eight contiguous U.S.

states, but they are most common east of the Mississippi, especially in the valleys of the Cumberland, Tennessee, and Ohio rivers. So by the time the Hopewell people were building their big houses for mortuary rituals, the general area had long been home to humans.

By the 1960s Hopewell-like human remains had been located in Michigan, Wisconsin, and throughout the Mississippi Valley, as well as in Illinois, where they seemed to be older than the Hopewell remains of Ohio. Hopewell-like artifacts had been discovered as far away from Ohio as Minnesota and Florida. Yet the geometric enclosures seemed limited to the valleys of the Ohio and its Scioto, Muskingum, and Miami tributaries, while Hopewell-like burial mounds seemed to diminish in height and richness of deposited grave goods the farther one got from what was apparently the Hopewell heartland. The creation of the geometrical enclosures had long argued for the involvement of a large number of well-organized people, but little evidence had been found near the enclosures that very many people had lived immediately among them for lengthy periods of time. By the 1960s, a key question for American archaeologists had become exactly where the Hopewell people went and how they lived when they were not gathering to cremate and bury their dead.

In 1959, while technically still a student at Harvard, Olaf H. Prufer arrived in Ohio to take a position at the Cleveland Museum of Natural History and become an instructor at what was then the Case Institute of Technology. Prufer had been born in 1930 in Germany. Due to the exigencies of World War II, Prufer had quit school at the age of twelve. Harvard accepted him in 1954 following time he spent in India where he had become interested in archaeology and gained practical experience in the field. At Harvard, Prufer studied Old World Paleolithic archaeology, but marriage to a Cleveland native brought him to Ohio, where he took up the task of organizing what was known about the Hopewell Culture and the vexing unsolved problem of the location of their settlements.

In 1962, Prufer hypothesized that Ohio's Hopewellians might have organized themselves like the ancient people of Middle

America. They might have constructed religious or spiritual centers that formed the nuclei of their communities, but which were
vacant when rituals were not being performed there. They might
have lived their daily lives as swidden agriculturalists, or very
small-scale farmers who tended plots they cleared by slashing and
burning, dwelling in small farmstead communities rather than
larger villages. The settlement pattern Prufer proposed came to
be known as the Vacant Center Pattern. Instead of searching for
large Hopewell villages in all the wrong places, Prufer advocated
searching for scattered hamlets along river bottomlands.

That same year a Ross County farmer named Alva McGraw,
who also happened to be an amateur archaeologist, drew Prufer's
attention to a floodplain on his property that was soon to become
the scene of road construction. He had already found some flint
chips and other fragments, but the site had no other indications of
having been occupied. What came to be known as the McGraw
site was located on a small rise above the Scioto River about two
miles south of Chillicothe and about a mile southeast of an earthwork that had been called the East Bank Work by Squier and Davis
but had since disappeared. Prufer tested the site by digging a
trench and a pit and discovered black soil packed with residential
debris. Prufer had made the sort of find that gladdened the heart
of any archaeologist. He had located a midden, or trash dump.

With financial support from the National Science Foundation
and the Cleveland Museum of Natural History, Prufer organized
a team of museum personnel and students from the Case Institute
of Technology, Western Reserve University, and the Cleveland
Museum of Natural History. Excavation began in the summer of
1963 and the results were published in a December 1964 article
in *Scientific American* and by the Cleveland museum in 1965. .

While the team failed to locate postholes that would have been
evidence of a dwelling, the trash in the dump had much to suggest
about daily life among the Hopewell. There were flint blades and
blade fragments as well as tools made from bone. There were
many other bones and bone fragments with signs of cutting and
scratching, which indicated that the tools had been used for

butchering meat. There were bits of mica, terracotta, and shell, and a single copper object that might have formed part of a drill.

The team discovered a most interesting charred ear of corn and separate individual corn kernels. At the time most scholars contended that the Hopewell people had been primarily hunters and gatherers, but Prufer was convinced they had been food producers engaging in agriculture. In the years since, archaeologists have agreed that maize constituted no major part of the Hopewellian diet, though it might have been known and used as an occasional religious offering. Other McGraw rubbish showed that the people who had lived there also dined on turtles, fish, and shellfish from the nearby river, as well as rabbits, turkeys, deer, waterfowl, nuts, acorns, and berries.

By the time Prufer and his team were excavating the McGraw site, the process of radiocarbon dating had been developed, enabling archaeologists to objectively date certain organic materials. Radiocarbon testing of materials from the McGraw site showed it had been occupied during the fifth century AD, possibly for a single generation. Radiocarbon dating of materials from other Hopewell sites showed that McGraw had been occupied relatively late in overall Hopewell history.

In his writings Prufer offered some speculation on the rise and fall of Hopewell society. Physical anthropology had already demonstrated that the people buried at the great Hopewell charnel houses had different types of skulls than those buried in older, simpler mounds. Prufer speculated that a new people might have immigrated into southern Ohio from Illinois via southern Indiana bringing with them new customs and beliefs, perhaps becoming a dominating minority among an indigenous population. Prufer was not enthusiastic about the ambiguous phrase "Hopewell Culture." He thought that "Hopewell complex," or "Hopewell cult," or specifically "Hopewell cult of the dead" more accurately described the obvious obsession with funerals attested to by the artifacts they had left behind. Their customs, which demanded exotic materials for grave goods, probably resulted in an exchange network which simultaneously spread the cult's beliefs among other Native Americans living great distances away.

So what had caused the Ohio Hopewell to cease building their ceremonial centers around AD 500? Recently archaeologists have speculated on societal changes incurred by the development of agriculture, but in an article titled "The Hopewell Complex of Ohio," published in a 1964 book titled *Hopewellian Studies*, Prufer wrote, "The impression gained is that the people rather suddenly took to the hills, abandoning their centers in the wake of some danger." In so supposing Prufer was more or less echoing the opinions that had been expressed by certain nineteenth-century observers, including William Henry Harrison and Josiah Priest. Prufer added that in this period the Iroquoian populations settled farther north had started fortifying their own sites with stockades. Prufer continued, "I am tempted to interpret these events in Iroquoian and in the Ohio heartland of the Hopewellians as the result of a common and unidentified cause which may have led to the violent end of the Ohio Hopewell, following a period of upheaval during which the hilltop enclosures were occupied." The same unrest might have made it difficult to obtain the raw materials from distant locations for Hopewell grave goods. In any case, it appeared to Prufer that by around AD 750 the cult had died, leaving earlier local traditions to reassert themselves.

In another article published in *Hopewellian Studies*, archaeologist Joseph R. Caldwell, then of the Illinois State Museum, tried to replace the phrase "Hopewell culture" with the phrase "Hopewell interaction sphere" to describe the phenomenon through which Hopewell communities acquired materials from all over North America. Caldwell wrote, "It is an interaction sphere of a special kind. The interactions and hence the connections among the various societies are in mortuary-religious matters but not, primarily, at least, in other departments of culture." In the same volume Stuart Struever, then at the University of Chicago, used the phrase to mean "relations of a still undetermined nature, though involving idea and goods exchange, between groups scattered over a broad area of eastern North America." He recommended that future research focus on exactly what kind of intercourse was taking place.

While archaeologists continued to be interested in how
diverse materials got into the hands of Hopewell craftsmen, over
the next twenty years it was Prufer's Vacant Center Pattern that
provoked the most discourse. In April 1992, the fifty-seventh
meeting of the Society for American Archaeology included a symposium titled "Testing the Prufer Model of Ohio Hopewell
Settlement Patterns." Most of the papers presented were published in a 1997 book titled *Ohio Hopewell Community Organization*.
Unfortunately, the symposium's organizers neglected to invite
Prufer, prompting him to pen a long letter expressing his disap-
pointment. The organizers apologized and Prufer became a major
contributor to the book.

In general the book dealt with evidence discovered in the mid-
to late 1980s and early 1990s. Findings generally reinforced
Prufer's hypothesis that the Hopewell occupied outlying hamlets,
but they apparently also established themselves at other dispersed
sites that could not be classified as hamlets, such as specialized
camps for hunting or other occupational purposes. It was also
likely that the Hopewell people did not stay in any one place for
too long, which might have been the result of having to find new
locations for their gardens.

In November 1993, Hopewell scholars gathered in Chillicothe
for a conference titled "A View from the Core." This time Prufer
was invited and he commented during a panel session following
the plenary. A resulting 1996 publication also titled *A View from the
Core* examined the Hopewell heartland of southern Ohio, though
both the book and the conference also included material on the
Hopewell suburbs, or "periphery." Once again Prufer's model
emerged relatively intact; the scholars concluded the Hopewell
people maintained their dispersed sedentary communities until
evolving lifestyles demanded true nucleated villages. The book
also explored possible explanations for the collections of refuse
that had since been discovered near the ceremonial earthworks.
Did these qualify as Hopewell hamlets or were they evidence of
itinerant workshops or camps where craftsmen gathered to make
items for the ceremonial centers?

In July 2000, yet another Hopewell scholars' conference led to yet another book: *Recreating Hopewell*, published in 2006. Discussion on Hopewellian settlement patterns again prevailed, and again Prufer's model was more or less accepted, though many archaeologists were by then trying to flesh out the details on how it may have worked. How often did Hopewellians visit their earthworks? Just how much did individual Hopewellians move around? Were they really farmers, primarily gatherers, or something in-between? Would construction of the earthworks have required laborers to relocate? Who fed and housed the laborers while they worked? Who scheduled the ceremonies once the ceremonial centers were built? Participants at the 2000 conference also revisited the Hopewell Interaction Sphere, hoping that in the future it would be possible to learn more about the nature and scale of what might have been multiple trade or interaction networks.

Archaeologists are still arguing about how sedentary or mobile the Hopewell people might have been. Floors with hearths have been excavated near Newark, Ohio, but no one has yet found what could be described as a Hopewell hamlet.

Bradley T. Lepper, a native Ohioan who is currently Curator of Archaeology at the Ohio History Connection (successor to the Ohio Historical Society and the Ohio State Archaeological and Historical Society), contributed a chapter to *Recreating Hopewell* on the Great Hopewell Road, which he described as a monumental work of construction stretching for miles across central Ohio. Caleb Atwater had been first to speculate that the parallel walls of earth discovered in various locations near Newark were part of a road leading out from the earthwork complex possibly toward defensive earthworks on the Hocking River. In the mid-nineteenth century, James and Charles Salisbury traced the supposed road over streams, fields, and swamps, speculating that it might have connected Newark and either Circleville or Chillicothe. By the late nineteenth century, the area in question had long been under cultivation, and traces of any such ancient road were well on their way to oblivion. In 1930 a Newark businessman named

Warren Weiant, Jr. went looking for parallel lines in the soil from an airplane, observing that the Hopewell Road seemed to connect Newark's Octagon and Chillicothe, and that it was punctuated by small circular enclosures at regular intervals along the way. He joked about Hopewellian gas stations or possibly hot dog stands.

Newark and Chillicothe were both well supplied with Hopewellian mounds and earthworks, and both had a circular earthwork that connected to an octagonal earthwork. In his *Recreating Hopewell* chapter, Lepper wrote, "The Hopewell builders were forging a dramatically new kind of connection between two distant places. The long, straight road would not have been simply a route of commerce and communication; it was a conduit of unifying ritual." Lepper also speculated that the Hopewell Road might have been one of a network of roads connecting ceremonial centers, possibly used by pilgrims in the same way that Mayans used their own sacred roads. Were this the case, then the possible habitation sites located nearest the earthworks might have been lodging for visiting pilgrims, and the objects and materials that were not native to Ohio might have been their offerings, while the Hopewellian objects found in distant locations might have been something like pilgrim badges, or souvenirs. The pilgrims might also have contributed their labor in constructing the earthworks and taken home religious and ceremonial knowledge.

Newark, at one terminus of the Hopewell Road, was one of the northernmost of the great Hopewellian ceremonial centers and one of the largest, covering over four square miles with corridors that intriguingly seemed designed to herd visitors into the earthwork in a certain way, and restrict their movements once they got there. Discovered in the early 1800s, Newark's earthworks had been illustrated by Caleb Atwater in his 1820 book as well as by Squier and Davis in *Ancient Monuments*, in which they classified the site as a "sacred enclosure," describing it as complex and as awe-inspiring as "passing the portals of an Egyptian temple, or gazing upon the silent ruins of Petra in the desert." Pidgeon's Native American friend had dubbed Newark the ancient "Prophet's Metropolis."

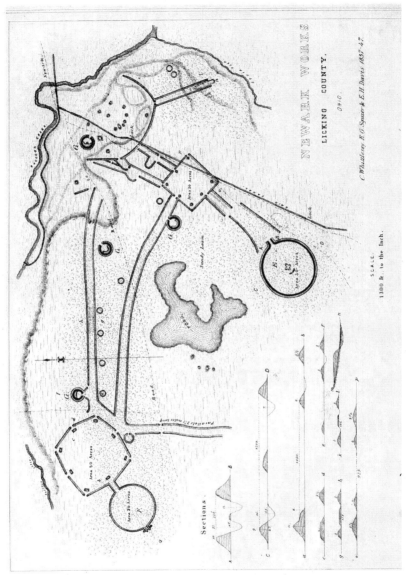

The extensive ancient remains at Newark, in *Ancient Monuments*. This complex originally extended over 3,000 acres. The structures that have survived and are visible
today include the Great Circle, over 1200 feet in diameter (center right); the Circle-
Octagon Complex, enclosing a total of 70 acres (lower left) that has now been incorporated into a golf course; and what is now known as the Wright Earthworks, part of
a square earthwork originally enclosing about 20 acres (center top).

This view shows the golf course and surrounding residential neighborhoods that have incorporated the Circle-Octagon Complex. The golf course helped preserve this ancient earthwork. (*Science Views*)

Paradoxically, the Newark region attracted little organized archaeological investigation in the period during which its remains were being quickly consumed by the growing city of Newark, where nearby Hopewellian mounds came in very handy for use as fill for railroad embankments. Newark's Great Circle became better known as the Fairgrounds Circle after the Licking County Fair, which was held there from 1854 to 1933. In 1910, an organization called the Moundbuilders Country Club leased Newark's Octagon from the Newark Board of Trade. The golf course they constructed actually helped preserve the earthwork in the ensuing years, but limited public access. In the 1930s the Great Circle and the Octagon were acquired for preservation by the Ohio Historical Society, but by then Newark's Hopewellian mounds had been mostly destroyed.

In the 1980s scholars began examining what was left of Newark's earthworks in a different way, to determine what they might reveal about the knowledge of astronomy and geometry among the Hopewell. In 1982 Ray Hively and Robert Horn of Earlham College in Indiana mapped the site, observing that it had been carefully constructed with an eye for symmetry and geometrical harmony. They also stated that its builders had oriented it to the northern maximum moonrise, allowing for the precise monitoring of an 18.6-year lunar cycle, so that its various parts could be used for sighting lunar alignments and observing lunar time. William F. Romain, who had similarly mapped the Serpent Mound, proposed that the design, layout, and possibly the use of the Newark earthworks had included a nearby feature called Geller Hill, the highest point on the plain that the earthworks occupied. Indeed high points and overlooks were probably where Hopewellian astronomers made their initial observations and established sightlines in order to build such large Hopewellian ceremonial centers.

At the time, the discipline of archaeoastronomy, which had originally been the avocation of astronomers and engineers, was attracting interest not only from scholarly anthropologists, but also book publishers and television producers eager to hawk ancient mysteries, which incidentally invited criticism from skeptics. The foremost of these was James A. Marshall, a civil engineer who had been surveying and mapping prehistoric constructions since 1965. He argued that archaeoastronomers tended to look for evidence supporting their foregone conclusions, while they examined too few sites to conclude much at all. Hively and Horn apparently were listening, for they followed up with a 1984 article on High Bank Works, Ohio's other circle-octagon earthwork complex located below Chillicothe at the Hopewell Road's presumed other end. They discovered that High Bank had astronomical alignments with the winter and summer solstice sunrise and sunset, as well as eight lunar standstills (maximum and minimum rise and set points of the moon), making it seem highly unlikely that such alignments had occurred by accident at two similarly constructed earthwork complexes, and also raising the interesting question of whether there might have been some grand regional plan for choosing locations for individual monuments.

On a warm, early summer day in 2013 we arrived at the Great Circle Museum on the outskirts of modern-day Newark. Inside, where one could watch a video, we found a group of preteens sitting on the floor of the exhibit area where they were being educated in "ancient skills." We also found a very busy executive director who was kind enough to take the time to answer our questions and impart the impressive statistics that the Great Circle Museum then welcomed thousands of visitors annually from thirty-three states, and thirteen foreign countries. He was busy because that evening the site would host something called the World Heritage Celebration, which would commemorate progress toward putting all of Ohio's earthworks on the UNESCO World Heritage list. He was expecting scholars, local civic leaders, and members of the Eastern Shawnee Tribe of Oklahoma, who had taken up the cause despite the lack of a demonstrable link between themselves and Mound Builder cultures. "I honestly don't know what to expect tonight," he admitted.

The preteens had preceded us outdoors but we soon lost sight of them in and around the Great Circle. The Great Circle, like Mound City, was an excellent place to get a feel for the oversize scale of Hopewellian earthworks. Its circular wall was high and steep, and its interior ditch was deep. We might have climbed the Eagle Mound at the circle's center (which the executive director had informed us was a reproduction), but we figured that by the time we walked all the way over to it in the summer sun, we would no longer have had the energy.

Just as Squier and Davis predicted, outside the Great Circle Museum we found a reproduction of the diagram from their 1848 book illustrating the extensive earthworks that once stood in this area, which also indicated which pieces of the original complex were left. We compared the model to an atlas and a map of modern Newark, as well as the driving directions between the existing earthworks provided at the museum. We were further impressed by the scale of the original works as we drove the blocks and blocks that separated their remains. If you imagine that

Inside the Great Circle at Newark. Human figures show the scale of the enclosure. Adjacent to this earthwork is a small museum offering interpretative information and directions to the other earthworks remaining in the Newark area. (*Author*)

Newark's vanished graded ways were built for processions, the parades must have lasted all day or all night.

The earthen walls seemed a little lower at what was known in Newark as the Octagon, actually part of a circle-octagon complex, inside and outside of which spreads the golf course of Moundbuilders Country Club. In the years since the Ohio Historical Society acquired the earthwork, the two organizations have worked out a way for the public to see it without bothering the golfers too much at this private club. We were able to follow a trail that went part way around the outside of the circle, and mount a viewing platform located just at the short avenue that joins the circle and the octagon. Once atop the platform I noticed that we had arrived on maintenance day. There were no golfers, just a lot of landscapers grooming the course. At first it was difficult for my eyes to separate the earthen walls from the greens and bunkers, but once I got oriented I could distinguish the curving walls of the circle from the straight walls of the octagon. The avenue between them had been cleverly turned into a tee.

In October 2005, moonrise over the main axis of this circle-octagon complex marked the northernmost moonrise at the end of an 18.6-year lunar cycle. The public was invited to attend. If you don't want to wait until 2023 to witness this phenomenon, you can find a reconstruction at ancientohiotrail.org. CERHAS, the Center for the Electronic Reconstruction of Historical and Archaeological Sites, an interdisciplinary laboratory founded in 1995 at the University of Cincinnati, also uses computer simulations to re-create the ancient earthworks of Ohio and their surrounding landscapes.

When we visited Newark, we stayed in neighboring Granville, a charming town that retained a lot of nineteenth-century and early twentieth-century architecture, including our hotel, the Granville Inn, constructed in 1922. When we dined in its elegant Oak Room I wondered whether Henry Clyde Shetrone had ever enjoyed a meal there, perhaps in the company of his mentor, William Corless Mills, when they were both working for the Ohio State Archaeological and Historical Society in nearby Columbus during the 1920s.

As we drove between Newark and Granville, I took another look at Squier and Davis's map, titled "Six Miles of the Newark Valley." I could see that we were probably traveling the same road they had illustrated linking these two towns. I identified the plateau where they had diagramed the Alligator Mound, which is still there if you know where to look for it. But just east of it, Squier and Davis had drawn a "Fortified Hill." I didn't see any fortified hill along the road, and later I learned that this monument had succumbed to agriculture long before suburban development had turned this general area into one of the nicest places to live in all of Ohio. I found a new appreciation for golf courses and county fairs and the random circumstances and interested people that preserved the remaining parts of what Squier and Davis had seen and recorded.

Not far from Newark stands the largest surviving Hopewellian construction, which has borne the popular name Fort Ancient since before that name was also applied to a culture that did not build it. Located on a mesa above the Little

Miami River, Fort Ancient's embankments surround an irregular space of about one hundred hilltop acres. The complex also includes mounds, crescents, circles, and paved areas.

Fort Ancient became the property of the state of Ohio in 1891, and its first professional excavators realized early on that the general vicinity had been inhabited by two different peoples. By the mid-twentieth century, an Ohio State Archaeological and Historical Society archaeologist named Richard Morgan concluded that the Hopewell people built Fort Ancient, but that Fort Ancient people later occupied it. In the 1980s and 1990s Patricia Essenpreis of the University of Florida and Robert Connolly of the University of Cincinnati excavated Hopewellian remains outside Fort Ancient's northern segment. Radiocarbon dating of the remains indicated that Hopewellians constructed and occupied Fort Ancient for about four hundred years from 100 BC to AD 300.

Throughout the nineteenth century and well into the twentieth, the leading scholars tended to agree that Fort Ancient was a fort. Caleb Atwater and John Locke (whose description was published by Squier and Davis) had classified Fort Ancient as a work of defense despite the large gaps or openings in its three and a half miles of earthen walls, which would have rendered it difficult to defend. In a letter to the editor of *Science* magazine published in 1886, Cyrus Thomas very definitely defined Fort Ancient as a fort, writing, "that it was built and intended as a work of defense is so apparent, that it is scarcely possible there should be conflicting opinions on this point." He also foreshadowed Prufer on the apparent retreat of Hopewellians from the floodplains to the hilltops, commenting, "These works were built by a populous tribe, which was being pressed step by step before a victorious foe."

In his 1858 book, *Traditions of De-coo-dah*, William Pidgeon suggested that Native Americans had other ideas. Pidgeon wrote, "Tradition assigns to this remarkable work the name of MOON CITY," adding that the moniker might have been inspired by a crescent-shaped earthwork near the entrance of its southern segment which, according to Pidgeon's Native American friend, was built before the northern segment. The entire project was "constructed by the successive labors of a long line of kings or rulers, whose pride of dominion led them to enlarge and extend the original work." It turns out that Pidgeon was correct about the length of construction and use, and recent discoveries show he may have been on to something with "Moon City," too.

Fort Ancient's northeastern corner has a large opening that once pointed toward a set of parallel walls extending toward a circular enclosure with a small mound. The diagrams in the publications of Atwater and Squier and Davis both illustrate this feature, though the description by John Locke notes that by the mid-nineteenth century, "It has been so much obliterated as to escape ordinary observation, and it is now traceable with difficulty." Around here amateurs discovered caches, one containing over a hundred sheets of mica, and stone and copper ornaments that seemed purposely broken or bent, the other containing what might have been valuable blades fashioned from Wyoming obsidian, Indiana chert, and clear quartz, altogether making this opening seem like an entrance to Fort Ancient where some sort of ceremony occurred.

Fort Ancient's northern segment also contained four stone-paved nonburial mounds positioned so that they formed a near perfect square. In the 1980s Patricia Essenpreis working with astronomer David Duszynski plotted astronomical alignments through the openings in the northeast corner of the northern segment of Fort Ancient. They discovered that someone standing on or near the westernmost mound would be able to sight through three openings to observe the annual summer solstice sunrise, plus the maximum and minimum northern moonrises, which occur 9.3 years apart. In the 1990s Robert Connolly studied and commented on Fort Ancient's intentionally constructed ponds and ditches that may have served as a drainage system or a way to collect potable water, possibly for ceremonial activities.

By 1995 when Jack K. Blosser and Robert C. Glotzhober wrote a book titled *Fort Ancient: Citadel, Cemetery, Cathedral, or Calendar?* the citadel conjecture was beginning to sound like the least likely possibility.

When we visited in 2007, we found a recently refurbished museum whose exhibits illuminated the broader topic of Native American prehistory, from the time the Paleoindians discovered Ohio until the time of first contact between Indians and Europeans. Exhibits and visual aids also showed how the interpretation of Native American life changed over time. We witnessed a large display on Hopewellian astronomy and a model of Fort Ancient that made its astronomical function easier to understand. Outside, the site was a pleasant park where quite a few visitors were picnicking on a summer afternoon. The earthworks were mainly identifiable by the signs warning people to stay off of them. The stone-paved mounds we saw had similar signs. The best view was from the north overlook where we could see far down into the ravine below us, and in the distance, Ohio's tallest bridge (which was identified by a sign).

It was very late summer when we were there and we probably just missed meeting the people working on one of the most exciting archaeological finds in Ohio in years. Very likely they had recently packed up their equipment and covered over their site to preserve it for further work the following season. In 2005, the Ohio Historical Society began a project to mitigate erosion of Fort Ancient's walls with some remote sensing just to make sure that their heavy equipment would not disturb or damage anything significant underground. No one was really looking for artifacts, but in the north segment, magnetometer readings indicated there had once been some sort of circular feature surrounding what seemed to be burned soil.

The Ohio Historical Society contacted Dr. Robert Riordan of Wright State University to manage the excavations that began in 2006 with a crew of students and volunteers. Riordan named the mysterious circular feature after Warren K. Moorehead, who had conducted the first systematic excavations at Fort Ancient and worked to make the site a state park. Riordan's excavations revealed that the Moorehead Circle was actually three concentric circles defined by wooden posts about ten to thirteen feet high planted firmly in the ground with an entrance on the southeast paved with limestone slabs. At the circle's center there was some

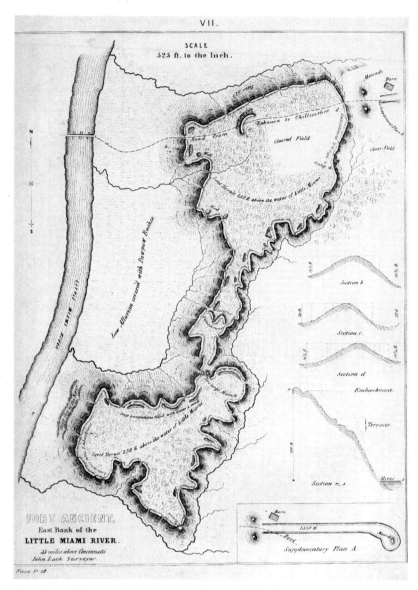

VII.

SCALE
525 ft. to the Inch.

FORT ANCIENT,
East Bank of the
LITTLE MIAMI RIVER.
33 miles above Cincinnati
John Lock Surveyor.

Fort Ancient from *Ancient Monuments*. This massive hilltop enclosure incorporates three and a half miles of earthen walls punctuated by mysterious gaps. Exhibits in a museum at the site help visitors understand how it might have functioned as an observatory.

reddish burned soil surrounded by the pieces of intentionally broken pots. In the southern half of the circle there were trenches suggesting seating for congregants. Riordan concluded that the Moorehead Circle, once the scene of ceremonial activity, had also been systematically dismantled rather than carelessly abandoned.

Over the last few years, folks have taken to calling the Moorehead Circle a "woodhenge," a name that has stuck to a similar structure discovered on the Little Miami River during salvage excavations in 1998. Archaeologists were using computer modeling to determine whether the Moorehead Circle has astronomical alignments similar to those of England's Stonehenge. As of 2012 Riordan reported that it appeared that the sun would rise in the gateway of the Moorehead Circle on the summer solstice, the longest day of the year. Today's archaeologists expect to discover additional previously overlooked evidence of timber circles and structures in other Hopewell enclosures and landscapes, as well as clues to their purposes.

If astronomically aligned earthworks are intriguing enough to make one wonder what religious and social life among the Hopewellians was really like, you can turn to the works of a number of anthropologists who apparently have overcome the hesitation of earlier scholars to try to read the minds of prehistoric people, or theorize about their religious beliefs, signaling an era when speculative hypotheses have become more acceptable in the field. A pair of authors produced *Gathering Hopewell: Society, Rituals, and Ritual Interaction* and a second book titled *The Scioto Hopewell and their Neighbors: Bioarchaeological Documentation and Cultural Understanding*. Christopher Carr is listed first on the cover of *Gathering Hopewell*; D. Troy Case got top billing on *The Scioto Hopewell*. A. Martin Byers recently completed a trilogy of lengthy works filled with hypotheses on Hopewell society, ceremonies, and interaction sphere. William F. Romain is responsible for the romantically titled *Mysteries of the Hopewell: Astronomers, Geometers, and Magicians of the Eastern Woodlands*, as well as *Shamans of the Lost World: A Cognitive Approach to the Prehistoric Religion of the Hopewell.*

Case was associate professor and director of the Anthropology Department at North Carolina State University and Carr was a professor in Arizona State University's School of Human Evolution and Social Change, which was the new name for what used to be the university's anthropology department. Case was one of Carr's students at ASU. About twenty more of Carr's graduate students also contributed to *Gathering Hopewell*.

The introductory material in both *Gathering Hopewell* and *The Scioto Hopewell* explains that Carr and Case employ a methodology they call "thick prehistory," which they define as a detailed reconstruction of Hopewellian society, or getting to know the Hopewell people on their own terms. Various reviewers of these books defined the term "thick prehistory" as the interpretation of social history through the study of artifacts, or analogous behavior in other Native American societies.

One reviewer linked this methodology to the British practitioners of "post-processual archaeology." Post-processual archaeology had followed processual archaeology, also called New Archaeology, when the methodology was introduced in the 1960s and 1970s. Processual archaeology emphasized scientific methods and dealt with processes that explained, rather than merely described, change in ancient society. Post-processual archaeology, also known as interpretive archaeology, was inaugurated in Britain in 1985 by a man named Ian Hodder. It was advocated by the critics of processual archaeology who were unsatisfied with how archaeology had been practiced up to that time. They argued that scientific detachment was impossible due to the cultural biases that archaeologists themselves brought to their interpretations. They believed that culture was created by the actions of people and could not be interpreted without examining the roles of previously neglected minorities such as women. (Over at the typical university's history department, the faculty was calling the same sentiment "history from the bottom up.") It's likely no coincidence that post-processual archaeology arose around the time that the radicals of the 1960s were becoming the tenured faculty of the 1980s, bringing their Marxist and feminist views into every academic discipline and refocusing the general curricula on race, class, gender, and sexual orientation. Today most archaeologists studying North America's prehistory would probably describe their methodology as processual or "processual plus," indicating that they also have an interest in social dynamics. I'm not sure I'll ever "get" thick prehistory, but at approximately eight hundred pages each, *Gathering Hopewell* and *The Scioto Hopewell* were certainly both thick.

The authors of *Gathering Hopewell* came up with some interesting reinterpretations of old conclusions. Instead of Hopewellians residing in dispersed hamlets and occasionally visiting a ceremonial center, à la Prufer's Vacant Center Pattern, the authors proposed that Hopewellians living in a single hamlet visited different ceremonial centers for different purposes, and that certain earthworks might have been constructed and used by multiple Hopewellian communities. They defined three types of possible communities: residential communities of neighboring households; "sustainable" communities, or regional social networks; and "symbolic" communities with a common purpose, be it religious, economic, or something else.

The authors more or less rejected previous interpretations of the Hopewell Interaction Sphere as too one-dimensional. They also questioned whether competition was natural in society, an assumption they defined as a bias of Western civilization. Could Hopewellian history have been a time of widespread human cooperation, and could the materials taken to or brought from great distances have been evidence of individuals traveling around for diverse, noncompetitive reasons including "Vision and power questing, pilgrimages to places in nature, the travels of persons and/or patients for healing, the buying and spreading of religious prerogatives, pilgrimages to a ceremonial center for tutelage in religious knowledge and ceremony, and occasional cases of long-distance spirit adoption or intermarriage." Other scholars have portrayed Hopewellian society as generally nonviolent, but any-

one who wants to characterize it as a time of total peace and harmony needs to explain the Hopewellian custom of making things
out of human skulls and bones and depositing them as grave
goods.

In order to understand Hopewellian society, Carr and Case
suggested that one must understand the social and ritual roles that
Hopewellians played in their local societies. To do this the authors
linked Hopewellian artifacts with ethnographically defined social
roles and used them to label the individuals they were buried with
as shamans, warriors, hunters, diviners, healers, or other leaders.
They included a table associating mica sheets with divination,
copper antler headdresses with public ceremonial leadership, and
mushroom effigies with "trancing and ceremony," among other
relationships. Carr and Case addressed gender issues, concluding
that women had more power in certain Hopewellian communities than others based on the number of artifacts buried with
women that they assumed to be evidence of leadership. Members
of academic cultural anthropology and sociology departments
sometimes speak of "multiple genders," or persons who are
accepted by their societies as being neither male nor female. The
authors sought evidence for such persons in the tombs of those
they assumed to be shamans and apparently they found some.
However they cautioned, "Our study is the only one known to
address the possibility of multiple genders within Hopewellian
society, and one of the first in archaeology."

The Scioto Hopewell, the companion volume to *Gathering
Hopewell* focusing more narrowly on the geographic area in the
valleys of the Scioto River and Paint Creek, was also a self-
described "thick prehistory," presented as "holistic description of
Scioto Hopewell cultural life." In identifying social roles and
clans, it covered a lot of the same ground as *Gathering Hopewell*.
There was also material speculating on the rather abrupt beginning and end of Scioto Hopewell culture, suggesting it was a spiritual phenomenon that began with "rapid development of a new
world view" and collapsed with "some form of perceived spiritu-
al-religious event or problem of major importance to
Hopewellian peoples."

Another author who weighed in with theories about Hopewell life was A. Martin Byers, an anthropology professor retired from Vanier College in Montreal and currently a research associate with McGill University's Department of Anthropology. The first installment of his trilogy was titled *The Ohio Hopewell Episode: Paradigm Lost, Paradigm Gained* published in 2004. The second and third were *Sacred Games, Death, and Renewal in the Ancient Eastern Woodlands: The Ohio Hopewell System of Cult Sodality Heterarchies*, and *Reclaiming the Hopewellian Ceremonial Sphere 200 B.C. to A.D. 500*, published in 2011 and 2015, respectively. If you can get past the jargon, which is no easy task, Byers argues that the Hopewell culture had two kinds of communities: clans into which members were born and sodalities that they joined the way modern people join clubs and fraternal organizations. Byers contends that sodality members constructed the Hopewell earthworks and used them for sacred games and world renewal rituals made necessary by their increasing reliance on agriculture and its damaging effects on the environment. The interaction of the sodalities across regions generated what Byers renamed the Hopewell Ceremonial Sphere.

The problem with the hypotheses set forth by these anthropologists is that they are just that: hypotheses. I recommend that you skip all five tedious tomes and pick up two books by William F. Romain, who is hands down the most eloquent and compelling writer and whose two works far surpass those of Byers, Case, and Carr in terms of crossover appeal to a general reading audience. In both his books, Romain admitted that his reconstruction of Hopewellian society is not the only one possible. In *Shamans of the Lost World*, Romain wrote, "The phenomenon that was Hopewell represents a 'lost world'—a world that has, in large measure, been erased by time and faded from memory. What I have offered in the preceding pages is not a map, but rather a sketch of that territory—an outline, if you will, limited to a few structural components. Others will view the same territory and draw a different picture."

William F. Romain holds degrees in both anthropology and archaeology. In his book *Mysteries of the Hopewell*, Romain mentioned that his academic training represented a career change following years of work as a business executive in New York City. Romain was a member of the Society of Professional Archaeologists, and had an academic affiliation with Ohio State University. He is currently associated with an organization called the Ancient Earthworks Project.

Romain defines his methodology as cognitive archaeology, or the idea that archaeologists can gain insight into prehistoric religious beliefs and rituals, cosmology, ideology, and iconography through a study of artifacts interpreted through a "lens of shamanism." Romain contends that a shamanistic worldview is common to humans living the lives of hunter-gatherers, where humans survive by killing animals and plants whom they believe willingly give their lives so that humans can eat. Such a universe is full of spirits that can be contacted and influenced, often through altered states of consciousness, a universe where humans, spirits, and animals can assume each other's forms, and one where all things have souls that are released upon death.

In *Mysteries of the Hopewell,* published in 2000, Romain studied Hopewellian earthworks and concluded that their designers were definitely familiar with the basic concepts of geometry, despite the fact that their enclosures were often imperfectly shaped. He observed that they tended to locate earthworks near places where the earth had offered humans special natural resources such as deposits of flint, pipestone, salt, and red ochre. Romain concluded that Hopewellian builders must have employed a standard unit of measure, and that they deliberately oriented a number of earthworks and graded ways to allow celebrants within to view summer and winter solstice events through certain openings, while they often aligned their charnel houses with lunar celestial events. Romain suggested that square-shaped earthworks symbolized the sky or the heavens while circular enclosures symbolized the earth. The Hopewellians combined these shapes in earthworks "used for ceremonies relating to passage from this world to the next, death and rebirth, world renewal, and creation."

In *Shamans of the Lost World*, published nearly a decade after *Mysteries of the Hopewell,* Romain filled in the details on the

Hopewellian worldview. Hopewellian life unfolded in a Middle Earth of people and animals poised between an Upper World of sun, moon, stars, and bird spirits, and a Lower World of snakes, fish, fantastical monsters, and spirits of the dead. The three worlds were connected by an "axis mundi," or a line through the earth's center around which the universe revolved. Even in the quotidian Middle Earth one might encounter dangerous creatures lurking in hidden places. The passage of time was measured by predictable events like the recurring seasons of the year.

The Wray figurine, discovered at Newark, depicts a shaman donning a bearskin, probably for a ceremony. (*Ohio History Connection*)

Hopewellians depended on their shamans to interact with the nonordinary or extraordinary events in their universe. Shamans could heal or cause illness and predict the future through divination, making it possible for communities to avert disasters that might be brought on by war, drought, or flood. Romain interpreted caches of artifacts as gifts or expressions of thanks that would have been deposited with ceremony under the direction of a community's shaman. Perhaps a shaman's most important responsibility was to guide community members through death, even those souls who were less than willing to depart. In this capacity, shamans presided over the physical disposal of corpses.

Some shamans could "turn" themselves into certain animals with which they enjoyed a special relationship. Like Carr and Case, Romain cited as evidence a small Hopewellian artifact called the Wray figurine, unearthed in Newark in 1881 and named for its former owner (now housed at the Ohio History Center's museum), depicting a shaman donning a bearskin and thereby changing into a bear. Early frontier settlers had noted that

Native Americans had a special affection for powerful, intelligent bears: animals that came closer to humans in appearance than any other. Settlers also recorded that certain individuals in Indian communities could don bearskins and very realistically mimic the characteristic actions of bears.

In both books Romain suggests that Hopewellians had means of traveling beyond their physical world on a basis less permanent than death. He mentions the mushroom wand discovered by Mills and Shetrone at Mound City and the powerful hallucinogenic properties of the *Amanita muscaria* that it depicts. A less perilous trip might be induced by smoking strong wild tobacco in pipes whose effigies might have represented an individual's spirit helper or guardian. For the most part, Hopewellian effigy pipes represented birds, bears, otters, beavers, or animals with desirable talents and traits, rather than animals that humans tended to consider repulsive like insects and snakes.

Romain's books received far fewer professional reviews than the works of Byers, Carr, and Case. *Mysteries of the Hopewell* attracted some mild criticism for reporting celestial alignments in earthworks that have yet to be accurately dated, since the apparent position of celestial bodies changes over time. I could not find any reviews of *Shamans of the Lost World* in professional journals, but it received a "highly recommended" rating in *Choice*, a journal for academic librarians. I can only say that Romain explained foreign concepts like soul flight in terms that made them perfectly reasonable activities for shamans of a hunter-gatherer society, and perfectly understandable to a nonanthropologist like myself.

Fascinating or pedantic, all the anthropologists' hypotheses may well be equally premature because archaeologists still lack sufficient dates to establish a chronology, or reliable timeline, of Hopewell civilization: a point made by Mark J. Lynott in his book titled *Hopewell Ceremonial Landscapes of Ohio*, published after its author died in 2014. Lynott was manager and supervisory archaeologist at the Midwest Archaeological Center in Lincoln, Nebraska, until 2013. He spent most of his career studying the National Park Service's Hopewell sites at Mound City, Hopewell

Mound Group (originally called Clark's Work), and especially Hopeton Earthworks.

Lynott's book includes much detail on the Hopeton Earthworks Project initiated in 2001 by the Midwest Archaeological Center and the National Park Service. The project focused on earthwork construction, as opposed to previous research, which tended to concentrate on what happened to be buried in or under Hopewell mounds. Lynott wrote, "The study at Hopeton was designed to provide data about three basic questions—which can be abbreviated into 'when, how and why?'"

The project employed geophysical and geoarchaeological, as well as traditional archaeological, methods. Its researchers were able to come up with a range of radiocarbon dates for the Hopeton Earthworks because their builders frequently made small fires during the construction process. Lynott concluded that it had taken Hopewellian construction workers four to six generations to build the Hopeton Earthworks, roughly between AD 100 and 250. The monument was later modified by other tenants around the year 1000. The original builders also had removed a great deal of topsoil before any embankment construction began, implying that the complex was built according to design, not organically grown, a fact that contradicts a hypothesis made by Byers that circular Hopewellian enclosures predated rectangular enclosures.

Lynott mentioned that the project revealed a lot about when and how Hopeton was constructed, but that we still can't be sure why. At this point we do not know what Hopewellians did at their enclosures besides build them. So far, archaeological research only confirms that Hopeton, at least, was not a habitation site or a cemetery.

When we visited the museum of the Ohio History Center in 2013 we could not help but notice the Ohio History Connection was also keeping the hypotheses and assumptions to a minimum. The exhibit on the ancient people of Ohio just grouped together in a category objects thought to have sacred meaning, like birdstones and pipes. As for Hopewellian earthworks, this exhibit simply suggested they were used "to remember, to gather, to include others, and to connect with the spirit of nature."

In today's fast-paced world it does not take long for the latest developments in science and technology to be adopted by those studying the prehistoric world. For example, the same break-throughs in DNA analysis that help the police solve crimes make it possible to study relationships among prehistoric populations. In an article titled "Migration and Social Structure among the Hopewell: Evidence from Ancient DNA," published in *American Antiquity* in 2007, authors Deborah A. Bolnick and David Glenn Smith studied mitochondrial DNA extracted from prehistoric skeletal material at two sites: the Pete Klunk Mound Group in Illinois and the Hopewell site in Ohio. Among the questions they were hoping to answer were where individuals resided following marriage and whether actual migration accompanied cultural exchange.

Besides southern Ohio, archaeologists had long acknowledged a second Hopewell "core" area in the Mississippi and Illinois river valleys in Illinois where high concentrations of Hopewellian-crafted artifacts had been recovered. Prufer had argued that the Hopewell tradition had spread from Illinois into Ohio, but since the early 1960s, other studies rendered the relationship between Illinois and Ohio Hopewell centers unclear. Bolnick and Smith discovered no evidence of mass migration between the two sites, just small numbers of people moving per generation, possibly the result of moving in with a new spouse, or consistent with the reasons Carr had suggested for long-range travel, such as pilgrimages or expeditions to acquire exotic goods. However Bolnick and Smith's conclusions showed that migration among the populations they studied occurred from Ohio to Illinois, not the other way around.

Studies like this show how our interpretation of life among the prehistoric Americans we continue to call the Hopewell is subject to change at any time. In the 2010s most scholars concur that the Hopewellians shared a culture and a worldview that caused them to bury their elite dead with considerable ritual and to value exotic raw materials obtained from distant regions. Today's scholars have dropped the phrase "Hopewell culture" in favor of "Hopewell tradition" to describe Hopewell society as a whole. This is because the dispersed but related Hopewell communities who settled throughout eastern and central North America practiced the ideology or religious beliefs they shared in subtly different ways and left behind artifacts with regional differences. Archaeologists now distinguish Hopewellistic groups by their location and may or may not add the word "culture," or another qualifier like "focus" or "complex." Those who left evidence of sharing the Hopewell tradition and participating in its exchange networks currently include prehistoric groups called the Armstrong Culture, the Copena Culture, the Crab Orchard Culture, the Goodall Focus, the Havana Hopewell Culture, the Kansas City Hopewell, the Laurel Complex, the Marksville Culture, the Miller Culture, the Montane Hopewell, the Point Peninsula Complex, the Saugeen Complex, the Swift Creek Culture, and the Wilhelm Culture.

If there was a Hopewell heartland, or capital, or pilgrimage center, it would have been located in southern Ohio, specifically in the Scioto River valley, where the greatest concentration of Hopewell ceremonial earthworks was found. There the Hopewell built geometrical enclosures on river terraces and hilltops where they probably gathered for ceremony and ritual, each carefully laid out according to plan and possibly aligned with celestial events, their walls restricting access and visibility. There they also constructed many "big houses" to serve as mortuaries and places of worship, and they may have constructed roads connecting their most important heartland sacred places.

Individuals probably resided in small hamlets in forest clearings where they hunted and gathered sustenance from the rivers and forests, also clearing small plots of land that they farmed with simple tools. They may have been linked by membership in a clan or other social units. They may have engaged in long-distance travel for various reasons including the acquisition of exotic raw materials. If so, the tales they might have told could have inspired pilgrims to visit their heartland and their enclosures, thus spreading their beliefs and bringing more exotic raw materials to Ohio.

Scholars are still debating whether it was the movement of people or trade goods that created what has been called the Hopewell Interaction Sphere.

Hopewellians seemed to have valued things that glittered, like mica. Innovative and artistic Hopewellian craftspersons created works of art in both naturalistic and abstract styles. They likely incorporated symbols that would have had meaning for those who shared their tradition. Some of the best Hopewell artwork survived in their animal effigy platform pipes. The custom of burying fine possessions no doubt created perpetual demand that kept the interactions going.

The fact that the Hopewell people buried some community members with rich gifts while others were buried with little or nothing suggests that some individuals and families held higher status in their communities than others. However Hopewell community leaders were probably not absolute rulers or tyrants, nor even in position to command their fellows.

We're still uncertain exactly when all this took place. Hopewell scholars date the onset of the tradition in a two-hundred-year period starting in about 200 BC. What earlier antiquarians might have called a golden age, which today's scholars prefer to call an efflorescence of material culture, persisted for several centuries until the Hopewell earthworks and traditional artistic endeavors were abandoned between AD 400 and 500.

New, less invasive, and more illuminating research methods are currently teasing more data out of the Hopewell landscape, even those sites that might have been considered long exhausted. A remote sensing technology called LiDAR, from the words "light" and "radar," uses laser pulses from a plane or helicopter to map land. It can also detect disturbances in topography like the remains of a Hopewell mound or earthwork no longer visible at ground level. So it is possible that the Hopewell earthworks may soon be able to tell us more about the people who built them.

9

The Eclipsed Adena

The intriguing Hopewell earthworks and associated mounds that yielded beautifully carved pipes and other items so engaged the American imagination that other Midwestern mounds known from prior experience to offer much less sophisticated artifacts were often labeled "unproductive" and summarily leveled. This nearly became the fate of a mound outside Chillicothe on property purchased around the turn of the twentieth century by Joseph Froehlich, who wanted to cultivate the tract of alluvial bottomland that the mound was sitting on and consign its soil to fill an old railroad cut.

Froehlich's land had been part of a larger tract that had long been owned by the heirs of Governor Thomas Worthington, known as the Father of Ohio Statehood, who had purchased it in

1798. In the early years of the nineteenth century this native Virginian and friend of Thomas Jefferson hired the acclaimed architect Benjamin Latrobe to design a mansion, which he surrounded with gardens and orchards. Worthington left intact the Indian mound on his estate, thinking that its summit might someday make a nice location for a summerhouse with a scenic view. Worthington named his estate Adena, a Hebrew word meaning delightful place.

In his capacity as curator of the Ohio State Archaeological and Historical Society, William Corless Mills arrived at Adena's mound in the summer of 1901. Froehlich had already removed the trees that had grown on it over the years, and Mills was permitted to examine the mound while it was simultaneously being demolished five feet at a time starting at the top. Mills failed to find any intrusive burials but quickly discovered that the mound was actually two mounds constructed during two different periods; there was an original mound about twenty feet high with a base diameter of about ninety feet beneath a second layer of sand and soil that had extended the mound's base mainly on its north side and made it twelve to fifteen feet taller.

Whenever Mills found a grave, demolition slowed down while the deceased was photographed in situ with his or her accompanying grave offerings. Mills unearthed thirty-three skeletons in all: twenty-one from the original mound and twelve from the mound expansion. The deceased in the original mound had been laid to rest in timber enclosures of varying sizes, some of them tall enough for a man to stand upright. At the center of the original mound was a large grave dug into the earth. The skeletons in the second, or expansion, mound were not protected by timber sepulchers and were therefore not as well preserved. There were fireplaces near the original mound's subterranean grave and among some ashes Mills found animal bones and mussel shells, which he interpreted as the "remains of a sacrifice."

Artifacts unearthed with the deceased of both the original mound and the expansion mound Mills described as "similar in every respect, but more abundant in the first period than in the second." Mills discovered copper rings and bracelets, weapon points, and beads made of shell. Mills also discovered what became an icon of Ohio prehistory now known as the Adena pipe. Carved of pipestone, the tubular pipe was the effigy of a man wearing ear spools and a loincloth with a feather bustle. The bowl of the pipe was between the figure's feet, and the mouthpiece was a hole on top of its head. It's unclear whether the pipe's ancient craftsman was depicting a stylized human form or creating a portrait of a specific person who happened to be a dwarf with a goiter. The figure has long been interpreted as a shaman in ceremonial regalia. The Adena pipe is unique and today occupies a place of honor in the museum of the Ohio History Center.

Since the contents of the mound on the Adena estate differed significantly from those of other Ohio mounds, Mills considered its builders to be members of a distinct culture which he named Adena. He further proposed that similar mounds covering similar burials with similar artifacts, such as the Grave Creek Mound in West Virginia and the Miamisburg Mound in southeastern Ohio were the legacy of this same Adena Culture.

Don't expect to see or even hear about the Adena Mound at the Adena Mansion and Gardens, which are now open to the public, having become the property of the state of Ohio in 1946 as the gift of the family of George Hunter Smith, who purchased the rest of the Adena estate from the Worthington family in 1903. When we visited in 2007, our tour guide was not entirely sure in which direction to point to indicate the mound's former location. We did enjoy the glimpse this estate gave us of an attempt to establish a home reminiscent of genteel Virginia on the frontier, as well as our guide's entertaining account of a visit to Adena by Tecumseh and his Native American entourage.

In 1920 when Henry Clyde Shetrone, Mills's successor at the Ohio State Archaeological and Historical Society, published an article in *American Anthropologist*, he was grappling with the chronological relationship among Ohio's known prehistoric cultures including the Hopewell, the Fort Ancient, and the Adena. Shetrone wrote, "It would be gratifying to find that the Adena type of mounds represent an earlier phase of the Hopewell culture," but at that time the Adena had not been studied sufficiently to support the assumption. By 1930 when Shetrone's book *The Mound-Builders* appeared, not much more had been learned. The Adena Culture was thought to be represented by only the Grave Creek Mound, the Westenhaver Mound in Pickaway County, and the Miamisburg Mound in Montgomery County, Ohio. Shetrone's list of the cultural characteristics of Adena mounds, burials, and grave goods (later called Adena traits) was short. Shetrone wrote that the Adena had left behind "shapely conical mounds, located singly or in groups; uncremated burials, in log cists, placed either below, above, or on the original surface; use of copper, mainly for ornaments; use of mica; admirable artistic ability in sculpturing small objects in the round; [and] use of tubular tobacco pipes." However Shetrone also acknowledged that the Adena were "least in evidence" among Ohio's prehistoric cultures. His book, which was nearly five hundred pages long, devoted all of three pages to the Adena Culture.

In the summer of 1930, Shetrone began excavating the Coon Mound assisted by Emerson F. Greenman. Born in Michigan, Greenman had studied archaeology at the University of Michigan and anthropology at Oxford and the University of Michigan, where he received a PhD in anthropology in 1927. He arrived at the Ohio State Archaeological and Historical Society in 1928 to take Shetrone's former position as curator. Greenman published an account of the Coon Mound excavation in the society's quarterly in 1932.

The Coon Mound, another structure named for its owner, Gabriel Coon, was located in an Ohio village called The Plains a few miles northwest of the city of Athens near the Hocking River. At one time there had been more mounds in this area, but many had succumbed to agricultural development, which was shortly to become the fate of the Coon Mound. During its excavation, the Coon Mound's soil was shoveled into trucks to be spread as topsoil for surrounding gardens.

Earlier descriptions recorded that the Coon Mound had once been about thirty feet high, but its excavators discovered that it contained only a single burial: that of a young adult male who had been laid to rest in a rectangular tomb about five feet below ground level. Its walls had been constructed of vertical timber posts apparently set upright in a trench. The tomb had a kind of foyer, or passageway, through which it was apparently entered. Greenman observed that this entrance was on the east and that the tomb was oriented with the cardinal points, factors he suspected had symbolic meaning. Greenman assumed that the tomb had been constructed with a timber roof. He included a "hypothetical reconstruction" to illustrate his article. Greenman thought that some time might have elapsed between the burial of the deceased and the construction of the mound over his tomb, perhaps for a period of mourning. Greenman wrote, "There is no way to estimate the time occupied in throwing earth over the tomb to a height of thirty feet. But with the accumulation of weight upon the roof it may have collapsed, and if so those engaged in the work were probably aware of it."

Greenman reported that the deceased had been buried wearing two copper bracelets and probably several strands of disc-shaped shell beads. Between his shins there was a hollow clay object filled with yellow powder, tiny spherical lumps of black clay, and decomposed pyrite, a mineral resembling gold. Greenman concluded, "While extreme caution is necessary in making deductions regarding social status from the manner in which the dead are buried, it seems worthwhile in the present instance to suggest that the individual entombed in the Coon Mound was a person of considerable importance."

Greenman also wrote, "The Coon Mound exhibits the characteristic features of the Adena culture in its purest form," because its subfloor burial so closely resembled those that Mills had discovered when he excavated the Adena Mound. In the same article Greenman expanded Mills's brief list of Adena cultural characteristics, or traits, to fifty-nine and the number of mounds that could be called Adena to seventy by including any mound that had two or more of those traits he had listed as belonging to the Adena Mound. But the trouble with Greenman's classification system was that fifty-seven of his seventy Adena mounds exhibited ten or fewer Adena traits, while the Miamisburg Mound, which was shaped like an Adena mound, had been inexpertly excavated in

1869, without yielding enough other material to be classified as Adena at all.

Among the new and interesting traits on Greenman's list was the use of red ochre to paint parts of skeletons, which seemed similar to a custom that eighteenth-century travelers had observed among the Choctaw Indians. Greenman also described stones with flat surfaces roughly rectangular in shape with incised designs that suggested written characters. These "grooved stones" were not unlike the Grave Creek Tablet, which by this time had been denounced as fake. Greenman observed, "It seems apparent that the Grave Creek Tablet was regarded as a fraud mainly because it was at first widely heralded as the work of Europeans who visited America before 1492, a claim for which there is little or no support. If the characters on this tablet had been compared with inscriptions found only in America, carved on rocks in various parts of the mound area, their fraudulent origin would have been less generally accepted."

To Greenman the evidence certainly suggested that the Adena and Hopewell Cultures were related, with the Hopewell Culture likely growing out of the Adena Culture. However Greenman quibbled with Shetrone that such a process must have taken a long time. "In the Hopewell new forms are presented suddenly and fully-developed," Greenman wrote, while declining to take a guess as to what had triggered this sudden revolution. When it came to dating both cultures, Greenman ventured only that both the Adena and Hopewell peoples had lived prior to 1492. He wrote, "Nothing ascribable to the period after 1492 has been found in a mound of the Hopewell type, nor in any burial mound in Ohio."

During the 1930s and the decade following World War II, events in modern America would bring to light a great deal more information about the Adena people who had constructed mounds south and east of Ohio. The federal government's Works Progress Administration authorized excavations of sites of supposed historic significance, particularly in those areas that would shortly be flooded by the reservoirs being constructed by the Tennessee Valley Authority. Once the war was over and industrial expansion was surging, business owners sometimes eased their consciences by encouraging archaeologists to excavate mounds while the bulldozers of their construction crews stood waiting to obliterate them so that something else could be built where they stood.

New interpretations derived from the excavation of a number of Adena mounds in Kentucky appeared in 1945 in a book titled *The Adena People* by two University of Kentucky professors: William S. Webb and Charles E. Snow. Born in Lexington, where he lived most of his life, Webb had been one of the leaders of the Tennessee Valley Authority's archaeological program. In 1929 he was appointed head of the University of Kentucky's Department of Anthropology and Archaeology after having taught in the university's Department of Physics since 1908. Snow came from Colorado and Harvard University where he had studied physical anthropology. Webb had hired him to work for the Tennessee Valley Authority's archaeological program in Alabama, then got him appointed to the faculty of the University of Kentucky in 1942.

Webb and Snow carried on Greenman's work by expanding the list of Adena traits to 218 and the list of Adena sites to 173, but because they had excavated mainly burial sites and skeletal remains, they did not speculate too much about the nature of Adena society or the daily lives of Adena individuals. In their preface they explained, "It is, therefore, recognized that the picture of these people and their culture, which this study is intended to portray, must, in the nature of the case, be incomplete." They did propose that the number and size of Adena mounds argued for large populations occupying relatively limited areas. They stated that, "Adena man built in this region the earliest known wooden houses" and explained that the Adena people might have obliterated the sites of former villages by building mounds over them, perhaps accounting for their scant remains. Webb and Snow found no evidence that the Adena people built forts or any structures serving military purposes, which might have meant that at the time they were living in their river valleys they had no need for protection against enemies. They did construct what Webb and

Snow called sacred circles. Webb and Snow wrote, "They are so numerous that one may infer that every large Adena community had at least two, or often more." Today's archaeologists interpret these as gathering places for Adena groups or social units associated with particular mounds.

The fact that both the Hopewellians and the Adena people constructed earthen enclosures was just one of a number of similarities between these cultures. The Adena people reserved their log tombs and mounds for special individuals, but like the Hopewellians, probably cremated most of their dead. Both cultures decorated and dressed up their dearly departed, sometimes burying individuals with severed human skulls that archaeologists had taken to calling trophy skulls, a trait more common among Hopewellian burials. The common features led Webb and Snow to argue that "Ohio Hopewell developed out of Adena," but they did not endorse Greenman's assertion that the Hopewell Culture had developed suddenly. They identified as early Adena those sites with no Hopewell characteristics, and late Adena those sites with "a few scattered, unique, and obviously Hopewellian artifacts." They were first to suggest that the Adena people and Hopewellians had lived as neighbors for a while in both space and time.

Snow, the physical anthropologist, described the Adena people as big, tall, round-headed individuals who had moved into the general area among an earlier people who did not build burial mounds, but ones who gradually adopted Adena customs. As for where the Adenas had come from, Webb and Snow suggested Middle America, specifically Mexico, where physically similar prehistoric people were known to have lived.

In 1957 Webb produced a sequel to *The Adena People* which had the descriptive but perhaps uninspired title *The Adena People No. 2*. Snow and other authorities contributed chapters, and Webb collaborated with Raymond S. Baby, a new coauthor. Baby was employed by the Ohio Historical Society where he had gained a great deal of experience practicing salvage archaeology, or excavating mounds earmarked for demolition, and occasionally mounds where demolition was already under way.

Besides once again expanding the lists of Adena sites and traits (to 222 and 241, respectively), the authors also teased a bit more social history out of recovered artifacts and skeletal remains. Snow contributed a chapter titled "Adena Portraiture" which included reconstructions of the heads of a typical Adena male and female. The images showed skull deformations that the Adena likely inflicted on their own young with the use of cradleboards and some sort of headbinding. The excavation of a mound in Kentucky by a University of Kentucky team had yielded the remains of an Adena man who had been buried with an artifact in his mouth made from the upper jaw of a wolf. Further study indicated that some of the man's teeth had been extracted during his lifetime, apparently so that the wolf jaw would fit more firmly among his own remaining teeth. Greenman had excavated a similar wolf jaw artifact from cremated remains in Ohio. The authors concluded that the deceased had been a shaman or medicine man venerated in his community. Naming him the Adena Wolf Man, the authors included a drawing showing what he might have looked like wearing a wolf mask. Although the evidence was scant, the authors suggested that the Adena people might have made and carried medicine bags containing materials they regarded as protective charms. What Greenman had called "grooved stones" the authors renamed engraved tablets. Dark red stains in some of their grooves suggested they might have been used to stamp symbols on human flesh or clothing, while also functioning as sharpening stones for the instruments used by shamans for bloodletting ceremonies.

The Adena People No. 2 included a chapter titled "Adena Occupancy of Rock Shelters in Eastern Kentucky." Rock shelters were not really caves but rather protected spots formed by rocky overhangs in the walls of cliffs. Anything deposited within them had long remained undisturbed due to the rock shelters' remote locations and the lack of interest in archaeology on the part of those backwoods dwellers who knew where to find them. A number of Kentucky rock shelters had been surveyed by University of Kentucky teams with assistance from the Smithsonian Institution between 1929 and 1935. In the 1940s the observation that some of their recovered artifacts bore Adena traits resulted in their reexamination in the early 1950s, and the confirmation that some Adena people must have been among the sequence of prehistoric persons using the rock shelters. The authors wrote, "This chapter is meant, in part, to be suggestive of a new source of Adena materials which undoubtedly will widen our knowledge of that culture. The complete and detailed analysis of the materials from the rock shelters of the entire Adena area of residence is yet to be done."

In June and July 1929 Webb had conducted his own rock shelter explorations with W. D. Funkhouser, cofounder of the Department of Anthropology and Archaeology at the University of Kentucky, and the two scholars published an account that year in a university periodical. They had traveled to Lee County where they hired as laborers local residents who otherwise worked as roustabouts in the coal, oil, and natural gas industries. They soon discovered that the locals were unfamiliar with archaeologists and therefore suspicious that the two professors had some ulterior motive. Webb and Funkhouser were suspected of being disguised revenuers out to locate and shut down lucrative moonshine stills, or the seekers of buried treasure with more intrinsic value than the stones and bones of prehistoric Indians. Apparently there was a local legend about an eighteenth-century man named John Swift who had discovered a silver mine and recorded its secret location together with that of a number of silver caches in a long-lost journal. A second legend held that hoards of silver and gold were waiting to be discovered in the "Great Shawnee Cave," whose location was also unknown. Once Webb and Funkhouser had convinced their team that they really were just seeking knowledge of Native American prehistory, they still faced the problem of unwittingly violating local customs. One day they made the mistake of burning sassafras wood in their campfire, which was considered extremely unlucky, nearly causing the rebellion and departure of their entire workforce.

The locals called the rock shelters "ash caves" because they were typically lined with layered beds of ash twelve to fifteen feet deep. The ash beds were the refuse of many different successive groups of Native Americans who had used the rock shelters during the winter as hunting lodges. When the ash beds became too deep for comfort, the campers would create a new surface by covering them with a layer of sand, grass, and leaves. Sometimes the hunters buried their own dead in hastily made graves in the ash beds or hid their possessions in holes dug into them. While the highly alkaline wood ashes tended to destroy human remains, they were remarkably good for preserving fabric, leather, and wooden artifacts. Webb and Funkhouser found coarsely woven homespun, leather moccasins, the remains of a pouch or bag, and pieces of string. At the time Webb and Funkhouser had concluded, "Two distinct cultures are represented—one which may be very old and which is responsible for the ash beds, the hominy holes, the flints and the burials; the other a later culture which is represented by the pottery and the fabrics." Today's archaeologists hesitate to identify any rock shelter artifacts as specifically Adena though they do recognize that the rock shelters were used by Paleoindians, or the very earliest aborigines to explore the area, and likely all their successors with the possible exception of Hopewellians, who seemed to have preferred hunting closer to home.

In the years between the publication of *The Adena People* and *The Adena People No. 2*, the big news in the discipline of archaeology was the advent of radiocarbon dating. Willard F. Libby, an American physicist, developed what he called the carbon-14 method, or C-method, in the mid-1940s. Carbon 14, or radiocarbon, was an isotope produced artificially in laboratories during the 1930s, before scientists discovered that it also occurred in nature. Living organisms cease to absorb radiocarbon upon death, when it begins to decay at a constant known rate. Measuring the amount of residual radiocarbon in a dead organism can therefore provide an estimated date of its death. So if an archaeologist discovered a piece of burnt wood at a site's hearth, radiocarbon-dating the wood would tell him roughly when it had been used by a human to make a fire. Radiocarbon dating finally gave archaeologists a way to objectively date sites and organic artifacts and study the rate of cultural evolution in various regions.

Libby and others began publicizing the method in the late 1940s, and a growing number of proponents resulted in the installation of radiocarbon dating equipment in the labs of several prestigious universities during the 1950s. The first radiocarbon dating of Mound Builder remains curiously suggested that the Hopewell Culture had preceded the Adena Culture, touching off some skepticism about the methodology in the archaeological community. Confidence was restored when it was learned that the Adena material first submitted for testing had come from late Adena sites. Subsequent testing put the Adena people back where archaeologists had assumed they belonged in relative time.

In their book, Webb and Baby used radiocarbon-dated artifacts to date the Adena Culture from approximately 800 BC to AD 900 and the Hopewell Culture from 600 BC to AD 1500. Carbon dating also suggested to Webb and Baby that there was a relatively short chronological gap between the Adena Culture and those that preceded it, known as Archaic Cultures. They also noted that local Archaic Cultures shared a number of traits with the Adena people and proposed that additional testing of artifacts would narrow the gap and support a theory of contact between the two peoples. However, *The Adena People No. 2* reinforced the assertion that these Adena people were newcomers to the area, probably from Middle America. In his chapter on portraiture Snow wrote, "Our current beliefs for Adena would suggest the more probable source down Mexico way."

In the following seven years another archaeologist reevaluated the Adena Culture based on his own excavation of a West Virginia mound that he regarded as this culture's "previously missing key." The mound was located in Marshall County, West Virginia, on the Ohio River a few miles southwest of Moundsville. The archaeologist was Don W. Dragoo, who had become interested in the Adena Culture at Indiana University where he had completed a master's dissertation in 1949 on its possible origin. In 1952 Dragoo started work for the Carnegie Museum of Natural History in Pittsburgh where he stayed until 1977, eventually becoming the museum's chief curator of anthropology. Dragoo began excavating his missing key mound in 1958. Two years after introducing his findings in a paper presented at the annual meeting of the American Anthropological Association, he published his reevaluation in a 1963 book titled *Mounds for the Dead: An Analysis of the Adena Culture.*

Dragoo's missing key mound had long stood on the West Virginia property of the Cresap family. When the family sold their land to the Hanna Coal Company, they tried to preserve the mound by deeding a small plot of ground to the West Virginia State Highway Department, which developed it as a rest area along Route 2 with the mound remaining undisturbed. However in 1958 when the state rerouted Route 2, they abandoned the road's former right of way, selling the adjacent rest area to the Hanna Coal Company, which planned to develop the site as an industrial plant. Moundsville native Delf Norona joined with the officers of the West Virginia Archaeological Society in meetings with the coal company, the highway department, and the Carnegie Museum to arrange for the so-called Cresap Mound to be scientifically excavated and its remains studied prior to its demolition. Hanna Coal agreed to this salvage operation, even offering their own laborers and machinery.

Excavation started in June and was completed by the end of August. The coal company supplied plastic tarps to prevent rain delays. Dragoo started with a trial trench, and the initial digging was done with hoes. Earth was worked to the edge of the mound where power machinery removed it. When the workers discovered a burial they switched to hand trowels and smaller tools.

When Dragoo hit bottom he discovered a circular fire pit surrounded by a circular clay floor about forty feet in diameter, itself surrounded by a ditch that seemed to have held upright poles. Although modern archaeologists would disagree, Dragoo decided that the original structure had been a house. A grave and a crematory basin had been dug through the clay floor, and two additional extended corpses had been lain upon the floor which had then been spread with earth deep enough to cover everything.

Dragoo was able to use what he had unearthed on the way down to reconstruct the history of the Cresap Mound. Following the initial burials, more human remains had been added and covered with earth until a small mound just under five feet was formed. At some point while this mound was growing, its builders dug a second grave and crematory basin in a yet bare portion of the clay floor, which they covered to form a sort of annex mound. Two other small mounds covered other burials before the structure surrounding the clay floor was burned. What was left of the entire complex was then covered with earth to form a conical mound about seven feet high. Other artifacts and burials were later added on top of this mound under another earth layer that grew it to just over eight feet. Then a cremation burial was placed in a depression dug into the top of the mound and roofed with logs before the mound was furnished with a new cap of earth raising it to thirteen feet three inches.

Following a period of apparent abandonment, the Cresap Mound became the scene of eight more Adena burials around a fire on the mound's summit, before the whole thing was capped with a "thick mantle of gravelly earth" making the mound seventeen feet high. It then gradually sank to a height of about fifteen feet. One last corpse was buried in a shallow pit at the top of the mound, but this individual had been laid to rest sometime between AD 1200 and 1600 by persons other than Adena people.

Altogether the Cresap Mound had held fifty-four burials and thirty-one of what Dragoo had called its "distinctive features," such as its crematory basins, fire pits, and tombs. Dragoo found traces of red ochre in twenty-three of the features and thirty-one of the burials. Thirty-four burials were honored with grave offerings including copper bracelets and shell beads, pipes, weapon points, tools, and engraved tablets, one of them shaped like a turtle.

The reason why Dragoo had conferred upon the Cresap Mound the title of "missing key" was because a population of Adena people had used it for many generations, and its relatively undisturbed layers therefore told the story of the evolution of Adena mortuary customs, which allowed Dragoo to separate the Adena Culture into two phases: an early-middle phase and a late phase. Early-middle Adena burials were relatively simple, with fire acting as an important element in funeral rites. Corpses might be processed in a variety of different ways, and the deceased were ultimately placed in pits lined with bark and covered with logs. There was likely a period of exposure, a viewing of sorts, when the corpse was painted with pigments and offerings were made, mostly consisting of objects that might have belonged to the deceased. The mounds grew gradually as burials were added. There had been what Dragoo called "sweeping and seemingly abrupt changes" between early-middle Adena and late Adena (also known as Robbins Complex Adena after a late Adena mound called the Robbins Mound in Kentucky). Simple pit burials evolved into elaborate log tombs which remained open for a period of mourning for the one or more persons' remains contained within. As burials were added, the conical Adena mounds could grow to impressive heights, like the Grave Creek Mound. De-fleshed and cleaned up trophy skulls, often placed in the laps of extended burials, were strictly a late Adena custom. Late Adena corpses wore more objects of adornment like copper bracelets and rings, and more varied stone gorgets. Effigies began appearing on the tubular pipes buried with individuals. In general, Dragoo perceived more attention being lavished on fewer individuals, possibly indicating that class distinctions had become more defined within Adena communities.

The Cresap Mound also allowed Dragoo to study the development of Adena engraved tablets. The mound had yielded twenty-two such tablets with the crudest examples in its lowest layers and the finest examples, including the tablet shaped like a turtle, in the upper layers. Since most of the tablets were stained with red ochre, Dragoo assumed they were used to prepare pigments to adorn the dead, then purposely consigned to a ceremonial fire following use. Dragoo also observed that Hopewellians apparently had not adopted the use of these engraved tablets.

What Dragoo recovered from the Cresap Mound also allowed him to reinterpret the contents of other Adena mounds that had been used for shorter periods of time. A decade earlier the Pittsburgh Plate Glass Company had acquired land just a few minutes away from the Grave Creek Mound where another mound called the Natrium Mound happened to be standing on property the company wanted to use to expand a chemical factory. A farmer had earlier reported finding Indian artifacts near the mound, and Pittsburgh Plate Glass had delayed their demolition plans for a few years at the request of Delf Norona, who had alerted the Smithsonian. In the winter of 1948-49 the Natrium Mound became another salvage archaeology operation. Supervising the excavation was an archaeologist from the Smithsonian's Bureau of American Ethnology, Ralph E. Solecki, who wrote about the effort in an article published by the Smithsonian in 1953.

Solecki had started with trial trenches, but the need to work quickly made this project the first to employ a bulldozer using recently developed salvage archaeology techniques. Work was completed in twenty days, undeterred by winter snow, rain, and freezing temperatures. In his article Solecki described his findings as a "curious assemblage of mixed items" in a mound he thought had not been used for very long. Most curious were two artifacts called a birdstone and a boatstone, both spear thrower weights named for their shapes, and both thought at the time to be Hopewellian objects. In light of his Cresap experience Dragoo did not regard Solecki's finds as all that anomalous. Dragoo had found a boatstone in the middle zone of the Cresap Mound while bird-stones had since been found in Archaic mounds and other Adena mounds, so neither of these artifacts necessarily indicated Adena-Hopewell contact. Acording to Dragoo, the features and artifacts that Solecki had found in the Natrium Mound resembled those of the middle and lower levels of Cresap, so he confidently classified Natrium as Early-middle Adena.

The perspective on Adena development that Dragoo had gained from Cresap also led him to take on Webb and Snow's theory of a Middle American origin for the Adena people. He could see that the remains at certain Mexican sites were similar to the burial traits of Late Adena, not Early-middle Adena. Back when Webb and Snow had put forth their theory, archaeologists had known little about North American Archaic Cultures. Dragoo looked into what had been learned about Archaic Cultures in the Northeast and Great Lakes regions and found similarities with

Early-middle Adena, including the use of red ochre in burials, animal masks, medicine bags, and tubular pipes. He concluded that the Adena Culture had developed on site from local Archaic Cultures by people who had come up with innovations and elaborations for their burial practices.

Dragoo also proposed an alternative to Webb and Snow's theory that the Hopewell Culture had developed from the Adena Culture. He proposed that the Hopewell Culture had originated among Archaic peoples living to the west and northwest of Adena territory, who had entered in and then come to dominate a portion of it, thrusting their Adena neighbors into their Late Adena or Robbins Complex transformation. Artifacts showed that Hopewellian influence had spread into southern Illinois and southwestern Indiana, but the fact that there were no major Hopewell complexes south of the Ohio River in Kentucky or West Virginia or in the upper Ohio Valley until Adena occupation ended, indicated they had encountered some Adena resistance.

Dragoo harbored misgivings about the breakthrough of radiocarbon dating. In his book he wrote, "It would seem that we are a long way from having the kind of dates that can be used to establish finely drawn chronological distinctions among sites. To attempt to use them for this purpose is now only misleading and confusing." He was willing to propose an end date for the Adena Culture in the Ohio Valley at AD 1 or earlier, with the Hopewell Culture overlapping the Adena for about two hundred years, then Hopewell continuing for several more centuries until it ended around the year 500.

In the 1930s construction workers building a seawall at a place called Sandy Point, north of Cambridge, Maryland, on the left bank of the Choptank estuary, found caches of cremated and uncremated remains buried with a great many curious artifacts. In the tidewater regions of Maryland and Virginia, it was not uncommon to unearth what were called ossuaries, or collections of human remains that had been deposited by Algonkian-speaking Native Americans around the time of early European contact. In a book published in 1897, Henry Mercer described his own excavation of two deposits of disarticulated human remains at the same location. Mercer wrote, "No implement or trinket or object of human workmanship—save for a simple fire-fractured pebble—was found in either of the bone deposits." So the presence of artifacts made the construction workers' find clearly different.

The construction workers soon discovered that the bones they had found tended to crumble when disturbed, but they brought some of the artifacts into Cambridge where they greatly interested a number of antiquarians. Over the following years, often at night, these pothunters returned to Sandy Point with picks and shovels. Since they were essentially looting this site, they failed to keep records, also discarding broken artifacts and cleaning up the ones they found intact. Eventually it became apparent that the antiquities turning up for sale out of Maryland seemed to have Adena traits. The artifacts included copper beads, perforated stone gorgets, a snake effigy pipe, and weapon points and blades made from raw material from Flint Ridge in Ohio, which is a chain of hills extending from Newark to Zanesville where erosion intermittently exposed a layer of fine flint.

In 1947 another group of workmen discovered eight more burials nearby accompanied with stone tubes and other artifacts, but this time more professional antiquarians preserved all the artifacts, broken or not, nor did they clean off remaining traces of red ochre. It was seven years later when bones, artifacts, and cremation pits were exposed by the erosion of a cliff on the Chesapeake's western shore that an anthropologist proclaimed the Maryland finds as definitely related to the Adena Culture.

The question became how Adena artifacts ended up so far away from Ohio. Were they evidence of trade, or the possessions of actual Adena people who had moved? Together with William A. Ritchie, a New York state archaeologist, Don Dragoo addressed the issue of a possible Adena diaspora in a 1959 article in *American Antiquity*, then repeated much of the same interpretation in *Mounds for the Dead*. Dragoo believed that the increasing domination of the Hopewell Culture in the Midwest had not only created the Late Adena transformation of their culture, it had sent other Adena people packing, taking their treasured possessions and burial customs with them. While in northern Kentucky and southwestern West Virginia, some Adena groups stayed put and clung to their ways for several hundred more years, other Adena people traveled up the Ohio River to Pittsburgh where they would have had to choose between the valleys of the Allegheny and Monongahela rivers. Some followed the Allegheny into western and central New York, while others migrated from the Monongahela to the Potomac Valley and thence to the Chesapeake Bay, a few of these folks eventually also reaching New York via Delaware and New Jersey. Adena-like remains had turned up in all these locations, not to mention places in New England and an island in the St. Lawrence River, which would have been the farthest-flung Adena outpost.

But isolated groups of Adena people, minority members in their new homes, probably lacked the manpower to continue the practice of building mounds, and within a generation or two, they would have buried with their dead all the prize possessions they had brought from Ohio. It would not have taken much longer for the wandering Adena people to become completely absorbed by the populations already residing where they had resettled.

Dragoo's and Ritchie's Adena Diaspora Theory sparked considerable new interest in prehistoric Indian burial sites in the mid-Atlantic and the Northeast, but it also drew criticism from scholars arguing that it had been objects, not people, migrating into these areas through trade. By the 1970s, Dragoo himself admitted that many materials recovered from supposed Adena outposts exhibited more Hopewellian traits than Adena traits, or a combination of Hopewellian and Adena traits. Evidence was also mounting that the people living in the East during earlier Archaic times had already developed burial cults, and had been laying their dead to rest with considerable ceremonialism before any Adena people could have arrived to inspire them. But if the Adena-like artifacts turning up in foreign contexts got there through trade, it would mean that the Hopewell Interaction Sphere got its start earlier than previously supposed, simply hitting its peak in Hopewellian times.

When we visited the small museum maintained by the Dorchester County Historical Society in Cambridge in 2011, it seemed like the proponents of the trade argument had carried the day. In one of the museum's rooms there was a glass case of pre-historic Native American artifacts identified as "Adena Related Material." A label read, "Although found on the Eastern Shore, the material that these artifacts are made from came from far away. These objects are approximately 2000 years old and are consid-ered trade goods."

A 2012 article published in the periodical *Archaeology of Eastern North America* by Darrin Lowery, a Smithsonian research associate, revisited information on recent discoveries indicating that the controversy is becoming more refined if not yet resolved. Those who possessed artifacts with Ohio origins in the Chesapeake Bay area now warrant a name: the Delmarva Adena Complex. Their culture's epicenter appears to be the watershed of the Murderkill River where the most extensive Delmarva mortuary site, called the Frederica site, was discovered in the 1960s. Other evidence suggests an interaction corridor from the Ohio Valley through the valleys of the Potomac and Patuxent rivers across the Chesapeake Bay and up the Choptank River to the drainages of the St. Jones and Murderkill rivers. This would have been in use mainly between 500 BC and AD 450, or from Adena into Hopewell times, though it might have originated earlier. It might also explain the marine artifacts that turn up in Ohio.

Throughout the twentieth century, as scholars amassed data on North American prehistory, they also sought to create an intellectual framework so that groups like the Adena people could be placed in context. This led to the development of various clas-sification systems and a great many professional debates that were lengthy, acrimonious, and arcane to a layperson. For some time many scholars had used the term Paleoindian to describe groups throughout North America whose members were nomadic hunters who crafted weapons like Clovis and Folsom points, but had no knowledge of making ceramics nor any need to haul heavy pots around. In the early 1930s, William A. Ritchie came up with the term Archaic to describe a culture he was studying in New

York State whose people were beginning to settle down and rely more on fishing and gathering to round out their diets. The term was soon extended to other similar cultures throughout deglaciated North America. Those who settled in the forests and floodplains of the Midwest's Mississippi, Ohio, Cumberland, and Tennessee river valleys from about 4000 to 1000 BC came to be collectively called the Central Riverine Archaic Cultures. In 1939 archaeologist W. C. McKern of the Milwaukee Public Museum came up with the Midwestern Taxonomic Method, which placed less emphasis on time and space and more on overall similarities among objects. In 1941 J. A. Ford and Gordon Willey came forth with a system to classify the cultures of eastern North America in a way that integrated time and space. Their system began with Paleoindians and Archaic, or preceramic and prefarming, cultures, which were followed by four stages of cultural development they called Burial Mound I, Burial Mound II, Temple Mound I, and Temple Mound II. A culture's pottery, burial practices, and earthworks or lack thereof, determined which stage they fell into.

The term Woodland had been used since the 1930s to describe the way of life of prehistoric hunter-gatherers in the eastern United States who did some gardening, made some pottery, and built burial mounds. In the 1940s and 1950s James B. Griffin developed a system that followed Paleoindian and Archaic stages with three Woodland periods: Early, Middle, and Late. The Adena people could be classified as an Early Woodland Culture concentrated in the Ohio Valley, mainly along the Scioto and Kanawha rivers with small communities in Indiana, Kentucky, and elsewhere in Ohio and West Virginia.

For a culture to be classified as Early Woodland, the original defining diagnostic criteria were plant cultivation, pottery manufacture, and mound construction coupled with mortuary ceremonialism validating group identity. Then yet more incoming data on various Archaic Cultures revealed that their way of life had incorporated all these practices to some extent. An Archaic Culture called Glacial Kame, whose practitioners had lived in northwestern Ohio and neighboring areas of Indiana and

Michigan, just on the edge of Adena territory, had buried their dead in natural ridges or hills of gravel deposited by Ice Age glaciers, decorating their remains with red ochre. The conical man-made mounds constructed by the Adena for their honored dead conceivably could be viewed as an outgrowth of this custom, which incidentally also marked a group's territory. Late Archaic peoples appear to have valued items from far off places which they passed between individuals and often buried with their owners. The Adena people traded items from a wider geographic area, the "Adena-Related Material" turning up in Maryland, New England, and elsewhere providing evidence of their expanding reach and cultural influence. Archaeologists have reasoned that this ritual exchange of valuable gifts created relationships that could help a group during leaner times.

Similarly, the Middle Woodland way of life, whose practitioners include the Hopewellians and whose hallmarks consist of advances in tool making, more refined and sophisticated pottery, more permanent settlements, and the beginning of a gradual transition from the use of spear throwers for hunting to bows and arrows, is now seen as a natural evolution from the Early Woodland way of life. In his book on Hopewellian shamanism, Romain notes that "many of the shamanic themes found in Hopewell are expressed in Adena using the same design elements," and he cites other archaeologists who consider Adena and Hopewell part of the same ceremonial system, viewing Adena as an early regional expression of Hopewell. Others have called Hopewell an elaboration on the Adena mindset, which did not affect all Adena communities. For a time the Adena and Hopewell cultures overlapped, but the relationship between them remains poorly understood.

When it comes to dating the Adena culture, the experts have yet to come to a consensus. The Wikipedia entry appearing online in the fall of 2012 says the Adena people lived from 1000 to 200 BC. The contemporary Britannica Online offered the dates 500 BC to AD 100. The *Oxford Companion to Archaeology* published in 1996 cites 500 BC to AD 200 while the *Concise Oxford Dictionary of Archaeology* published in 2002 cites 1000 to 100 BC. I'll cast my vote with a website called Ohio History Central maintained by the local experts at the Ohio History Connection and their "online encyclopedia" which dates the Adena culture from 800 BC to AD 1.

Archaeologists also express date ranges followed by the letters "BP," which are used for radiocarbon ages. BP stands for "before present," where the present is defined as 1950. Radiocarbon dating measures the amount of time between when plant or animal tissue dies and the present. Because the present changes every year, radiocarbon dating labs have arbitrarily adopted 1950 as a permanent present because it was close to the time that Willard Libby published the first radiocarbon dates.

Although a great many Adena mounds were leveled during the nineteenth and twentieth centuries, about a thousand remain. Many are standing on private property, but enough are located in places where interested visitors can get a good close look, like those preserved in modern cemeteries or those in residential communities such as Chillicothe's Story Mound, the Enon Mound in the village of Enon, and the Wolf Plains Group northwest of Athens.

Vying with the Grave Creek Mound for the title of America's largest Adena mound is the Miamisburg Mound standing on a ridge above the Great Miami River in Montgomery County, Ohio. This mound was excavated in 1869 by amateurs who sank a shaft from the top to the base through layers of ash and stone to discover one skeleton about eight feet below the summit, and further down some flat stones and logs that might have formed part of a burial vault. Its paucity of burials made archaeologists of the early twentieth century suppose the huge mound might have actually been a place for lighting signal fires. No modern-day systematic excavation has ever been done, but the site became a park in 1920 and the property of the Ohio State Archaeological and Historical Society in 1929. Known today as the Miamisburg Mound State Memorial, it is open throughout the year and equipped with picnic facilities.

The waitress at the Miamisburg bar where we stopped for lunch on a summer day in 2013 gave us directions to the Miamisburg Mound. "Just turn left at the Dairy Queen and follow the road around," she said. "Believe me, you can't miss it."

We followed her directions past the new office buildings of Mound Advanced Technology Park and found ourselves, as we had while seeking some of the remaining earthworks of Newark, at the edge of a golf course. That day ours was the sole car in the parking lot and we were the only ones in the park surrounding the mound, except for two guys throwing a Frisbee around.

The mound was impressive from the distance of the parking area and it loomed ever larger as I approached. The mound itself was protected by a cyclone fence, which left free only the stone staircase to its summit. Though our waitress had informed us that a climb up its 116 steps was a healthful activity that she often added to her morning run, the temperature was in the nineties that day, so I decided to admire the enormous thing from its base. Signage reported its scant excavation history as well as its more recent history, including a reclamation project initiated by the city of Miamisburg in 2009 as well as the controlled burn conducted each year to rid the mound of nonnative vegetation and encourage the growth on its surface of native grasses.

The Buffington Island Mound also stands in a state park, located about twenty miles east of Pomeroy. However, its small memorial park commemorates not the mound but the only significant Civil War battle fought in Ohio. The mound is essentially unstudied. Apparently some person or persons dug into it during the early nineteenth century but they kept no records of what they found, if anything. Visitors can climb concrete steps to the top.

A few miles northwest of Columbus visitors can find the Shrum Mound in the Campbell Memorial Park named for Governor James E. Campbell, who later served as president of the Ohio State Archaeological and Historical Society. A winding trail leads to the mound's summit. The Taft Reserve outside Newark is home to the Hoffman Mound (also called the Tippett Mound). Indian Mound Campgrounds near Athens was probably so named thanks to its Straight Mound.

The Adena Mound at Miamisburg, one of the two largest conical mounds in North America. Located in the Miamisburg Mound State Memorial, this sixty-five-foot mound has never been professionally excavated. (*Author*)

The materials found in Adena mounds that were more or less professionally excavated can be found in various museums, most notably the one at the Ohio History Center in Columbus. In fact, the Adena pipe was the very first thing we saw at the entrance to the exhibit called Following in Ancient Footsteps. And in a separate case right beside it stood the Wray figurine of the Hopewell Culture, plus works representing the artistic achievements of the Fort Ancient Culture and those of Native Americans in later times. We found this museum to be the best place to compare and contrast the artifacts of Ohio's various ancient cultures and understand their relationship with even earlier ones. The exhibit was balanced in other ways, too. Items thought to have sacred meaning could be contrasted with the artifacts of daily life like pots and textiles. Ancient history was juxtaposed with the history of its discovery, from the work of early archaeologists to the latest discoveries like the Moorehead Circle at Fort Ancient. Most artifacts were displayed so that they can be viewed from all angles with excellent lighting. And if you want to study Adena weapons, tools, and pottery without visiting Columbus, check out the Ohio History Connection's online exhibit called Virtual First Ohioans.

For mystery lovers, there remain some relatively unexplained aspects of Adena Culture. Although some smaller buildings beneath Adena mounds might have started as houses where a family member was buried in a hole in the earthen floor, most architecture associated with Adena mounds is now interpreted as having been constructed for mortuary purposes. For the most part we can only guess where the Adena people lived or what their dwellings looked like. No one has fully explained the uses of Adena engraved tablets. The Adena also fashioned little cones and

The iconic Adena pipe greets visitors at the Ohio History Center's museum. It was discovered by William Corless Mills in his excavation of the Adena Mound in 1901. (*Ohio History Connection*)

hemispheres out of hematite, limestone, sandstone, and pipestone, among other materials. No one really knows what they used these for, either. My guess would be something to aid them in counting, either for sophisticated calculations—or maybe just the prehistoric equivalent of poker night. In any case, Adena craftsmen obviously took a lot of time and went to a lot of trouble to manufacture them, and some Adena people considered them important enough to take to the grave.

10

Fort Ancient

I n the early years of the twentieth century, while William Corless Mills directed excavations at the Edwin Harness, Seip, Tremper, and Adena mounds, he was also studying the remains of two village sites that happened to be located near Hopewell monuments. The first of these lay on a terrace above Paint Creek in Ross County near the borough of Bourneville. Mills called it the Baum Prehistoric Village after the Baum family who had owned the land for over three quarters of a century. In 1899, 1902, and 1903 Mills systematically examined remains surrounding what Squier and Davis had called a "square, truncated mound" where they mentioned having found "quantities of coarse, broken pottery" just north of a square-circle complex. Mills located many burial sites, subterranean storage pits filled with refuse, and what he described as "forty-nine teepee sites."

His second prehistoric village site, located in Scioto County north of Portsmouth, Mills named the Feurt Village after the Feurt family who had long owned this particular tract of land. Mills's excavations commenced in 1916 and followed Warren K. Moorehead's limited examination in 1896 of three mounds located in the village. The Feurt Mounds and Village were just across the Scioto River from the Tremper Mound, which Mills had excavated with Henry Clyde Shetrone the prior year.

Mills and Shetrone were both naturally very interested in ascertaining whether the Feurt remains and the Tremper Mound had been "contemporaneous." However, the pipes Mills unearthed in the Feurt Village were very different from the magnificent Tremper Mound pipes. In a report published in 1917 Mills wrote, "The portrayal of life forms is not so realistic and the sculptures lack detail, so that outside of the human face sculptures, it would be difficult to determine what kind of bird or animal the primitive artist had in mind. On the other hand, the Tremper Mound peoples were able to produce sculptures with such realistic and minute detail, that not only the animal or bird is readily identified, but its habits and characteristics are fully portrayed." Mills concluded that the inhabitants of the Feurt Village seemed to have lived far more primitive lives than those of Hopewellians.

So if two very different groups had lived at the same time and in such close proximity, the question became: had they lived in peace? Mills sought an answer in the position and condition of artifacts located at both Feurt and Tremper. Over at the Tremper Mound some objects had been discovered that seemed to belong to a less sophisticated, non-Hopewellian culture. There weren't many, but Mills reasoned that the superior Hopewellians would not have coveted the possessions of their lowlier neighbors. In two Feurt burials Mills found necklaces: one made of shell and copper beads, the other made of bear teeth and pieces of wood shaped like bear teeth covered in copper. These appeared to be Hopewellian artifacts that the Feurt people had prized, which would argue for a friendly relationship. But the Feurt village site also yielded copper objects that had been hammered to smithereens and seemingly tossed away as refuse, as one might treat the spoils of war in a fit of anger or rage. Perhaps the two groups had lived in peace for a while, then fallen out. A nearby pipestone quarry that both groups had mined seemed like a possible source of contention between them.

Recovered artifacts indicated that another prehistoric village had been located on the Little Miami River just below the earthwork in Warren County that had long been called Fort Ancient, which had been earlier excavated by Moorehead. Mills concluded that all these village communities represented the same culture, noting in his article on the Baum site, "At one time the valleys of southern and central Ohio were peopled by a culture which was quite uniform throughout the entire section." Mills proposed to name the culture the Fort Ancient Culture, a name that would prove to be mighty confusing once it was accepted that the earthwork called Fort Ancient had been built by Hopewellians.

Mills might have made a better choice had he named the culture after another site where its separate identity had been recognized about forty years earlier by Frederic Ward Putnam, then director of Harvard University's Peabody Museum of Archaeology and Ethnology. Putnam's interest had been piqued by the published accounts of work funded by an antiquarian organization called the Madisonville Literary and Scientific Society describing the finds of one of its members: a Madisonville doctor named Charles Metz. In 1878 Metz had been exploring land owned by the Ferris and Stites families a few miles up the Little Miami River from its confluence with the Ohio River near the town of Madisonville. This largely uncultivated tract had been long known locally as Pottery Field because beneath its old growth trees one could easily find ceramic potsherds, no doubt worked to the surface by the hogs that local farmers routinely set loose in the woods to root for food.

In March 1879 Metz and his workman discovered a very decayed skeleton buried about two feet below the earth's surface. Metz began digging trenches eastward from this point and soon found other burials. Eventually hundreds of skeletons would be recovered from what had been a large prehistoric cemetery.

In 1881 Putnam traveled to Madisonville, where members of the Madisonville Literary and Scientific Society received him. In a report published by the *Harvard College Bulletin*, Putnam described the "burial ground, which has now become famous in American archaeology," where "very much of interest has been discovered." When some of the original society members discontinued their financial support of the excavation, Putnam worked out a funding deal in which the Peabody would hire Metz and pay some of the excavation expenses in return for some of the recovered material.

When Phoebe Ferris died in 1896, she left Harvard a sizable piece of the Madisonville site, where the university's anthropology students continued to conduct excavations into the first decade of the twentieth century. Her will was contested and Harvard lost, but not before thousands of implements, pipes, ornaments, and ceramic bits and pieces recovered from the site's burials and the trash-filled pits (originally constructed for storage) of its residential area were shipped to the Peabody. In 1920 the Peabody published a comprehensive report by anthropologist Earnest A. Hooton and curator Charles C. Willoughby on the site and its artifacts.

Don't wander into the Peabody today expecting to see those artifacts on display. Some of the recovered artifacts ended up at the Smithsonian as part of a trade negotiated by Putnam. The Peabody later exchanged other Madisonville artifacts with other museums and eventually simply discarded bulkier items during the early to mid-twentieth century. In the more recent past the Peabody renovated its public exhibition of North American Native artifacts along the theme of "Change and Continuity," or an interpretation of how Indians responded to the arrival of Europeans, which sent the earlier Madisonville artifacts into permanent storage. When we visited in 2012, an assistant curator informed us that today's emphasis in the discipline overall is on the ethnographic rather than the archaeological. However she did take the time to walk us over to an annex where we descended a long metal stair in a three-story, partly subterranean storage space furnished with shelving. There we witnessed an entire aisle of material recovered from Ohio housed in little boxes and often accompanied by the field notes handwritten in pencil by Putnam and Metz. The Peabody can and does arrange study sessions.

Over several following decades, after many similar sites had been excavated and studied, most published scholars generally echoed Mills's conclusions that the so-called Fort Ancient Culture had been widespread in Ohio and its adjacent states, and that daily life among the Fort Ancient people appeared to have been very different from that of the Hopewellians. Research had shown that instead of isolated hamlets, the Fort Ancient people lived in larger villages outside the old Hopewell heartland where separate dwellings surrounded a central plaza, the village itself often surrounded by palisades or deep ditches. Instead of processing their dead at ceremonial centers, Fort Ancient people buried their dead in village cemeteries under small stone mounds or in stone-lined cists, or sometimes even in graves dug in refuse middens. The Fort Ancient people cleared and cultivated more land where they raised domesticated plants, most significantly maize. They crafted simpler and more practical tools, using locally available chert rather than flint from a distant quarry, and they acquired far fewer items crafted from mica or seashells.

They were more efficient hunters thanks to their widespread adoption of the bow and arrow, which allowed hunters to carry more ammunition and fire faster from many positions to bring down the game that also formed part of their diet. They used rock shelters as hunting camps to a greater degree and became such successful deer hunters that some scholars speculate their over-hunting reduced the average size of deer. Their lethal bows and arrows also made it much easier for them to murder one another, possibly due to competition for resources to support their growing populations, hence their need to hunker down in palisaded villages.

By the middle of the twentieth century, Fort Ancient archaeologists had joined other scholars in their enthusiasm to classify things. For his 1943 book titled *The Fort Ancient Aspect*, James B. Griffin of the University of Michigan studied Fort Ancient artifacts preserved in various museums that had come from over thirty Fort Ancient sites in Ohio, Indiana, and Kentucky. He developed a classification system based on differences and similarities in ceramics and other artifacts and separated the culture into four geographical foci: Baum, Feurt, Anderson (a village site on the Little Miami River north of Fort Ancient), and Madisonville.

Then following a period of nearly three more decades when few Fort Ancient excavations had been conducted, Olaf Prufer collaborated with Orrin C. Shane on a book about the excavation of a Fort Ancient site called Blain Village on the Scioto River near Chillicothe. Prufer and Shane pronounced, "It seems to us, in the light of the evidence that has accrued since the publication of Griffin's study, that the old four-focus scheme of classification is no longer adequate to understand the dynamics of Fort Ancient." By that time they had radiocarbon dates for various Fort Ancient sites, so Prufer and Shane attempted to relate Griffin's four geographical foci to chronological time. Defining Fort Ancient overall as a "tradition," they identified three phases within it: Early, Middle, and Late. Their Early Fort Ancient phase lasted from AD 950 to 1250, having arisen in regions including the Baum site. Middle Fort Ancient dated from 1250 to 1450 and was evident in the Feurt and Anderson areas. Late Fort Ancient dated from 1450 to 1750 and encompassed the entire region drained by the Ohio River in southern Ohio, Kentucky, and West Virginia.

If the radiocarbon dates were correct, then precisely what had been going on for about four centuries after AD 500 when the Hopewell culture was acknowledged to have ended? James B. Griffin seemed to be searching for another culture to fill the apparent gap. In a chapter in a book published in 1952 called *Prehistoric Indians of the Ohio Valley*, Griffin mentioned the recent recognition of the Newtown culture whose artifacts suggested continuity with the Hopewell culture, but whose villages were in some respect similar to Fort Ancient villages. In his 1966 book, Griffin asked, "Is the Intrusive Mound Culture a cultural as well as chronological step to the Fort Ancient culture?" referring to certain groups and cults who buried individuals in Hopewell mounds with offerings of tools, pipes, and red ochre as though they deliberately wanted to claim for themselves the Hopewell monuments. Prufer and Shane regarded the differences between the Hopewell and Fort Ancient Cultures as a "sharp break," arguing that there was some evidence to support a theory of invasion of the Hopewell homeland. In the intervening years, archaeologists have largely ignored this period where the Ohio Valley's population continued to grow minus the Hopewellian glamour and drama. The most recent theory to be advanced was that of Case and Carr, who leaned toward some seminal, possibly religious event that undermined Hopewellian beliefs and dissolved alliances, but it's unclear just what sort of shock wave could have caused so many prehistoric people to change their worldview at the same time. Recent evidence from Hopeton Earthworks and the Hopewell Mound Group suggests that some people repaired or remodeled these particular sites around the year 1000, but the relationship of those people to the earthworks' builders is unknown.

Had the Hopewell homeland indeed been invaded, the logical invaders would have been members of a Native American tradition that began to flourish in areas to the south, southeast, and southwest of Fort Ancient villages around the Mississippi River valley from about AD 700–800 to 1500. Called Mississippians, these people built large ceremonial centers with earthwork truncated pyramid mounds, sometimes called platform mounds, that served as bases for charnel houses and the residences of community leaders. One of their largest settlements had been described by the traveler Henry Marie Brackenridge when he crossed the Mississippi at St. Louis and witnessed the group of mounds now known as Cahokia. But had these Mississippians actually formed an army and mounted an invasion? Was a site such as Marietta, where Mississippian-like platform mounds stood within what seemed to be Hopewellian enclosures, evidence of a literal conquering of one people by another?

In a 2008 book titled *Sunwatch: Fort Ancient Development in the Mississippian World*, Robert A. Cook of Ohio State University's Department of Anthropology addressed the nature of the relationship between Mississippian and Fort Ancient peoples. One of the key elements of Mississippian society was its hierarchical

chiefdom structure; archaeologists could readily identify important people by the characteristics of their burials, and important
households by their locations. Fort Ancient society did not seem
as rigidly ranked. Cook argued for interaction of Mississippian
and Fort Ancient people at a retail level, where Mississippian individuals or small groups might have moved into Fort Ancient villages. The persons involved would have hailed not from the centers of Mississippian culture like Cahokia, but from smaller, more
free-wheeling villages on its frontier. They would have made contact with fellow frontiersmen of the Fort Ancient Culture, a phenomenon Cook termed "periphery peer interactions."

Archaeologists had already acknowledged that the rivers and
tributaries on which Fort Ancient villages tended to be located
had likely served as transportation corridors linking the communities of southern Ohio, northwestern Kentucky, and parts of
Indiana and West Virginia. Cook concluded it may have been
mainly ideas spreading from Mississippian to Fort Ancient territory, causing the two cultures to evolve along similar lines.

And one of the subjects of discussion may well have been how
to plant and grow the Mexican corn whose cultivation and adoption as a dietary staple might have been the real agent of cultural
change. The tropical grass that was the ancestor of maize originated in Mexico, and by 5000 BC local hunter-gatherers were culti-
vating it on a small scale. By 2100 BC the Archaic peoples of the
American Southwest recognized its advantages and began to cultivate it. Maize cultivation slowly spread to the American
Southeast and became the basis for a new way of life while its
farmers invented means for its storage and cooking and discovered that growing it required a more sedentary life than their
prior cultivation of native plants. In a chapter in the 1996 book
View from the Core, William S. Dancy, an Ohio State University
anthropologist, suggested that the end of the Hopewellian way of
life was really an evolution of the Darwinian kind, as a new agri-
culturally focused way of life proved to be "more reproductively
successful." Population growth and the resulting larger settlements might have precluded the need for isolated communities to
come together at ceremonial centers as the Hopewellians had

done, so the Hopewellian Tradition could have ended peacefully and gradually without any violent collapse.

As for Marietta, in 1990 a proposed library expansion occasioned an excavation of the mound which had long stood beneath the public library. The project yielded a number of Hopewellian artifacts showing that Marietta was largely a Hopewell Tradition site that happened to have rare but not unknown Mississippi-esque platform mounds. Around the same time, Tennessee's Pinson Mound Group, previously considered a Mississippian site because of its flat-topped mounds, had most of its construction reassigned to the Hopewell Tradition, thanks to new radiocarbon dating. Both sites may well argue for a peaceful and gradual transition.

Cook had focused his study on a village known in modern times as Sunwatch Indian Village and Archaeological Park, citing as one reason the fact that it had been extensively excavated and analyzed. Located in Dayton on the Great Miami River, the site had long been known as a good place to hunt for Indian relics, particularly weapon points. To the Vance family, who had owned the property since 1869, the points, bones, and other artifacts turned up by their annual spring plowing had always been mainly a fascinating sort of nuisance.

When the last Vance moved off the family farm in 1941 and the city of Dayton acquired the property where they opened a "Workhouse Farm," the site began to attract more focused relic hunters. Kenneth McNeal and his wife collected many artifacts in the decades prior to 1970, including weapon points from the Archaic, Adena, Hopewell, and Fort Ancient Cultures. At meetings of the Ohio Indian Relic Collectors' Society, McNeal met John C. Allman, an amateur archaeologist whose day job was credit manager for Sears and Roebuck but whose prior experience included building bridges and dams for the Illinois Highway Department, where he had learned surveying and excavation. Unlike McNeal who was loathe to disturb possible Indian graves, Allman was eager to learn what might lie beneath the plowed fields. After retiring from Sears and Roebuck in 1963, Allman surveyed the site and obtained permission to dig trenches in his efforts to locate an Indian camp. Allman was later joined by Charles J. (Chuck) Smith, a Sears and Roebuck sales manager who had served in the Engineer Corps while in military service.

Between them, Allman and Smith located a number of storage pits and several burials, then in 1968 Smith and his son discovered a number of post holes. Over the following weeks, Smith worked with Allman in unearthing what appeared to have been a dwelling, with two hearths and a heavily charred area hinting that the house had burned down. Smith also discovered human remains: apparently those of some poor soul who had died trying to escape the conflagration when the house collapsed on him. John Allman had been calling the village the Incinerator Site, after an incinerator building that the city of Dayton had located near there, and the discovery of the burned house seemed to make the impromptu name particularly appropriate.

Smith brought the Incinerator Site to the attention of J. Heilman, the new curator of anthropology at the Dayton Museum of Natural History in 1969 when it appeared that the opportunity for research was about to abruptly end. In 1970 the city planned to upgrade a nearby sewage treatment facility, a project that would have included the construction of sludge ponds that would have obliterated all the prehistoric remains. In 1971 the city issued the museum a contract to begin salvage excavations but retained the right to bring in their bulldozers on three days' notice.

Grasping the potential importance of the site, Heilman devoted himself full-time to its excavation, beginning with a massive trench and exploration to expose house patterns, burials, and storage pits. The city renewed the museum's contract and work continued until 1974 by which time the major features of a Fort Ancient village had emerged, including a stockade and a central plaza. By the end of 1974 enough had been learned about the site to merit its being placed on the National Register of Historic Places, saving it forever from the construction of sludge ponds. Salvage archaeology could end and more deliberate excavations begin.

By the early 1980s local groups joined forces to reconstruct some of the village's features and plant an "Indian garden" at the site where they planned to receive visitors and reenact the daily lives of village residents. Since a name like the Incinerator Site was hardly likely to draw a crowd, the village clearly needed to be called something else. A name-the-village contest came up with Sunwatch. When the site formally opened to the public in 1988, large-scale excavation ceased but limited exploration and analysis continues at Sunwatch to this day.

All the years of excavation revealed that Sunwatch had been a village of clustered dwellings whose contents indicated a certain homogeneity in lifestyle. Most Sunwatch houses were examples of rectangular pole construction, which was widely employed throughout the Fort Ancient Culture, but Sunwatch also held a single example of a Mississippian-style wall trench house, perhaps the home of an immigrant or trade partner who might have been an example of the "periphery peer interactions" Cook wrote about. The clustered houses appeared to be associated with nearby burial plots, perhaps indicating that families liked to keep their deceased members nearby. Sunwatch storage pits were three to five feet deep, either pear-shaped or cylindrical and mostly filled with debris.

The village also contained several unique structures including one with fire-cracked rocks on its floor and in the area around it, which scholars interpreted as the first sweat lodge to be unearthed in Ohio. In 1978 archaeologists unearthed a structure whose floor was strewn with lithic material, or the waste product of stone tool making. They interpreted this as a men's lodge located in an area of the village where the guys might have hung out to bond while crafting tools.

There were clues at Sunwatch that at least some residents had an affinity for, or a fascination with, wolves. The site yielded an unusual effigy pipe with a stylized wolf's head on one side and a human face on the other, where the human mouth formed the hole for the insertion of a pipe stem. In 1981 researchers found the carcass of a young male wolf apparently ritually buried in an area where several human burials had been previously discovered accompanied by wolf teeth and wolf jaws. The Sunwatch wolf clan neighborhood, perhaps?

In 1973 at the center of the Sunwatch's plaza the excavation crew located a heart-shaped chunk of red cedar sunk deep in the ground. They concluded that a towering red cedar post over thirty feet tall and over two feet in diameter had once dominated the village. After holes for smaller poles had been discovered around it, J. Heilman and Roger Hoefer, then the Dayton Museum of Natural History's curator of astronomy, suspected that the pole complex had some astronomical function related to telling time. At Sunwatch the remains of maize had been found in nearly every soil sample, making its importance to the community obvious and suggesting that the pole complex might have functioned as a calendar telling the residents when it was safe to plant.

Heilman and Hoefer extended sight lines in various directions from the pole complex, and to its southwest they found the remains of a dwelling constructed at an odd angle. They then discovered that the village's central post hole and the rising sun aligned with the dwelling's hearth twice a year: around April 29 and August 14, which happened to coincide with advisable dates for planting and harvesting corn in this region.

The central post hole also aligned with the hearth of another house at sunrise on the winter solstice, a time when the villagers could look forward to longer days, but the pole complex yielded no evidence that the summer solstice was any sort of special occasion. No alignments were found anywhere at Sunwatch to indicate that the villagers observed lunar events, but at that time Sunwatch was thought to have been occupied just slightly longer than a single 18.6-year lunar cycle.

Trash found in the pits on the western side of the pole complex included burned corn, pipes, and tools, unlike the less valuable refuse found in other Sunwatch pits. Perhaps the central pole also marked a part of the village that might have been holy ground where villagers made sacrifices. In historical times, other Native Americans were known to have offered corn to a sacred fire during what was known as a Green Corn ceremony.

Back in the late 1960s, John Allman had identified Sunwatch as a Fort Ancient site based on the potsherds and weapon points it had yielded. He placed it within the Anderson focus based on a further examination of pottery artifacts, confirming his theory with James B. Griffin. Allman and Smith contacted the Ohio Historical Society, which arranged for the radiocarbon dating of carbon samples from the site. The results placed Sunwatch in the latter half of the 1100s AD. The fact that the remains of its houses, pits, and burials did not overlap one another argued for a short period of occupation of around twenty and not more than thirty years.

The initial radiocarbon dates were contradicted by subsequent testing of other Sunwatch samples, which yielded dates ranging from AD 1000 to 1500. In his 2008 book Cook explained the anomaly by suggesting that Sunwatch might have been occupied twice: initially in the late 1100s, then again in the late 1300s when the Mississippian-style house might have been constructed. Cook accounted for the lack of overlapping features by suggesting that Sunwatch's second population might have been able to make out the locations of earlier houses and pits and reuse them, just as they would have reused the Sunwatch fields which had long lain fallow. Sunwatch's current administrators simply call it a Fort Ancient Native American village.

We arrived at Sunwatch Indian Village and Archaeological Park just as a group of senior citizens on a bus tour was leaving, while several vans loaded with grade-school-age children followed us into the parking lot. The staff at the Heilman-Kettering Interpretive Center were very accommodating about giving us the run of their museum while the kids watched the interpretive film, then allowing us to watch the film alone.

We thought the museum did an excellent job of illustrating the various aspects of daily life among the Fort Ancient people. I had found it difficult to visualize the underground storage pits I had read about, but the museum had a cross section clearly showing their general size, depth, and how the ears and kernels of corn would have been arranged. There were many stone and bone tools on display, and the exhibits had also juxtaposed the various components of a hunter's tool kit, including his good luck charms. The film explained what scholars meant when they described the settlement pattern of Fort Ancient villages as "matrilocal clusters."

Imagine the roughly round palisaded village as a pie cut into slices where each slice contains related family households. When a guy married he moved into his wife's family's slice of the village. No wonder the village needed a men's lodge; it would have been a place to escape the in-laws.

There were no guides outdoors in the reconstructed village, but the Interpretive Center did rent audio guides one could listen to while walking around. Not all of the buildings for which there was archaeological evidence had been reconstructed, but there was a diorama in the museum showing how densely the village would have been settled. From almost every point in the village we could see the complex of poles forming the calendar that gave Sunwatch its modern name. It's easy to imagine its prehistoric residents regarding them daily as they waited for the real warmth of planting season. When we lived in Ohio twenty years back it was late winter and early spring. Our favorite café in Lebanon daily noted the number of days until the vernal equinox on the chalkboard near the door right above the soup du jour. We looked forward to seeing that number go down as much as the news that prime rib was the daily special.

Over the last twenty years there's been no excavation of a Fort Ancient site as extensive as Sunwatch, but the use of new technologies has brought new information to light, and the most recent interpretations have focused on changes over time, often within a specific region. Current scholars tend to agree with Prufer and Shane on a tripartite Fort Ancient chronology with an Early Fort Ancient phase dating from AD 1000–1050 to 1200–1250, Middle Fort Ancient dating from 1200–1250 to 1400–1450, and Late Fort Ancient dating from 1400–1450 to 1650–c. 1700. Some scholars prefer to replace the Early, Middle, Late terminology with the names of certain type sites; you may hear scholars referring to Fort Ancient Culture in southern Ohio as having Turpin, Schomaker, and Mariemont phases, but the time scale is roughly the same.

The Early Fort Ancient phase is when Hopewellian hamlets began to be replaced by Fort Ancient's nucleated villages. There appear to be more villages in Fort Ancient's early than its middle

A model at Sunwatch's Interpretive Center, top, suggests what the village looked like to its Fort Ancient inhabitants. Sunwatch village, below, reconstructed. The poles off the central path at Sunwatch Indian Village form the calendar that gave the village its modern name. (*Author*)

phase, which scholars attribute either to a population decline, or a great many Middle Fort Ancient villages still waiting to be discovered. During the middle phase, the Fort Ancient people seem to have moved away from Ohio River tributaries to locations closer to the Ohio River proper. Over time the village dwellings grew larger.

It's not yet possible to discern a trend in the building of palisades that surrounded many Early and Middle Fort Ancient villages, since most Fort Ancient sites have not been excavated extensively enough to determine whether they were thus protected. For the same reason it's not currently possible to proclaim a trend in the development of the central plazas that characterize Fort Ancient villages of all phases.

At the onset of the Early Fort Ancient phase, villagers had replaced Hopewellian gardens with deliberately cleared fields where they grew maize together with beans and squash, with maize comprising the bulk of their diet. This pattern remained stable over time. So they could keep eating their corn over the winter, Fort Ancient villagers developed underground storage pits to store shelled corn. Early Fort Ancient pits were often shallow and irregularly shaped. By the middle phase of the Fort Ancient Culture, the villagers were building cylindrical pits with straight sides and flat bottoms, often lined with mold-resistant grasses. When the pits were empty they were reused for trash disposal. Early Fort Ancient villagers continued some distinctly Hopewellian customs. The custom of building burial mounds persisted until around 1250 to 1300, but the trend was toward box-like shallow graves lined with stone. Fort Ancient villagers also continued interacting with other communities at distant locations, their interaction networks extending to the west, the south, the Lake Erie shore, and the upper Mississippi Valley.

The Fort Ancient villagers might have been influenced by Native Americans settled in southern Wisconsin and parts of Illinois, Iowa, and Minnesota who had taken mound building in a new direction between 650 and 1300 by erecting burial mounds shaped like animals. It is estimated that at least 10,000 animal effigy mounds were constructed by this culture yet to be named, mainly west of Lake Michigan. The Fort Ancient villagers constructed two effigy mounds that have survived in Ohio: the Serpent Mound and the Alligator Mound, which stands in Licking County between Granville and Newark overlooking Raccoon Creek at what would have been the northern frontier of Fort Ancient territory.

Squier and Davis included a diagram and description of the Alligator Mound in their 1848 *Ancient Monuments*, and William

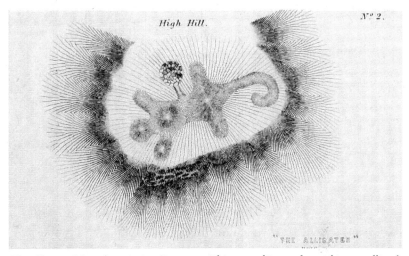

The Alligator Mound, in *Ancient Monuments*. This mound is now located in a small park surrounded by a residential community between Granville and Newark. Two scholars have suggested that it represents not an alligator bur a mythical creature called the Underwater Panther in Native American tradition.

Pidgeon recorded his own observations in *Traditions of Dee-Coo-Dah*, both noting the similarities between the Serpent Mound and the Alligator Mound. Both had been constructed on elevated ground with a commanding view. Like the Serpent effigy, the Alligator effigy conforms to the land. Squier and Davis wrote, "The hill or headland is one hundred and fifty or two hundred feet in height; and the [Alligator] effigy rests upon its very brow, conforming to its longitudinal as well as lateral curve." Both effigies had an elevated appurtenance covered with stones that appeared to have experienced fire. When Moorehead examined the Alligator, he described this presumed altar as "scarcely three feet wide and a foot high." It was connected to the effigy by a graded way ten feet wide.

The Alligator Mound was never really excavated until a local resident conducted a study in the 1980s after a developer acquired the property on which it stood. The developer donated the mound to the Licking County Historical Society in 1991 and surrounded the hill on which it was constructed with a circular lane, making it into a little park around which building lots were surveyed. There's no sign along the road connecting Granville and Newark indicating where to turn to see the Alligator Mound, but if I owned one of the houses on Bryn Du Drive that sell for upward of half a million dollars, I wouldn't want a whole lot of sightseers in the neighborhood, either. In 2013 we used an atlas to locate the site, parked our car on the circular lane, and climbed to the top of the hill. Then we looked in vain for the effigy. Unlike the Serpent Mound's park, there's no observation tower, and all we could make out from ground level were a few bumps and indistinct ridges on the ground. According to the executive director at the Great Circle Museum whom we met later that day, "The Alligator Mound is not doing too well."

In an article published in the *Cambridge Archaeological Journal*, Bradley Lepper and Tod A. Frolking wrote, "No one seriously disputes that Alligator Mound was built to depict some long-tailed quadrupedal animal, but there is little consensus about what animal it represents." Squier and Davis called it an alligator because that's what local folks called it, but Lepper and Frolking suggested a clue to the effigy's true identity might be found in Native American oral tradition. Perhaps the mound represents a being of the underworld called the Underwater Panther to whom Native Americans made sacrifices to ensure good fishing and safe river travel.

When the Alligator Mound was listed on the National Register of Historic Places in 1971 it was attributed to the Hopewell Culture, possibly because of its proximity to the Hopewellian earthworks of Newark. In the 1990s, charcoal samples recovered from the Alligator showed it had been constructed between AD 1170 and 1270, placing it at the end of the Early Fort Ancient phase.

We can assume that Ohio's effigy mounds were constructed by many persons cooperating in their design and construction, and we can assume they were used by shamans for religious purposes, but exactly what went on there we can only guess. In any case, effigy mound construction seems to have ceased around the same time that the Fort Ancient people stopped building burial mounds, making the Early Fort Ancient phase the official end of what was once known as Mound Builder civilization.

Although Madisonville did not lend its name to the Fort Ancient Culture, it did become the type site for a very important part of it, namely the "Madisonville Horizon." This term was coined in 1986 at a meeting of Fort Ancient scholars to refer to the Late Fort Ancient phase, sometimes also called the protohistoric period. Besides the Fort Ancient Culture and the Mississippian Culture, the eastern half of what is now the United States and southern Canada was home to two other contemporary major Native American protohistoric cultures: the Oneota Culture (or Upper Mississippian Culture) of southern Wisconsin, Minnesota, Iowa, and Illinois; and the Iroquoian Culture of southern Ontario and Quebec plus New York and parts of Pennsylvania.

In the Ohio Valley this period was a time of flux and contraction, judging by the evidence its residents left behind in their settlement patterns and burial practices. In general there were fewer settlements and villages appear to have become less formally organized around central plazas, with dwellings becoming larger, perhaps to house more than a single family. Storage pits were more frequently located inside dwellings. At Madisonville itself, which was likely occupied for about a century, though possibly not continuously, Hooton and Willoughby had observed that villagers were reusing grave sites by heaping the bones of the long deceased aside to make room for new occupants. Grave goods were more frequently left with the dead including pipes and small pots presumably holding food for the journey to an afterlife. Human remains from Madisonville differed physically from those of other persons buried in the region from the Archaic through the Late Woodland periods, so some of these changes might have resulted from a migration of Native Americans from elsewhere to this part of Ohio.

It's also possible that the region's climate cooled by several degrees throughout the 1500s and 1600s, bringing late spring frosts that affected maize agriculture. This phenomenon is sometimes called the Little Ice Age, which persisted into the nineteenth century. It caused grasslands to expand eastward, bringing into the region the bison and elk that became part of the Fort Ancient diet and whose bones and antlers the Late Fort Ancient people increasingly used as raw materials to be crafted into tools. Climate change could also account for villagers leaving the Ohio's tributary valleys for the Ohio River valley itself.

Meanwhile Europeans were establishing settlements on the eastern edges of the continent. The French made settlements on the St. Lawrence River in Quebec and southern Ontario. Hernando DeSoto ventured into parts of North Carolina, Arkansas, and Tennessee, while the Spanish founded missions in Georgia and Florida, including St. Augustine. The English made an attempt to settle at Roanoke but were more successful at Jamestown, Virginia, and Charleston, South Carolina, also taking over Swedish and Dutch settlements on the Delaware and Hudson rivers. Although no one residing in the Ohio Valley had yet experienced direct contact, by 1550 European goods including metal and glass objects were making their way into Fort Ancient villages, probably through the agency of other Native Americans.

In 1997 Penelope Drooker published a book titled *The View from Madisonville: Protohistoric Western Fort Ancient Interaction Patterns* in which she reevaluated the artifacts and excavation reports from that site, one of her goals being the identification of interaction networks of the protohistoric Ohio River valley. Describing Madisonville as a "gateway community," she noted that by 1600 the community had well-developed exchange patterns with points west and south. Madisonville also had exchange networks extending to the northeast and northwest. According to Drooker, Madisonville residents obtained European goods through Native American intermediaries from at least two directions, northeast and south, including brass bells, iron kettle lugs, and iron dagger guards.

Unfortunately, something else may have been moving along the inland trade routes: contagious diseases to which Native

Americans had no natural resistance. Mass and group burials were discovered at Madisonville, and scholars have estimated that 50 to 80 percent of Ohio's then population might have succumbed to diseases such as smallpox, measles, and scarlet fever. Although no one knows exactly how many Native Americans were living in North America in 1492 or how many died in the following centuries, academics have treated the assumed epidemics as the beginning of five centuries of catastrophe for Native American culture, some even calling for Columbus Day to be changed from a day of celebration to one of national mourning.

By the time Europeans came to explore and settle the Ohio River valley in the eighteenth century, they found a kind of buffer zone between Iroquois territory and other Native American groups into which several tribes had drifted. The English long claimed that the Iroquois drove the local population out of the area during the so-called Beaver Wars: mid-seventeenth-century conflicts in which the Iroquois pushed other tribes west and south in order to dominate the European fur trade after having overhunted their own ancestral land. Some modern scholars question what they refer to as the "myth of Iroquois conquest," citing a lack of evidence of mass violence in the region.

An earlier scholarly tendency to reflexively attribute most cultural change to invasions and migrations led scholars of the late twentieth century to lean toward cultural development in situ, as though the Indians didn't move around too much once the Paleoindian hunters settled down. Recent studies based on new access to ancient DNA suggest that prehistoric mass migrations were not uncommon. And migration might be the best guess for the ultimate fate of the Fort Ancient people. Many probably died of various epidemics and the decimated survivors probably moved of their own accord, perhaps closer to established trading partners. Whatever happened to them likely happened after 1674, the year an English trader named Gabriel Arthur was captured by Indians who brought him to their settlements at what was possibly the confluence of the Ohio and Kanawha rivers, and whose lifestyles he later described. European artifacts that can be dated much later are not to be found in Fort Ancient remains.

Historians had long been trying to link the mysterious vanished Mound Builders with historic tribes. Griffin suggested that the Shawnee, whose presence early settlers noted, might have been returning in historic times to what they regarded as an ancestral home, a place where their tribal identity might have been formed, but no one has so far made a definite and quantifiable link between the Fort Ancient people and the Shawnee or any other known historical Native American group. According to Drooker, "The most promise for the future probably lies in newly developed techniques such as DNA analysis, but availability of mortuary populations for testing is problematical under current legislative mandates such as the Native American Graves Protection and Repatriation Act."

11

So What's the Alternative?

In the fields of American anthropology and archaeology the key questions historically have been: Who are the Native Americans? Where did they come from? How and when did they get here? In 1590 the Jesuit scholar Joseph de Acosta proposed that both humans and animals migrated to North America from Asia across a land bridge. Acosta's theory today is pretty much accepted by scholars who have since managed to fill in many more details.

Scholars now believe that modern humans, or Homo sapiens, emerged from Africa about 100,000 years ago to begin exploring and settling Europe and Asia. About 40,000 to 35,000 years ago, these Stone Age hunter-gatherers had reached central Asia and Siberia, where a landscape that might have looked forbidding and bleak actually supported a healthy population of game animals. About 25,000 to 11,000 years ago, climate change dropped the earth's sea levels, exposing a large land mass between Siberia and Alaska that was given the name Beringia by a Swedish geologist in 1937. Humans then living in Asia discovered Beringia and began migrating across it not long after the big game they hunted started doing so. It is likely that humans representing a number of cultures from different parts of northeast Asia migrated east in successive waves, some groups successfully establishing themselves in the Western Hemisphere, others dying out. Some scholars now entertain multiple migrations via multiple routes.

For a long time scholars believed that Alaska was as far south as anyone got until after 12,000 BC when more climate change opened an ice-free corridor through the gigantic ice sheets covering Canada, called the Laurentide and Cordilleran glaciers. It is now thought that the corridor might have been open and passable earlier, though it might not have been very inviting to humans. However, humans would not have needed to wait for ice to melt if they knew how to build and operate a boat. It is now believed that pioneers had been using boats to reach places like Australia as early as 40,000 years ago. So the hunter-gatherers of coastal Asia might have constructed boats made from hides and followed the coast of Beringia to the American Pacific coast. As they traveled south, on their port side they would have discovered that the formidable Cordilleran Glacier was punctuated with ice-free harbors where they could fish and hunt seals while they sought a suitable place to land and settle or move farther inland.

This may be the prevailing wisdom currently available in college textbooks and lecture halls, but prevailing wisdom does not necessarily prevent people from proposing alternative answers to the key questions. Some of these stubborn seekers are credentialed faculty at respected universities whose theories appear in scholarly publications. Others conduct research and publish outside academia, as if in revolt from the hidebound self-proclaimed elect they disdain. Frequently the public votes with their dollars in favor of the more imaginative and thrilling theories, sometimes but not always provoking a backlash of damning reviews penned by professional archaeologists and anthropologists intended to dispel the nonsense. But the wheels turn very slowly in academia and any response can take years. Sometimes, one of the alternative theories survives the criticism and makes its way into the accepted canon.

One of the most creative alternatives for a route to America and an origin for those who became our Native Americans was proposed by Ignatius Donnelly, a Philadelphia native who took up residence in Minnesota: a lawyer, politician, and member of the Populist Party who served several terms in the US House of Representatives and twice ran for US vice president. While in Washington, DC, he frequented the Library of Congress and in 1882 he published his research in the form of a book titled *Atlantis: The Antediluvian World.*

Atlantis was supposed to have been a large island in the Atlantic Ocean whose people had been rich and powerful, trading all over the ancient world, until the island was destroyed by cataclysmic earthquakes and floods, causing it to sink below the sea. Historically, the story of Atlantis came from Greece, specifically from the philosopher Plato who first put the story in writing c. 350 BC, claiming that his source was the Greek statesman Solon, who got the information from Egyptian priests. In the mid-twentieth century, some scholars theorized that the Atlantis story had been inspired by the historical destruction of Minoan civilization on Crete due to the explosion of the volcanic island of Thera in the Mediterranean. But since then, scholars have discovered that Thera blew up before the fall of Knossos and other palaces on Crete. So there is really nothing to link the Atlantis tale to any actual event in the ancient world. And after Plato died, the Greeks considered his written account to be an invention or allegory.

Atlantis was very real to Ignatius Donnelly, however. He wrote, "The fact that the story of Atlantis was for thousands of years regarded as a fable proves nothing. There is an unbelief which grows out of ignorance, as well as a skepticism which is borne of intelligence." Pompeii and Herculaneum had been considered mythical, he declared, until someone discovered their remains.

To Donnelly, Atlantis was "the region where man first rose from a state of barbarism to civilization." As such it was the birthplace of all the world's great civilizations, of Egypt, the Near East, North Africa, and the Americas, including the Mound Builders. Like other lost civilization proponents before him, Donnelly rested his argument on perceived similarities in the artifacts and practices among widely separated groups, in this case those civilizations that Atlantis supposedly spawned. He wrote, "If then, we prove that, on both sides of the Atlantic, civilizations were found substantially identical, we have demonstrated that they must have descended one from the other, or have radiated from a common source." Specifically he cited as evidence Native American legends about a great flood similar to the flood described in the Bible. To Donnelly it made sense that the destruction of Atlantis had inspired both. As for the Mound Builders, they had crafted pipes decorated with animals that looked like elephants and constructed a mound shaped roughly like an elephant in Wisconsin. Plato had mentioned that elephants had thrived in Atlantis. Perhaps the descendants of Atlantean refugees who had settled in Mexico had carried with them their ancestral legends and what they remembered about elephants when they discovered the Mississippi and traveled north into Mound Builder country.

Donnelly hoped that Atlantis would be rediscovered by some explorer like Jules Verne's Captain Nemo who had already gazed upon its temples and towers in science fiction. Donnelly wrote, "Scientific investigation is advancing with giant strides. Who shall say that one hundred years from now the great museums of the world may not be adorned with gems, statues, arms, and implements from Atlantis, while the libraries of the world shall contain translations of its inscriptions, throwing new light upon all the past history of the human race, and all the great problems which now perplex the thinkers of the day?"

Donnelly's book was immensely popular, going through fifty printings and numerous translations. It inspired a number of followers including H. Spencer Lewis, an executive of the Rosicrucian Order, and Helena P. Blavatsky, founder of the Theosophical Society. It remains popular today despite the fact that no museum has yet to display a single Atlantean artifact recovered in the intervening hundred-some years. Scanned texts of Donnelly's book are readily available on the Internet via Google Books and the Internet Archive.

One of Donnelly's most interesting followers was a Kentucky farm boy born in 1877 named Edgar Cayce. As a young man he had experienced visions and, after finding employment in several bookstores, discovered he had the ability to memorize the contents of books simply by sleeping on them. He was also able to psychically diagnose medical problems and suggest treatments. Some people who came to consult with him were experiencing psychological problems which he was able to trace to traumas that they had suffered in past lives. These so-called "life readings" sometimes included Cayce's version of human prehistory and quite a bit about Atlantis. In the 1940s he predicted that Atlantis would rise again as part of the great upheavals that would destroy America's East Coast sometime in 1968 or 1969.

Cayce lived on through the nonprofit foundation he founded called the Association for Research and Enlightenment (ARE) located in Virginia Beach. His more modern disciples included Gregory L. Little and his wife who, together with John Van Auken, have produced books about Cayce's readings and predictions titled *Edgar Cayce's Atlantis* and *Mound Builders: Edgar Cayce's Forgotten Record of Ancient America*. Gregory and Lora Little have also gone searching the Bahamas for the actual ruins of Atlantis.

The Littles et al. relate that Cayce revealed Atlantis had been destroyed in successive disasters occurring in 50,700 BC, 28,000 BC, and 10,014 BC, with a final blow around 9,600 BC (Plato's date). As Donnelly proposed, they think its survivors migrated west to America as well as east to Egypt, the Mediterranean, and Iberia. The authors propose that they arrived in America to promulgate the Clovis Culture, offering this as proof of Cayce's accuracy, since at the time he was making his revelations little was known among the nonscholarly public about the Clovis Culture and the artifacts they left behind in so many parts of North America.

Mound Builder Culture developed much later, when the descendants of the earliest Atlantean refugees (who had arrived c. 50,000 BC) mixed with the Lost Tribes of Israel (who came to America in boats c. 3,000 BC). Immigrants from a few other cultures also blended in. According to the authors the Hopewellian earthworks demonstrate sophisticated Atlantean influence, while the Lost Tribes built the altars that Squier and Davis thought they had located beneath certain mounds.

Among the others contributing to Mound Builder Culture, Cayce mentioned refugees fleeing the destruction of Mu, who also arrived around 50,000 BC. Officially named Lemuria, the island of Mu is Atlantis's eclipsed country cousin, which supposedly once existed in the Pacific Ocean somewhere between Hawaii and Fiji before it too succumbed to natural disasters.

Although born in the minds of two nineteenth-century French antiquarians, Mu came to the attention of twentieth-century readers thanks to author James Churchward, an immigrant to the United States from his native Great Britain, which he had served as a colonel in India. While stationed there he discovered sacred tablets with the help of an old priest who had been his mentor in ancient languages. They revealed the former existence of Mu as well as its amazing place in the world's ancient history. Churchward wrote, "The Garden of Eden was not in Asia but on a now sunken continent in the Pacific Ocean. The Biblical story of creation – the epic of the seven days and the seven nights – came first not from the peoples of the Nile or of the Euphrates Valley but from this now submerged continent, Mu – the Motherland of Man."

After succumbing to earthquakes, volcanic eruptions, and tidal waves, Mu's few survivors clung to its remaining specks of land, but managed to regroup sufficiently to colonize India, Egypt, the Near East, and the entire western portion of North America. It was Cayce, not Churchward, who brought the Muvian refugees to Ohio. Churchward claimed only that they had been the ancestors of the Pueblos and the Cliff Dwellers of the American Southwest. Churchward wrote, "In fact, the rock writings and pictures of the Cliff Dwellers, except those drawn for artistic effect, are permeated with references to Mu, both before and after her submersion."

An early twenty-first-century argument for a different origin and route to America for at least a percentage of Native Americans came from the science of genetics and geneticists who identified several mtDNA haplogroups, or human populations sharing a common ancestor, which they identified with letters of the alphabet. They studied the haplogroups and Y chromosome groups of Native Americans and generally confirmed the Asian origin of Native Americans. Most Native Americans belong to haplogroups A through D, while haplogroup X is much rarer and confined to Native Americans of North America. Other concentrations of people belonging to haplogroup X are spread around the globe in the Near East, the Caucasus, and Mediterranean Europe. In Asia, members of haplogroup X include the Altai people of southwestern Siberia who possibly arrived there from the Caucasus. Seeing that the tools crafted by the Clovis Culture bear interesting similarities to those of the Paleolithic Solutrean Culture of France and Spain, where modern haplogroup X members live, Bruce Bradley and Dennis Stanford in a 2004 article proposed a North Atlantic alternative to Berengia as another gateway to the Western Hemisphere. Gregory Little argued that haplogroup X had its origin in Atlantis, whose refugees would have migrated to both America and Europe. Little also proposed that haplogroup B, frequently found in East Asia, China, and southern Siberia, may have originated on Mu.

Within a decade further analysis of ancient DNA prompted other scientists to explain the anomaly by proposing that a race of Ice Age hunter-gatherers in northern Eurasia migrated both west into Europe and east, eventually to America, before other immigrants from Asia took over their home territory.

Today the orthodox dogma among American archaeologists and anthropologists is that the civilizations of the Western Hemisphere developed completely independently of those of the

Eastern Hemisphere, with no significant contribution of tradition or technology prior to 1492. But since the middle of the twentieth century, a number of people who were willing to accept the orthodox answers on where the bulk of Native Americans came from and how they got to America were less inclined to believe that the hunting and gathering pioneers from Beringia evolved into farmers and builders all by themselves. Most of these theorists are not proposing to revive the lost civilizations theories of the nineteenth century; they're just searching for some sort of developmental spark or catalyst. Others would like to come up with contrarian evidence to make some tangential point of their own. The anthropological and archaeological communities call these folks modern-day diffusionists.

One of the twentieth century's most interesting diffusionists was the dashing and handsome Thor Heyerdahl, a Norwegian fascinated with Polynesia and the subject of ancient seafaring. His book *Kon-Tiki*, which sold over thirty million copies, documented his 1947 journey from South America across the Pacific to Polynesia on a handmade raft equipped with sails to prove his theory that the Polynesian Islands might have been colonized by immigrants from ancient Peru.

Inspired by perceived parallels between Inca and Egyptian civilizations, Heyerdahl planned another ocean voyage in the 1960s, this time in an ancient Egyptian-style vessel constructed from reeds. In his 1971 book on the subject titled *The Ra Expeditions*, Heyerdahl questioned, "What had really happened in Mexico and Peru before Columbus and his followers turned up in America? Was the ignorant Stone Age man from the Arctic tundra alone responsible for planting the seeds of all that the Spaniards found? Or were there other roads to ancient America?" While his adventure could hardly prove that Egyptians taught Native Americans how to construct pyramids, it might at least demonstrate whether Egyptians could construct a vessel as seaworthy as those that later did bring Europeans across the Atlantic. In Heyerdahl's words, "I wanted to find out if the ancient Egyptians had originally been able boatbuilders and seafarers, before they settled down along the Nile to become sculptors, Pharaohs and mummies."

In his vessel named *Ra,* Heyerdahl and his ethnically diverse crew left the port of Safi in Morocco in May 1969. Though he abandoned his sinking boat six hundred miles off Barbados, Heyerdahl captained a second vessel named *Ra II* and successfully completed a two-month voyage from Morocco to Barbados in 1970.

Credible evidence of Egyptian diffusion to the Western Hemisphere has yet to turn up, but today's scholars are finding some evidence to support Heyerdahl's Kon-Tiki thesis. DNA analysis of humans, sweet potatoes, and chickens currently found in Polynesia and South America does seem to argue for some sort of ancient contact between these locations.

No doubt inspired by the civil rights movement and the struggle for independence among African nations, in the 1960s and 1970s there arose in American academia a trend called Afrocentrism. Its adherents believed that civilization began with black Ethiopians of the Upper Nile who had instructed Egyptians, whence civilization spread by diffusion to other peoples. A book called *Black Athena* by Martin Burnal discussed the relation of ancient Greece with its African and Asiatic neighbors and the purported racist denial of their influence on Western civilization from the eighteenth century on.

In 1976, a professor of Africana studies at Rutgers University who had been born in Guyana while it was still a British colony published a book titled *They Came Before Columbus: the African Presence in Ancient America.* Author Ivan van Sertima proposed an African, specifically Nubian, influence on Mesoamerican cultures. Among other things, he argued that certain massive stone sculptures found in Central America dating from around 1,200 BC looked like Nubians.

Afrocentrists received the book enthusiastically and van Sertima's theory is still taught as fact in some Africana Studies programs and schools that have adopted an Afrocentric curriculum. Archaeologists and anthropologists largely ignored the book, nor did any professional journal review it until 1997 when a team of academics concluded, "There is hardly a claim in any of van Sertima's writings that can be supported by the evidence found in the archaeological, botanical, linguistic, or historical record. He employs a number of tactics commonly used by pseudoscientists including an almost exclusive use of outdated secondary sources and a reliance on the pseudoscientific writing of others."

So far genetic evidence has offered nothing to support significant pre-Columbian migration to America by Africans. Perhaps Africana scholars may one day the address the far more interesting question of why it seems the various political entities of pre-Columbian Africa did not seem inclined to venture across the Atlantic, which would have been for them a relatively short journey with favorable winds.

In 1970 in a book titled *Chariots of the Gods?* Erich von Daniken suggested cultural diffusion in the ancient world from yet another direction: outer space. His technique was to suggest mysterious alien origins for some of the world's more impressive antiquities whose origins had already been explained more mundanely, though not widely outside the scholarly community. Although *Chariots of the Gods?* has been repeatedly debunked, the book is still available in hardback, paperback, and e-book editions.

Von Daniken left out the Midwestern Mound Builders, but the producers of a History Channel series called *Ancient Aliens* that had been inspired by his book addressed them in a 2011 episode called "Aliens and the Old West." They argued that the Serpent Mound, like the Nazca lines of ancient Peru, seems designed to be viewed from the air. The producers made much of its location near the spot where a crashing meteorite had fractured the bedrock. They contended that the same meteorite might also have created a natural deposit of the element iridium. Perhaps the Serpent Mound had been constructed to guide extraterrestrials to a place where they could find iridium in case they needed it for spaceship repair.

The producers used Ross Hamilton (see Chapter 1) as a commentator, explaining his theory of the Serpent Mound's alignment with the constellation Draco. In the show, Hamilton points out what he calls the Serpent Mound Stone which he believes was once set like a totem in the middle of the Serpent's egg where it might have attracted lightning strikes as part of an alien technology. When the Serpent Mound is one day "reactivated," Hamilton suggested, it will mark the beginning of the restoration of the world.

The possibility of European diffusion was revived in the late 1970s and 1980s by Barry Fell who published three books suggesting that the Atlantic Ocean had been crossed by various Celts, Basques, Phoenicians, Egyptians, and others sailing to the Western Hemisphere as early as 3000 BC. Fell was born in England, grew up in New Zealand, and served in the British army. Holding a PhD from the University of Edinburgh, he came to the United States in 1964 to take a position at Harvard's Museum of Comparative Zoology and soon received a tenured professorship from Harvard University.

Fell's interest in American archaeology started in 1975 with a visit to the so-called Mystery Hill in New Hampshire, a complex of stone chambers sometimes called America's Stonehenge, more likely several root cellars constructed in a British vernacular architectural style by early settlers of New England. Having long been interested in inscriptions and petroglyphs, Fell translated the rock inscriptions he thought he had found at Mystery Hill and at other sites in North and South America, publishing his theories in 1976 in what became a very popular book titled *America BC*. Fell followed up with *Saga America* in 1980 and *Bronze Age America* in 1982.

When it came to Mound Builders, Fell revived some old assertions and came up with a few new ones. He claimed that the Grave Creek Tablet had been engraved in Tartessian, the language of the people living in and around Tartessus, a harbor city on the south coast of Iberia who had been trading partners with the Phoenicians. In West Virginia Fell claimed he found rocks with inscriptions carved in an old Irish script called Ogham, dating from the sixth to eighth centuries AD. Fell wrote, "The builders of the original Hopewell Mounds appear initially to have been mainly Libyans," citing as evidence the African styling of their pipes which sometimes depicted African animals. He also claimed that a race of pygmies had once inhabited Tennessee, just as John Haywood had long ago proposed.

Skeptical scholars questioned Fell's linguistic expertise and the similarities he professed to have found between European and Native American languages. They also wondered why all those Bronze Age explorers had left behind so many inscriptions but no other evidence of their occupation such as tools, weapons, refuse middens, and the remains of dwellings.

Diffusionists often complain that their theories are routinely and cavalierly dismissed, but that's not true of the theory of the discovery of America by Vikings, now acknowledged as among the greatest explorers of the Middle Ages, particularly in the North Atlantic. Several Scandinavian sagas and historical works inspired the theory by mentioning a place called Vinland, discovered by Leif Ericson, the son of Erik the Red. Leif was probably born on Iceland, but his father had traveled farther west to a place he named Greenland where he established the first permanent settlement in AD 986. Leif heard from a merchant who had been blown off course on the way to Greenland that there was land still farther west. Leif found the place and made several landings, the third at a spot he named Vinland for its grapes and vines. He and his crew built a small settlement and wintered over, returning with a cargo of grapes and timber. Several hopeful colonists followed and stayed a few years but left when they concluded they could not withstand the hostilities of Native Americans.

The literary references were finally confirmed in 1960 by Norwegian explorer Helge Ingstad and his archaeologist wife Anne who identified the remains of a Norse settlement on the northern tip of Newfoundland. Years of excavation uncovered the remains of buildings much like the structures of Iceland and Greenland in Viking days, as well as artifacts of Norse origin. The site's refuse indicated a short occupation. Known as L'Anse aux Meadows, the site has now withstood several decades of professional scrutiny, and the theory of pre-Columbian Vikings in America is now accepted knowledge.

It's also possible that following the failed attempt to settle Vinland, Vikings continued exploring America where they could obtain the timber that was scarce on Greenland, but made no further attempts at permanent settlement. In 1958 two amateur archaeologists found a coin they thought was an English penny at a site near Blue Hill in Maine. It was later discovered to be an eleventh-century Norwegian coin in which a hole had been drilled, making it into a pendant and very likely something Vikings had traded with Native Americans. It is also evidence that despite Viking presence in pre-Columbian America, their influence was very scant. Native Americans might have valued a curiosity like a metal coin, but they did not learn any Viking metalworking or boat building technology.

Unlike diffusionists seeking an outside source of knowledge to transform the ignorant hunter-gatherers, other alternative theorists believe that the ancient hunter-gatherers were not so ignorant. Instead, they possessed secret and sacred knowledge that could benefit modern people if we could just recapture it.

John Michell, an English writer well known to hippies of the 1960s as well as New Agers later on, founded what may be called the Earth Mysteries Movement in 1969 with the publication of his book *The View over Atlantis.* Part of his book dealt with the location of prehistoric sites in England, and the odd fact that when plotted on modern maps, the sites seemed to have been constructed along perfectly straight lines. This same phenomenon had been earlier observed by Alfred Watkins, who called the straight lines "leys" and suggested that those who followed their paths would find their lives enriched and energized. Michell added that the ley system seemed universal in the ancient world; in that era the Chinese also seemed to have aligned their sacred places along what they called "Paths of the Dragon."

Michell thought that the ancient builders' site selections had been driven by the earth's invisible currents of magnetic energy. Michell wrote, "All the evidence from the remote past points to the conclusion that the earth's natural magnetism was not only known to men some thousands of years ago but provided them with a source of energy and inspiration to which their whole civilization was tuned." While they might have forgotten this wisdom of the ancients, modern people still found themselves subconsciously drawn to ancient sacred sites. Michell continued, "The powers of the earth are reasserting themselves, as if demanding that we recognize anew the vital part they play in our existence and welfare. If one responds to that appeal by seeking to locate the springs and veins of the serpentine earth currents, one discovers ancient predecessors. Others have been there before, and the modern dowser's rod twitches in response to emanations from the earth at those very spots where they located their shrines and monuments."

Michell cited others' observations that those straight lines or leys across the earth's surface seemed to attract UFO activity. Perhaps the aliens were responding to, or somehow utilizing, the earth's flow of energy. Unless, of course, the aliens brought their own archaeologists who simply wanted to study our ancient remains.

In a 1990 book called *The People of the Web*, Gregory Little came up with a different explanation for modern day UFO sightings in the places that earth-generated magnetic forces had made special to ancient man, particularly Mound Builders. Little wrote, "It has long been recognized that sacred sites were often found in areas where strong magnetic anomalies occurred. In recent years, researchers have found that many sacred mound sites are located on top of powerful magnetic anomalies." Little revealed that his own fascination with Indian mounds began with dreams about them. During the 1980s, he and his wife visited thousands of such sites. Little wrote, "During this long period I gradually became aware that a huge mystery existed in the origins of the mound builder culture and the purposes of the mounds. And it was painfully apparent that mainstream archaeology's simple but absolute answers were not only insufficient, they were a cover for a great void in our knowledge of the past."

According to Little, when shamans performed certain mind-expanding rituals at places where the magnetic anomalies occurred, their eyes were opened to the appearance of "archetypes," or the physical entities of psychic energy which have interacted with humans since time immemorial. What do these archetypes look like? Whatever one expects them to look like, that is to say, whatever makes sense in one's own time and culture. To the ancient Mound Builders the archetypes might have appeared as the birds or birdmen so frequently represented in their art. To modern people, especially Erich von Daniken's reading audience, they might have looked like extraterrestrials. And maybe to folks in the Ohio River town of Point Pleasant, West Virginia, deep in the heart of Mound Builder country, they had looked like Mothman, a mysterious bird man creature with glowing eyes.

Ross Hamilton made a contribution to the Earth-mysteries-secret-knowledge genre with his 2012 book *Star Mounds: Legacy of Native American Mystery*, which is mainly about Midwestern Mound Builder earthworks, not mounds, despite the title. He proposes that many earthworks had information encoded in their structures and were physically oriented to ancient celestial constellations. Some served as "a resource for acquiring and holding subtle magnetic flows of energy." Hamilton contends that the mysterious Serpent Mound functioned as a hub or power center among geographically surrounding earthworks, forming a sort of zodiac. It all sounds intriguing, but only if you believe that the Hopewellian earthworks and the Fort Ancient effigy mounds were constructed at roughly the same time as part of one grand project.

In the last four decades scholars both orthodox and alternative have revisited the question of when Native Americans got here. By the middle of the twentieth century, professional archaeologists and anthropologists had accepted the "Clovis First" model. The Clovis Culture was long thought to be the prevailing way of life for the Paleoindians who were first to migrate south from Beringia from about 11,000 to 10,000 BC, around the time it was thought that an ice-free corridor had opened a path through frozen Canada. In the 1960s Dr. Louis Leakey, already famous for his work on human development in Africa, was among the first to express belief in a much greater antiquity of humans in America based on excavations that had yielded stone artifacts in southern

California. He created controversy in the anthropological world that lasted long after his death in 1972.

In 1980, George Francis Carter challenged the Clovis First model with a book titled *Earlier Than You Think: A Personal View of Man in America*. Born in San Diego, Carter developed an interest in anthropology early in life, though his PhD was in geography. He taught at Johns Hopkins and later at Texas A&M. Based on field work he had done in the 1930s for the San Diego Museum of Man, Carter had already argued for an early presence of humans in California in a 1957 book titled *Pleistocene Man at San Diego*, which had been dismissed by critics long before Leakey joined in the argument.

Carter believed that Beringia had indeed been the gateway to the Western Hemisphere for ancient people, but he also believed that ice-free corridors to the south had been open much earlier, possibly 155,000 years ago. Anyone arriving in California that early would have been a member of what European archaeologists called the Middle or Lower Paleolithic stages of development, who would have used broken rocks for tools and weapons: nothing nearly as sophisticated at the fluted Clovis point.

Carter also believed that the long time frame would have allowed people of many different races to migrate to the new world, including "Negritoids, the various Europoids, and belatedly the Mongoloids." They might even have been preceded by Neanderthals.

Critics attacked an experimental technique Carter had relied upon for dating human skeletal remains from California. The crude stone tools Carter claimed as evidence of human occupation they dismissed as "geofacts," or rocks that might look like they had been worked by ancient humans but actually had been formed by natural weathering processes. Carter's critics invented a new word—Cartifacts—to describe his dubious artifacts.

More recently archaeological sites have been discovered whose radiocarbon dated remains also seemed to challenge the Clovis First model. These included Caverna da Pedra Pintada and a rock shelter called Pedra Furada, both in Brazil; Cactus Hill in Virginia; the Gault site in Texas; the Paisley Five-Mile Point Caves in

Oregon; and the Pandejo Cave in New Mexico. Generally speaking, these sites provoke interest for about a decade but fail to stand up to rigorous scrutiny.

The latest such discovery was announced in the spring of 2016 by Jessi J. Halligan, an assistant professor of anthropology at Florida State University, and her colleagues. The research team excavated stone tools found together with llama and mastodon bones in an undisturbed geological context in a sinkhole in Florida's Aucilla River called the Page-Ladson site. Earlier researchers had discovered stone tools and a mastodon tusk bearing cut marks at the same location back in the 1980s and 1990s. Radiocarbon dating suggests that the artifacts are 14,550 years old, making Page-Ladson the first pre-Clovis site in southeastern North America. Research continues and the findings will no doubt undergo more examination. However, there are two sites that have survived the attention of fellow scholars.

In Chile, at a riverside site called Monte Verde some ten thousand miles from Beringia, a University of Kentucky archaeologist discovered what appeared to be the foundations of wooden huts plus artifacts and the remains of plants and animals. The radiocarbon dating of these remains suggested occupation that was pre-Clovis by about a thousand years. Following a determined assault by naysayers, the evidence slowly became accepted by the late 1990s.

The second site is the Meadowcroft Rockshelter, located above Cross Creek which flows into the Ohio River. Created by forces of nature, this overhang would have been visible to prehistoric people using the creek to guide them between the Ohio River valley and the uplands of western Pennsylvania. What with its southern exposure and easy access to fresh water, it probably would have been regarded by them as five-star accommodations for a temporary hunting camp.

Modern hunters left their empty beer cans in the same shelter, and its general area was long known as a good place to come across arrowheads. The rockshelter's twentieth-century owner, Albert Miller, discovered its archaeological potential in 1955 when he widened a groundhog hole and discovered an intact flint knife. Miller kept his find secret while he searched for a professional archaeologist. Years passed before he found J. M. (James) Adovasio, who directed the first professional excavation of the Meadowcroft Rockshelter with the Cultural Resource Management Program of the University of Pittsburgh starting in 1973. The original idea was to use the site as a training field school for budding archaeologists.

Beneath the beer cans on the floor of the shelter, Adovasio and his team began finding old-fashioned beer cans and bottles, then pieces of colonial glass bottles. Initially they thought they might find human remains dating as far back as 1200 to 1300 BC, but it soon became apparent that bedrock was farther down than anyone expected. In the season of 1974, the team plowed through many layers of prehistoric fireplaces, finding spear points classified as Archaic more than 10,000 years old. Then they found a layer of rocks from a natural rockfall sealing off layers containing even earlier artifacts. Among them was an intact spear point that appeared to be 12,000 years old. In a 2002 book called *The First Americans*, Adovasio wrote, "So we immediately decamped to our favorite bar in town and polished off ten kegs of beer. We named the point the Miller lanceolate to honor Albert Miller, the generous owner of a site that now looked as if it was going to make a lot of waves."

Below the Miller lanceolate there were even more remains buried with even earlier fireplaces. Radiocarbon dating of associated charcoal showed they had unearthed materials dating as early as 12,900 BC and 13,170 BC, that is, three or four thousand years before the Clovis Culture. In the words of the John Heinz History Center, which now oversees the site, Meadowcroft Rockshelter "served as a campsite for prehistoric hunters and gatherers 16,000 years ago."

Critics immediately began searching for ways in which the Meadowcroft radiocarbon dates could be wrong. In *The First Americans*, Adovasio documents their assault and his long years of defense. Adovasio had the advantage of being a credentialed professional and a meticulous excavator, but at the time he made his discovery he was also a relatively young man. Sample the textbooks currently used for teaching college level North American archaeology, and while Meadowcroft generally rates a mention, you'll see that most cite dates for the first successful colonization of continental America around 13,500 years ago. In either case, the Clovis First model has been overturned. Before the Clovis Culture formed and its distinctive fluted points were in widespread use, humans were already venturing south by various means, discovering and establishing routes, and leaving behind evidence of their passing. In Adovasio's words, "So, for now at least, the humans who stopped off at Meadowcroft represent the pioneer population in the upper Ohio River Valley and perhaps the entire Northeast."

Meadowcroft Rockshelter is now protected and interpreted for visitors by the John Heinz History Center. Archaeologist J. M. Adovasio discovered artifacts suggesting it had been used as a campsite approximately 16,000 years ago. (*Author*)

The Meadowcroft Rockshelter might have been easy enough for Paleoindians to find by following the course of Cross Creek, but the site eluded us on a 2013 trip in Washington County, Pennsylvania. We stopped at the Breezy Heights Bar and Grill to inquire whether we were even in the town of Avella, which is its mailing address. Since we did not look like the establishment's usual clientele of bikers and shale gas industry workers, the proprietress inquired as to our origin and destination. While we had lunch she asked around among the other patrons and gave us detailed directions, also mentioning in passing that this bar had been open for eighty-seven years and that she had worked there for sixty of them, making me wonder whether we were at the very bar where James Adovasio had celebrated the discovery of the Miller lanceolate.

We followed her directions to what had been originally open to the public as the Meadowcroft Village, where the Miller family had reconstructed the various buildings of a nineteenth-century rural town. While we waited for our tour to begin we visited its recently added sixteenth-century Indian village.

In 2008 the Meadowcroft Rockshelter was fitted with a roof and an observation deck reached by a long staircase. This allowed the public to get an up-close look at an exposed archaeological dig without disturbing anything. One could see how archaeologists label their layers and how very thin those layers can be, while a video introduced both Adovasio and Miller and summarized their findings and interpretations. We saw no archaeologists at work at Meadowcroft, but there was a guide stationed on the observation deck to answer questions. One of the things she pointed out to us was the part of the site left intentionally unexcavated for future archaeologists.

What I took away from Meadowcroft was the sense that while we still have a lot to learn about early humans on our continent, we have not run out of evidence, which can turn up in unexpected places. Nor have we run out of ways to examine the evidence and make it tell us more.

I got an equally exhilarating feeling at a small museum in Portsmouth, Ohio, nor far from where the Tremper Mound still stands. According to Squier and Davis, Portsmouth once had some impressive earthworks, but today they live on only as an artist's interpretation painted on the floodwalls that obscure a view of the Ohio River.

The Southern Ohio Museum located downtown had an exhibit titled "Art of the Ancients." It was a collection of over ten thousand Native American objects collected by a local resident named William Wertz and donated to the museum by his wife, Madeline, after his death. Possibly because Wertz was an amateur, his collection was an eclectic combination of tools, ornaments, and whatnot between 1,500 and 8,000 years old. Since this museum is primarily an art museum, and quite probably because Wertz never kept records about the provenance of his finds, the objects were displayed and interpreted simply as works of art. Personal ornaments like necklaces were grouped together, as were points and tools. There were some artifacts I had not seen elsewhere, like the tiny bone flutes designed for emitting high-pitched sounds. Several glass cases were chock full of items that were completely unlabeled, but elegantly housed and extremely well lighted, as if the exhibit designer was inviting viewers to take a close look and judge for themselves.

I asked the museum receptionist for more information on the collection and she introduced a staff member who was an amateur collector himself. He explained that while there was no formal archaeological excavation going on in the area at the time, around Portsmouth the prehistoric past didn't exactly wait for professionals to come on the scene in order to reveal itself. Finding Native American artifacts remained a common and almost inevitable occurrence after farmers completed the spring plowing that worked them to the surface, just as the act of plowing soil had been doing since before Ohio became a state. "Not long ago," he said, "I found a pipe. And once you find that first thing, you start seeing that these kinds of things are everywhere."

So even though the scholars and professionals might like to retain their closed-shop system and keep all the fun to themselves, it's nice to know that discovery can happen to anyone.

Bibliography

Abrams, Elliot M. "Hopewell Archaeology: A View from the Northern Woodlands." *Journal of Archaeological Research*, 17, no. 2 (June 2009): 169–204.

Adovasio, J. M. *The First Americans*. New York: Random House, 2002.

Allman, John C. "The Incinerator Village Site." *Ohio Archaeologist*, 18, no. 2 (1968): 50–55.

Anderson, Jerrel C. "The Circleville Earthwork and Hopewell." *Ohio Archaeolgist*, 61, no. 1 (2011): 18–29.

Applegate, Darlene and Mainfort, Robert C. Jr. *Woodland Period Systematics in the Ohio Valley*. Tuscaloosa: University of Alabama Press, 2005.

Ashe, Thomas. *Travels in America Performed in 1806, for the Purpose of Exploring the Rivers Alleghany, Monongahela, Ohio and Mississippi, and Ascertaining the Produce and Condition of their Banks and Vicinity*. London: R. Phillips, 1808.

Atwater, Caleb. "Description of Antiquities Discovered in the State of Ohio and Other Western States." *Archaeologia Americana*, 1 (1820): 110–267.

Baldwin, John D. *Ancient America in Notes on American Archaeology*. New York: Harper & Brothers, 1872.

Bancroft, Hubert Howe. *The Works of Hubert Howe Bancroft*. Vol. 26: *History of Utah*. San Francisco: History Company, 1889.

Barton, Benjamin Smith. "Observations and Conjectures Concerning Certain Articles Which Were Taken out of an Ancient Tumulus, or Grave, at Cincinnati." *Transactions of the American Philosophical Society*, 4 (1799): 181–215.

———. *Observations on Some Part of Natural History*. London: C. Dilly, 1787.

Bartram, William. *The Travels of William Bartram*. Edited by Francis Harper. New Haven, CT: Yale University Press, 1958.

Blosser, Jack and Glotzhober, Robert C. *Fort Ancient: Citadel, Cemetery, Cathedral, Or Calendar?* Columbus: Ohio Historical Society, 1995.

Boewe, Charles, ed. *John D. Clifford's Indian Antiquities; Related Material by C. S. Rafinesque.* Knoxville: University of Tennessee Press, 2000.

———. "Who's Buried in Rafinesque's Tomb?" *Pennsylvania Magazine of History and Biography*, 111, no. 2 (April 1987): 213–235.

Brackenridge, Henry Marie. "On the Population and Tumuli of the Aborigines of North America." *Transactions of the American Philosophical Society*, n.s. 1 (1818): 151–159.

———. *Views of Louisiana Together with a Journal of a Voyage up the Missouri River, In 1811.* Pittsburgh, 1814; reprint ed., Chicago: Quadrangle Books, 1962.

Bradley, Bruce and Stanford, Dennis. "The North Atlantic Ice-Edge Corridor: A Possible Palaeolithic Route to the New World." *World Archaeology*, 36, no. 4 (2004): 459–478.

Brew, John Otis. *Early Days of the Peabody Museum of Harvard University.* Cambridge, MA: The Museum, 1966.

———, ed. *One Hundred Years of Anthropology.* Cambridge, MA: Harvard University Press, 1968.

Brinton, Daniel G. *The Lenape and Their Legends; With the Complete Text and Symbols of the Walam Olam, A New Translation, and an Inquiry into Its Authenticity.* Philadelphia: By the Author, 1885; reprint ed., New York: AMS Press, 1969.

Brose, David S.; Cowan, C. Wesley; and Mainfort, Robert C., Jr., eds. *Societies in Eclipse.* Washington, DC: Smithsonian Institution Press, 2001.

Brose, David S. and Greber, N'omi, eds. *Hopewell Archaeology: The Chillicothe Conference.* Kent, OH: Kent State University Press, 1979.

Bryant, William Cullen. *The Poetical Works of William Cullen Bryant.* Edited by Henry C. Sturges. "The Prairies." New York: D. Appleton and Company, 1910.

Bushnell, David I. "Evidence of Indian Occupancy in Albemarle County, Virginia." *Smithsonian Miscellaneous Collections*, 89, no. 7 (1933): 1–24.

————. "Five Monacan Towns in Virginia." *Smithsonian Miscellaneous Collections*, 82, no. 12 (1930): 1–38.

Byers, A. Martin. *The Ohio Hopewell Episode: Paradigm Lost, Paradigm Gained*. Akron, OH: University of Akron Press, 2004.

————. *Reclaiming the Hopewell Ceremonial Sphere: 200 B.C. to A.D. 500*. Norman: University of Oklahoma Press, 2015.

————. *Sacred Games, Death, and Renewal in the Ancient Eastern Woodlands: The Ohio Hopewell System of Cult Sodality Heterarchies*. Lanham, MD: AltaMira Press, 2011.

Byers, A. Martin and Wymer, DeeAnne. *Hopewell Settlement Patterns, Subsistence, and Symbolic Landscapes*. Gainesville: University Press of Florida, 2010.

Carr, Christopher and Case, D. Troy. *Gathering Hopewell: Society, Ritual and Ritual Interaction*. New York: Springer, 2006.

Carter, Edward C., II. *One Grand Pursuit: A Brief History of the American Philosophical Society's First 250 Years, 1743–1993*. Philadelphia: American Philosophical Society, 1993.

Carter, George Francis. *Earlier Than You Think: A Personal View of Man in America*. College Station: Texas A&M University Press, 1980.

Carver, Jonathan. *Travel Through the Interior Parts of North America in the Years 1766, 1767, and 1768*. London: J. Walter and S. Crowder, 1778.

Case, D. Troy and Carr, Christopher. *The Scioto Hopewell and Their Neighbors: Bioarchaeological Documentation and Cultural Understanding*. New York: Springer, 2008.

Cayton, Andrew R. L. "Marietta and the Ohio Company." In *Appalachian Frontiers: Settlement, Society and Development in the Preindustrial Era*, pp. 187–200. Edited by Robert D. Mitchell. Lexington: University Press of Kentucky, 1991.

Chambers, S. Allen. *Poplar Forest and Thomas Jefferson*. Forest, VA: Corporation for Jefferson's Poplar Forest, 1993.

Charles, Douglas K. and Buikstra, Jane E., eds. *Recreating Hopewell*. Gainesville: University Press of Florida, 2006.

Chenoweth, Avery. "The Lost Tribe." *UVA Alumni News*, 93, no. 1 (Spring 2004): 16–21.

Churchward, James. *The Lost Continent of Mu*. New York: Ives Washburn, 1931.

Cockrell, Ron. *Amidst Ancient Monuments: The Administrative History of Mound City National Monument/Hopewell Culture National Historical Park, Ohio.* Washington, DC: National Park Service, 1999.

Cook, Robert A. "Single Component Sites with Long Sequences of Radiocarbon Dates: The Sunwatch Site and Middle Fort Ancient Village Growth." *American Antiquity*, 72, no. 3 (July 2007): 439–460.

————. *Sunwatch: Fort Ancient Development in the Mississippian World.* Tuscaloosa: University of Alabama Press, 2008.

Cowan, C. Wesley and Corson Hirschfeld. *First Farmers of the Middle Ohio Valley: Fort Ancient Societies, A.D. 1000–1670.* Cincinnati: Cincinnati Museum of Natural History, 1987.

Curry, Dennis C. *Feast of the Dead: Aboriginal Ossuaries in Maryland.* Myersville: Archaeological Society of Maryland, 1999.

Dahl, Curtis. "Mound-Builders, Mormons, and William Cullen Bryant." *New England Quarterly*, 34, no. 2 (June 1961): 178–190.

Dancey, William S. and Pacheco, Paul J. *Ohio Hopewell Community Organization.* Kent, OH: Kent State University Press, 1997.

Darrah, William Culp. *Powell on the Colorado.* Princeton, NJ: Princeton University Press, 1951.

Donnelly, Ignatius. *Atlantis: The Antediluvian World.* New York: Harper and Brothers, 1882.

Dragoo, Don W. "Adena and the Eastern Burial Cult." *Archaeology of Eastern North America,* 4 (Winter 1976): 1–9.

————. *Mounds for the Dead: An Analysis of the Adena Culture.* Pittsburgh: Carnegie Museum, 1963.

Drake, Daniel. *Natural and Statistical View; or Pictures of Cincinnati and the Miami Country.* Cincinnati: Looker and Wallace, 1815.

Drooker, Penelope Ballard. *The View from Madisonville: Protohistoric Western Fort Ancient Interaction Patterns.* Ann Arbor: University of Michigan Museum of Anthropology, 1997.

Drooker, Penelope B. and Cowan, C. Wesley. "Transformation of the Fort Ancient Cultures of the Central Ohio Valley." In *Societies in Eclipse*, 83–106. Edited by David S. Brose, C. Wesley Cowan, and Robert C. Mainfort, Jr. Washington, DC: Smithsonian Institution Press, 2001.

Dunham, Gary; Gold, Debra; and Hantman, Jeffrey L. "Collective Burial in Late Prehistoric Virginia: Excavation and Analysis of the Rapidan Mound." *American Antiquity*, 68, no. 1 (January 2003): 109–128.

Egloff, Keith and Woodward, Deborah. *First People: The Early Indians of Virginia*. Richmond: Virginia Department of Historic Resources, 1992.

Epstein, Jeremiah, et al. "Precolumbian Old World Coins in America: An Examination Of the Evidence." *Current Anthropology*, 21, no. 1 (February 1980): 1–20.

Fagan, Brian M. *Ancient North America; The Archaeology of a Continent*. New York: Thames and Hudson, 1995.

———. *Ancient North America*. New York: Thames and Hudson, 2005.

———. *The First North Americans*. New York: Thames and Hudson, 2011.

Fagan, Garrett G. *Archaeological Fantasies*. New York: Routledge, 2006.

Feder, Kenneth L. *Frauds, Myths and Mysteries: Science and Pseudoscience in Archaeology*. Mountain View, CA: Mayfield Publishing Co., 1990.

———. *Linking to the Past: A Brief Introduction to Archaeology*. New York: Oxford University Press, 2004.

Fell, Barry. *America BC*. New York: New York Times Book Company, 1976.

———. *Bronze Age America*. Boston: Little, Brown, 1982.

———. *Saga America*. New York: Times Books, 1980.

Fiedel, Stuart J. "Older than We Thought: Implications of Corrected Dates for Paleoindians." *American Antiquity*, 64, no. 1 (January 1999): 95–115.

Fifth Annual Report of the Bureau of Ethnology to the Secretary of the Smithsonian Institution by J. W. Powell, Director. Washington, DC: Government Printing Office, 1887.

Figgins, J.D. "The Antiquity of Man in America." *Natural History*, 27, no. 3 (1927): 229–239.

Fletcher, Robert V.; Cameron, Terry; Lepper, Bradley T.; Wymer, DeeAnne; and Pickard, William. "Serpent Mound: A Fort Ancient Icon?" *Midcontinental Journal of Archaeology*, 21, no. 1 (1996): 105–143.

Ford, T. Latimer Jr. "Adena Sites on the Chesapeake Bay." *Archaeology of Eastern North America*, 4 (Winter 1976): 63–89.

Fourth Annual Report of the Bureau of Ethnology to the Secretary of the Smithsonian Institution by J. W. Powell, Director. Washington, DC: Government Printing Office, 1886.

Fowke, Gerard. *Archaeological Investigations in James and Potomac Valleys*. Washington, DC: Government Printing Office [for Smithsonian Institution], 1894.

———. *Archaeological History of Ohio*. Columbus: Press of Fred. J. Heer, 1902.

Funkhouser W. D. and Webb, W. S. "The So-called 'Ash Caves' in Lee County, Kentucky." *Publications of the Department of Anthropology and Archaeology*, 1, no. 2 (December 1929): 37–112.

Glotzhober, Robert C. and Lepper, Bradley T. *Serpent Mound: Ohio's Enigmatic Effigy Mound*. Columbus: Ohio Historical Society, 1994.

Goodman, Jeffrey. *American Genesis*. New York: Summit Books, 1981.

———. *The Genesis Mystery*. New York: Times Books, 1983.

Goss, Charles Frederick. *Cincinnati, the Queen City*. Chicago: S. J. Clarke Publishing Co., 1912.

Graybill, Jeffrey R. "Marietta Works, Ohio and the Eastern Periphery of Fort Ancient." *Pennsylvania Archaeologist*, 50, no. 1–2 (April 1980): 51–60.

Greenman, E. F. "Excavation of the Coon Mound and an Analysis of Adena Culture." *Ohio Archaeological and Historical Quarterly*, 41, no. 3 (1932): 369–523.

Griffin, James Bennett. *The Fort Ancient Aspect*. No. 28: Anthropological Papers. Ann Arbor: University of Michigan, Museum of Anthropology, 1966.

Halligan, Jessi J. et al. "Pre-Clovis Occupation 14,550 Years Ago at the Page-Ladson Site, Florida, and the Peopling of America." *Science Advances*, vol. 2, no. 5 (May 13, 2016).

Hamilton, Ross. *Mystery of the Serpent Mound: In Search of the Alphabet of the Gods*. Berkeley, CA: Frog LTD, 2001.

———. *Star Mounds: Legacy of Native American Mystery*. Berkeley, CA: North Atlantic Books, 2012.

Hantman, Jeffrey L. "Archaeology and [Virginia] Indian History." *Quarterly Bulletin, Archaeological Society of Virginia*, 63, no. 2 (2008): 69–71.

———. "Between Powhatan and Quirank: Reconstructing Monacan Culture and History in the Context of Jamestown." *American Anthropologist*, 92 (September 1990): 676–690.

Hantman, Jeffrey L.; Wood, Karenne; and Shields, Diane. "Writing Collaborative History." *Archaeology* (September-October 2000): 56–61.

Hardman, Clark Jr. and Hardman, Marjorie H. "The Great Serpent and the Sun." *Ohio Archaeologist*, 37, no. 3 (1987): 34–40.

Harrison, Lewell H., and Klotter, James C. *A New History of Kentucky*. Lexington: University Press of Kentucky, 1997.

Harrison, William Henry. *A Discourse on the Aborigines of the Ohio Valley*. Chicago: Fergus Printing Company, 1883.

Haven, Samuel F. *Archaeology of the United States or Sketches, Historical and Bibliographical, of the Progress of Information and Opinion Respecting Vestiges of Antiquity in the United States*. Smithsonian Contributions to Knowledge, vol. 8. Washington, DC: Smithsonian Institution, 1856; reprint ed., Cambridge, MA: Harvard University Press, 1973.

Haywood, John. *The Natural and Aboriginal History of Tennessee*. Nashville: George Wilson, 1823; reprint ed., Kingsport, TN: F. M. Hill Books, 1973.

Heart, Major Jonathan. "Containing Observations on the Ancient Works of Art, the Native Inhabitants &c. of the Western-Country." *Transactions of the American Philosophical Society*, 3 (1793): 214–222.

Heckewelder, John. *An Account of the History, Manners, and Customs of the Indian Nations Who Once Inhabited Pennsylvania and the Neighboring States*. Philadelphia: Abraham Small, 1819.

Hedman, Matthew. *The Age of Everything: How Science Explores the Past*. Chicago: University of Chicago Press, 2007.

Heilman, James M.; Lileas, Malinda C.; and Turnbow, Christopher A. *A History of Seventeen Years of Excavation and Reconstruction – A Chronicle of Twelfth Century Human Values and the Built Environment*. Dayton, OH: Dayton Museum of Natural History, 1988.

Heyerdahl, Thor. *The Ra Expeditions*. Garden City, NY: Doubleday, 1971.

Hively, Ray and Horn, Robert. "Geometry and Astronomy in Prehistoric Ohio." *Archaeoastronomy: The Journal for the History of Astronomy*, 12: 1–20.

———. "Hopewellian Geometry and the Astronomy at High Bank." *Archaeoastronomy: The Journal for the History of Astronomy*, 15: 85–100.

Hooton, Earnest A. and Willoughby, Charles C. *Indian Village Site and Cemetery Near Madisonville, Ohio*. Cambridge, MA: Peabody

Museum of Archaeology and Ethnology of Harvard University, 1920.

Houck, Peter W. *Indian Island in Amherst County*. Lynchburg, VA: Warwick House, 1993.

Howe, Eber D. *Mormonism Unvailed*. Painesville, OH: By the Author, 1834.

Howe, Henry. *Historical Collections of Ohio*. Cincinnati: By the Author at E. Morgan & Co., 1851.

Hrdlicka, Ales. *Skeletal Remains Suggesting or Attributed to Early Man in North America*. Washington, DC: Government Printing Office, 1907.

Hurt, R. Douglas. *The Ohio Frontier: Crucible of the Old Northwest, 1720–1830*. Bloomington: Indiana University Press, 1996.

James, Peter and Thorpe, Nick. *Ancient Mysteries*. New York: Ballantine Books, 2001.

Jefferson, Thomas. *Notes on the State of Virginia*. Edited by William Peden. Chapel Hill: University of North Carolina Press, 1995.

———. *The Papers of Thomas Jefferson*. 32 vols. Edited by Julian Boyd. Princeton, NJ: Princeton University Press, 1950–1990.

Jennings, Jesse David. *Prehistory of North America*. New York: McGraw-Hill, 1968.

Jones, David. *A Journal of Two Visits Made to Some Nations of Indians on the West Side of the River Ohio in the Years 1772 and 1773*. Burlington, NJ: Isaac Collins, 1774.

Kelso, William M. *Archaeology at Monticello: Artifacts of Everyday Life in the Plantation Community*. Charlottesville, VA: Thomas Jefferson Memorial Foundation, 1997.

Kennedy, Roger G. *Hidden Cities: The Discovery and Loss of Ancient North American Civilization*. New York: Free Press, 1994.

King, Rufus. *Ohio: First Fruits of the Ordinance of 1787*. New York: Houghton Mifflin, 1888.

Lepper, Bradley T. *Ohio Archaeology*. Wilmington, OH: Voyageur Media Group, Inc., 2005.

Lepper, Bradley T. and Frolking, Tod A. "Alligator Mound: Geoarchaeological and Iconographical Interpretations of a Late Prehistoric Effigy Mound in Central Ohio, USA." *Cambridge Archaeological Journal*, 13, no. 2 (2003): 147–167.

Lewis, R. Barry. *Kentucky Archaeology*. Lexington: University Press of Kentucky, 1996.

Little, Gregory. *People of the Web.* Memphis, TN: White Buffalo Books, 1990.

Little, Gregory L.; Van Auken, John; and Little, Lora H. *Edgar Cayce's Atlantis.* Virginia Beach, VA: ARE Press, 2006.

————. *Mound Builders: Edgar Cayce's Forgotten Record of Ancient America.* Memphis, TN: Eagle Wing Books, 2001.

Loth, Calder, ed. *The Virginia Landmark Register.* Charlottesville: University Press of Virginia, 1999.

Lowery, Darrin. "The Delmarva Adena Complex." *Archaeology of Eastern North America,* 40 (2012): 27–58.

Lynott, Mark J. *Hopewell Ceremonial Landscapes of Ohio.* Havertown, PA: Oxbow Books, 2014.

Mainfort, Robert C. and Sullivan, Lynne P. *Ancient Earthen Enclosures of the Eastern Woodlands.* Gainesville: University Press of Florida, 1998.

Malone, Dumas. *Jefferson and His Time.* 6 vols. Boston: Little. Brown, 1948–1981.

Marshall, Humphrey. *The History of Kentucky: Exhibiting an Account of the Modern Discovery, Settlements, Progressive Improvement, Civil and Military Transactions, and the Present State of the County.* Frankfort, KY: Robinson, 1824.

Marshall, James A. "A Rebuttal to the Archaeoastronomers; Science Begins with the Facts." *Ohio Archaeologist,* 49, no. 1 (1999): 32–49.

————. "Astronomical Alignments Claimed to Exist on the Eastern North American Prehistoric Earthworks." *Ohio Archaeologist,* 45, no. 1 (1995): 4–16.

Mathews, Cornelius. *Behemoth: A Legend of the Mound-Builders.* New York: J. & H. G. Langley, 1839.

Mauss, Armand L. *All Abraham's Children: Changing Mormon Conceptions of Race and Lineage.* Urbana: University of Illinois Press, 2003.

Mettzer, David J. "Why Don't We Know When the First People Came to North America?" *American Antiquity,* 54, no. 3 (July 1989): 471–490.

Michell, John. *The New View over Atlantis.* New York: Thames and Hudson, 1969.

Mills, William C. *Certain Mounds and Village Sites in Ohio.* Columbus, OH: F. J. Heer Printing Co., 1917.

————. "Excavations of the Adena Mound." *Ohio State Archaeological and Historical Quarterly,* 10 (April 1902): 452–479.

————. "Exploration of the Gartner Mound and Village Site." *Ohio State Archaeological and Historical Quarterly*, 13, no. 2 (April 1904): 5–65.

————. "Exploration of the Mound City Group." *Ohio State Archaeological and Historical Quarterly*, 31 (October 1922): 423–584.

————. "Exploration of the Seip Mound." *Ohio State Archaeological and Historical Quarterly*, 18, no. 3 (July 1909): 269–321.

————. "Exploration of the Tremper Mound." *Ohio State Archaeological and Historical Quarterly*, 25 (July 1916): 263–398.

————. "Explorations of the Edwin Harness Mound." *Ohio State Archaeological and Historical Quarterly*, 16 (April 1907): 113–193.

Milner, George R. *The Moundbuilders: Ancient Peoples of Eastern North America*. London: Thames and Hudson, 2004.

Moorehead, Warren K. "The Hopewell Mound Group of Ohio." *Field Museum of Natural History Publications* 221, Anthropological Series 6, no. 5. Chicago: Chicago Natural History Museum, 1922.

————. *Primitive Man in Ohio*. New York: G. P. Putnam's Sons, 1892.

Morgan, William N. *Precolumbian Architecture in Eastern North America*. Gainesville: University Press of Florida, 1999.

Norona, Delf. *Moundsville's Mammoth Mound*. Moundsville: West Virginia Archaeological Society, 1954.

O'Donnell, James H., III. *Ohio's First Peoples*. Athens: Ohio University Press, 2004.

Ohio Department of Natural Resources. "Unique South-Central Ohio Rock Structure is Probably the Result of Ancient Meteorite Striking the Earth." Columbus: Press Release from Ohio Department of Natural Resources, December 16, 2003.

Pacheco, Paul J. *A View from the Core: A Synthesis of Ohio Hopewell Archaeology*. Columbus: Ohio Archaeological Council, 1996.

Page, Jake. *In the Hands of the Great Spirit*. New York: Free Press, 2003.

Pauketat, Timothy R. and Loren, Diana DiPaolo, eds. *North American Archaeology*. Malden, MA: Blackwell Publishing, 2005.

Pidgeon, William. *Traditions of De-coo-dah and Antiquarian Researches*. New York: Horace Thayer, 1858.

Potts, Louis W. "Visions of America, 1787–1788: the Ohio of Reverend Manasseh Cutler." *Ohio History*, 3 (Summer-Autumn 2002): 115–140.

Priest, Josiah. *American Antiquities and Discoveries in the West: Being an Exhibition of the Evidence that an Ancient Population of Partially Civilized Nations, Differing Entirely from those of the Present Indians, Peopled America, Many Centuries before its Discovery by Columbus.* Albany, NY: Hoffman & White, 1833.

Prufer, Olaf H. "The Hopewell Cult." *Scientific American*, 211, no. 6: 90–102.

————. *The McGraw Site: A Study in Hopewellian Dynamics.* Cleveland: Cleveland Museum of Natural History, 1995.

Prufer, Olaf H. and Shane, Orrin C., III. *Blain Village and the Fort Ancient Tradition In Ohio.* Kent, OH: Kent State University Press, 1970.

Putnam, Frederic Ward. "Iron from the Ohio Mounds: A Review of the Statements and Misconceptions of Two Writers of Over Sixty Years Ago." *Proceedings of the American Antiquarian Society,* n.s. 2 (1882–83): 349–363.

————. "Prehistoric Remains in the Ohio Valley." *Century*, 39, no. 5 (March 1890): 698–703.

————. "The Serpent Mound of Ohio." *Century*, 39, no. 6 (April 1890): 871–888.

Rafinesque, Constantine Samuel. *A Life of Travels and Researches In North America and South Europe or Outlines of the Life, Travels and Researches of C.S. Rafinesque, A.M. PhD.* Philadelphia: By the Author, 1836.

————. *The American Nations, or, Outlines of Their General History, Ancient and Modern.* 2 vols. Philadelphia: F. Turner, 1836.

Randall, E. O. *The Serpent Mound: Adams County, Ohio.* Columbus: Ohio State Archaeological and Historical Society, 1907.

Randall, Emilius O. and Ryan, Daniel J. *History of Ohio: The Rise and Progress of an American State.* 5 vols. New York: Century History Company, 1912.

Rasmussen, Morton et al. "The Ancestry and Affiliations of Kennewick Man." *Nature*, 23, no. 7561 (July 2015): 455–458.

Reps, John W. *Town Planning in Frontier America.* Princeton, NJ: Princeton University Press, 1969.

Ritchie, William A. and Dragoo, Don W. "The Eastern Dispersal of Adena." *American Antiquity*, 25, no. 1 (July 1959): 43–50.

Romain, William F. *Mysteries of the Hopewell: Astronomers, Geometers, and Magicians of the Eastern Woodlands.* Akron, OH: University of Akron Press, 2000.

————. "The Serpent Mound Map." *Ohio Archaeologist*, 37, no. 4 (Winter 1987): 38–39.

————. *Shamans of the Lost World: A Cognitive Approach to the Prehistoric Religion of the Ohio Hopewell*. New York: Rowman & Littlefield, 2009.

Royal American Magazine or Universal Repository of Instruction and Amusement, 2, no. 1 (January 1775): 29–30. "A Plan of an Old Fort and Intrenchment in the Shawanese Country."

Salmon, John S. *Guidebook to Virginia's Historical Markers*. Charlottesville: University Press of Virginia, 1994.

Saraceni, Jessica E. "Redating Serpent Mound." *Archaeology*, 49, no. 6 (Nov/Dec 1996): 16–17.

Sargent, Winthrop. "A Letter from Colonel Winthrop Sargent to Dr. Benjamin Smith Barton, Accompanying Drawings and some Account of Certain Articles, Which Were Taken out of an Ancient Tumulus, or Grave, in the Western Country." *Transactions of the American Philosophical Society*, 4 (1799): 177–180.

Seeman, Mark F. "Ohio Hopewell Trophy-Skull Artifacts as Evidence for Competition In Middle Woodland Societies Circa 50 B.C.-A.D. 350." *American Antiquity*, 53, no. 3 (July 1988): 565–577.

Shetrone, Henry Clyde. "The Culture Problem in Ohio Archaeology." *American Anthropologist*, 22 (1920): 144–172.

————. *The Mound-Builders*. New York: D. Appleton and Company, 1930.

Short, Charles W. "Description of an Indian Fort." *Transactions of the American Philosophical Society*, n.s. 1 (1818): 310–312.

Silverberg, Robert. *Moundbuilders of Ancient America: The Archaeology of a Myth*. Athens: Ohio University Press, 1986.

Smith, Claire and Wobst, H. Martin. *Indigenous Archaeologies: Decolonizing Theory and Practice*. New York: Routledge, 2005.

Smith, Joseph Jr. *The Book of Mormon*. Palmyra, NY: For the Author by E. B. Grandin, 1830.

Smith, Joseph, translator. *The Book of Mormon*. Salt Lake City: Church of Jesus Christ of the Latter-day Saints, 1920.

Smith, Thomas. H. *The Mapping of Ohio*. Kent, OH: Kent State University Press, 1977.

Snow, Dean R. *Archaeology of North America*. New York: Prentice-Hall, 2010.

Spaulding, Albert C. "The Origin of the Adena Culture in the Ohio Valley." *Southwestern Journal of Anthropology*, 8 (1952): 260–268.

Spaulding, Solomon. *Manuscript Found*. Edited by Kent P. Jackson. Provo, UT: Religious Studies Center, Brigham Young University, 1996.

Squier, E. G. and Davis, E. H. *Ancient Monuments of the Mississippi Valley*. Smithsonian Contributions to Knowledge, Vol. 1. Washington, DC: Smithsonian Institution, 1848.

Stiebing, William H., Jr. *Ancient Astronauts, Cosmic Collisions and Other Popular Theories about Man's Past*. Buffalo: Prometheus Books, 1984.

Symmes, John Cleves. *Papers of Charles Thomson*. Collections of New York Historical Society, 11 (1878): 233–239.

Taylor, R. E. *Radiocarbon Dating: An Archaeological Perspective*. New York: Academic Press, 1987.

Thomas, Cyrus. "Catalogue of Prehistoric Works East of the Rocky Mountains." *Bulletin of the Smithsonian Institution*, 12 (1891): 1–246.

―――――. "The Circular, Square, and Octagonal Earthworks of Ohio." *Bulletin of the Smithsonian Institution*, 10 (1889): 1–33.

―――――. "The Problem of the Ohio Mounds." *Bulletin of the Smithsonian Institution*, 8 (1889): 1–50.

―――――. "Report on the Mound Explorations of the Bureau of Ethnology." Twelfth Annual Report of the Bureau of Ethnology (1890–1891): 3–742.

―――――. *Report on the Mound Explorations of the Bureau of Ethnology*. Reprint ed., Washington, DC: Smithsonian Institution Press, 1985.

―――――. "Work in Mound Exploration of the Bureau of Ethnology." *Bulletin of the Smithsonian Institution*, 4 (1887): 1–15.

Thompson, Daniel P. *Centeola; And Other Tales*. New York: Carleton, 1864.

Transactions of the American Philosophical Society, 4 (1799): 37–39. "Circular Letter . . ."

Turner, Wallace. *The Mormon Establishment*. Boston: Houghton Mifflin, 1966.

Twelfth Annual Report of the Bureau of Ethnology to the Secretary of the Smithsonian Institution by J. W. Powell, Director. Washington, DC: Government Printing Office, 1894.

Van Sertima, Ivan. *They Came Before Columbus*. New York: Random House, 1976.

Von Daniken, Erich. *Chariots of the Gods?* New York: Putnam, 1969.

Wallace, Anthony F. C. *Jefferson and the Indians*. Cambridge, MA: Belknap Press, 1999.

Washington, George. *The Diaries of George Washington*. 6 vols. Edited by Donald Jackson. Charlottesville: University Press of Virginia, 1976–1979.

Wauchope, Robert. *Lost Tribes and Sunken Continents*. Chicago: University of Chicago Press, 1962.

Webb, William Snyder and Baby, Raymond S. *The Adena People, no. 2*. Columbus: Ohio State University Press, 1957.

Webb, William S.; Baby, Raymond S.; and Griffen, James B. *Prehistoric Indians Of the Ohio Valley*. Columbus: Ohio State Archaeological and Historical Society, 1952.

Webb, William Snyder and Snow, Charles E. *The Adena People*. Knoxville: University of Tennessee Press, 1974.

Weslager, C.A. "Ossuaries on the Delmarva Peninsula and Exotic Influences in the Coastal Aspect of the Woodland Pattern." *American Antiquity*, 8, no. 2 (October 1942): 142–151.

Whitney David S. and Dorn, Ronald I. "New Perspectives on the Clovis vs. Pre-Clovis Controversy." *American Antiquity*, 58, no. 4 (October 1993): 626–647.

Williamson Ray A., ed. *Archaeoastronomy in the Americas*. Los Altos, CA: Ballena Press, 1981.

Writers' Program of the Works Progress Administration in the State of Ohio. *Cincinnati: A Guide to the Queen City and Its Neighbors*. Cincinnati: Wiesen-Hart, 1943.

Zeisberger, David. *History of the North American Indians*. Edited by Archer Butler Hulbert and William Nathaniel Swarze. Columbus, OH: Press of F. J. Heer, 1910.

Acknowledgments

I am grateful to all those who helped me research and write this book. My husband, Mat Treese, accompanied me on all my treks to Mound Builder sites and shared his opinions about what we saw and heard. I thank the staff members of all the libraries I visited, in particular those of the Philadelphia Area Consortium of Special Collections Libraries (PACSCL) who helped me access the appropriate, and often arcane and rare, texts. In particular, the collections and staff members at the Haverford College Library and the Bryn Mawr College Libraries were extremely helpful. Bryn Mawr College, where I worked for over twenty years, is now my headquarters for research, and I extend my sincere thanks to my former coworkers in the Interlibrary Loan, Circulation, Special Collections, Reference, and Technical Support Departments of its libraries. I am particularly grateful to Dr. Richard S. Davis, professor emeritus of anthropology at Bryn Mawr College, who read my drafted manuscript and offered his advice and insightful comments.

I would also like to thank the many guides, docents, volunteers, and site managers at the many museums and historic sites that we visited who conducted tours and kindly and patiently answered my questions.

Finally, I would like to thank the staff at Westholme Publishing, including publisher Bruce H. Franklin, manuscript editor Noreen O'Connor-Abel, cartographer Tracy Dungan, and Trudi Gershenov, who designed the intriguing cover.

Index